T0256198

EVOLUTIONARY ALGORITHMS FOR MOBILE AD HOC NETWORKS

NATURE-INSPIRED COMPUTING SERIES

Albert Y. Zomaya, *Editor*
Mary Mehrnoosh Eshaghian-Wilner, *Editor*

Bio-Inspired and Nanoscale Integrated Computing
Edited by Mary Mehrnoosh Eshaghian-Wilner

Evolutionary Algorithms for Mobile Ad Hoc Networks
Bernabé Dorronsoro, Patricia Ruiz, Grégoire Danoy, Yoann Pigné, and
Pascal Bouvry

EVOLUTIONARY ALGORITHMS FOR MOBILE AD HOC NETWORKS

Bernabé Dorronsoro
University of Luxembourg

Patricia Ruiz
University of Luxembourg

Grégoire Danoy
University of Luxembourg

Yoann Pigné
University of Le Havre

Pascal Bouvry
University of Luxembourg

Published by John Wiley & Sons, Inc., Hoboken, New Jersey.
Published simultaneously in Canada.

For general information on our other products and services or for technical support, please contact our
Customer Care Department within the United States at (800) 762-2974, outside the United States at
(317) 572-3993 or fax (317) 572-4002.

Wiley also publishes its books in a variety of electronic formats. Some content that appears in print may
not be available in electronic formats. For more information about Wiley products, visit our web site at
www.wiley.com.

Library of Congress Cataloging-in-Publication Data:

Dorronsoro, Bernabe.
Evolutionary algorithms for mobile ad hoc networks / Bernabé Dorronsoro, Patricia Ruiz,
Grégoire Danoy, Yoann Pigné, Pascal Bouvry.
    pages   cm. – (Nature-inspired computing series)
  Includes bibliographical references.
  ISBN 978-1-118-34113-1 (hardback)
1. Mobile communication systems.   2. Evolutionary computation.   3. Genetic algorithms.   I. Title.
  TK6570.M6D65 2014
  621.382′1201519625–dc23

                                                                          2013031419

Printed in the United States of America

10   9   8   7   6   5   4   3   2   1

To our families

CONTENTS

Introduction to Wiley's

NATURE-INSPIRED COMPUTING SERIES

Wiley's *Nature-Inspired Computing Series,* edited by Professor Albert Y. Zomaya and Professor Mary Mehrnoosh Eshaghian-Wilner, is intended as a forum for researchers to explore different facets of nature-inspired computational paradigms and their impact on computing in the new millennium. The proliferation of computing devices in every aspect of our lives increases the demand for better understanding of such computing paradigms.

The following is a nonexhaustive list of topics that will be covered by the series:

Cellular Automata
Computational Methods for Biological Systems
Computational Synthesis
DNA Computing
Evolutionary Paradigms
Fuzzy Logic

Genetic Algorithms
Machine Learning Techniques
Molecular Computing
Neural Networks
Quantum Computing
Swarm Algorithms

This list serves as a guide to the diversity of series topics covered hoping that such diversity will thereby motivate readers to think of the applications of nature-inspired computing paradigms in their respective disciplines.

The series also publishes books related to technologies that are relevant to nature-inspired computing: Silicon Neuron Processing, Molecular Scale Computers and Nanotechnology, Optics, Evolvable Hardware, Quantum Hardware, Reconfigurable Hardware, and many others.

Moreover, the series targets application domains which employ nature-inspired techniques, including but not limited to:

Agents Technology
Bioinformatics
Cognitronics
Computational Challenges in Structural and
    Functional Genomics
Financial Applications
Grid Computing
Mobile Computing
Nanomedicine
Nanorobotics

Networking
Numerical Algorithms
Parallel Computing
Security and Cryptography
Simulations, Climate Modeling
Synthetic Biology
Tele-immersion
Ubiquitous Computing
Virtual Environment and
    Teleoperator Systems

The series advisory committee currently consists of: Professor Enrique Alba, University of Malaga, Malaga, Spain; Professor Azzedine Boukerche, University of Ottawa, Ontario, Canada; Dr. Robert A. Freitas, Institute for Molecular Manufacturing, Palo Alto, California; Professor Alice C. Parker, University of Southern California, Los Angeles, California; Dr. Mikhail Prokopenko, CSIRO, Clayton, Victoria, Australia; Professor John Reif, Duke University, Durham, North Carolina; Professor Franciszek Seredynski, Polish Academy of Sciences, Warsaw, Poland; and Professor El-Ghazali Talbi, Lille University and INRIA, Lille, France.

PREFACE

Recent advances in wireless and mobile technologies make communication possible anywhere and anytime with any device ranging from smartphones, tablets, to vehicles. We can envision a wide range of applications where the deployment of these ad hoc networks is key; for example, in remote locations coordinating the evacuation and rescue of people where the infrastructure is nonexistent or destroyed due to a disaster, assisting drivers or alerting them of a danger ahead. We can also think of the deployment, as a complimentary network, in dense areas to alleviate the already congested cellular network. Through these few cases we can already glimpse the importance of mobile ad hoc networks.

The specific features of ad hoc networks make it a very timely research topic since reusing existing protocols tailored for other type of networks are impossible or inefficient. As a consequence, their redefinition, redesign, and optimization are needed in order to create new optimal architectures.

Providing efficient and accurate communication protocols, topology management, or mobility models, to answer the aforementioned challenges, are difficult optimization problems. This book demonstrates how metaheuristics and, more precisely, evolutionary algorithms (EAs), can provide low-cost operations in the optimization process and allow the designer to put some *intelligence* or sophistication in his design. EAs have extensively proved their ability to solve complex, real-world problems, thanks to their capability to provide accurate (and possibly optimal) solutions in a reasonable time. Despite huge research potential, these nature-inspired algorithms are still seldom applied to solve problems in mobile ad hoc networks. In many cases, engineers do not use them or do not use them properly because of a lack of know-how. We focus on explaining how to identify, model, and solve such problems using advanced and cutting edge evolutionary algorithms.

The book is targeted to a wide audience, such as novel researchers looking for emerging research lines, senior researchers facing real problems, and parts of the book can be used in undergraduate or Ph.D. courses on optimization, advanced search techniques, multi-objective optimization, and mobile networks. Readers will find a highly self-contained book, with uniformly designed contents, chapters that can be accessed independently, and up-to-date/current topics in traditional research as well as in current lines in the world of mobile networks.

Researchers in the field of mobile networks will find highly interesting content in the book, addressing several examples on how to identify and solve problems in their research fields using advanced EAs. Additionally, the book will be of great interest for the optimization community, since researchers will find very interesting comparisons of three important kinds of EAs on a bench of complex, real-world problems, both single- and multi-objective ones. Finally, this book is highly recommended for engineers working on the design and standardization different kinds of mobile networks.

B. Dorronsoro
P. Ruiz
G. Danoy
Luxembourg   Y. Pigné
April 2014   P. Bouvry

PART I

BASIC CONCEPTS AND LITERATURE REVIEW

I

INTRODUCTION TO MOBILE AD HOC NETWORKS

The first wireless communication network between computers was created in 1970 by Norman Abramson at the University of Hawaii, the AlohaNet [11]. It was composed of seven computers distributed over four islands that were able to communicate with a central node on Oahu using radio communication. Additionally, the most well-known random-access protocol, ALOHA, was also developed and presented at that time [12]. The ALOHA channel is used nowadays in all major mobile networks (2G and 3G), as well as in almost all two-way satellite data networks [58].

Thanks to the reduction in the cost and size of the hardware needed, the wireless technology widely extends in our everyday life. The huge number of devices that provide wireless technology nowadays, as well as the increasing number of people that not only carry a device with wireless capabilities but actually use it, make the field of wireless technology a key topic in research.

The current mobile wireless networks consist of wireless nodes that are connected to a central base station. When a device moves to a different

Evolutionary Algorithms for Mobile Ad Hoc Networks, First Edition. Bernabé Dorronsoro, Patricia Ruiz, Grégoire Danoy, Yoann Pigné, and Pascal Bouvry.
© 2014 John Wiley & Sons, Inc. Published 2014 by John Wiley & Sons, Inc.

geographical area, it must connect to a different base station in order to continue with the service. This means that two nodes located in the same region cannot communicate unless there is a base station associated to that area. Researchers envisioned a possibility for communicating devices where the fixed infrastructure was not available, that is, remote or disaster areas. This kind of network is called an ad hoc network.

The term *ad hoc* has been extensively used during the last decade. According to the *American Heritage Dictionary of the English Language*, it has two different meanings: (1) form for or concerned with one specific purpose and (2) improvised and often impromptu. These two definitions of the term *ad hoc* describe the purpose of a new kind of network that emerged with the wireless technology.

Definition 1 Ad hoc Network. *It is a decentralized and self-configuring network spontaneously created between neighboring devices with communication capabilities, without relying on any existing infrastructure.*

In an ad hoc network, all devices may also act as routers and forward packets to enable communication between nodes that are not in range. Two nodes are said to be in range when they are able to receive and properly decode packets sent by the other node.

Some examples where the deployment of an ad hoc network can be used and actually can be very useful are relief in disaster areas, battlefield deployment, sensing areas, social events (like a concert), and the like. In those cases, devices can create a temporary network for a specific purpose, that is, an ad hoc network. When devices are mobile, they are called mobile ad hoc networks.

Ad hoc networks suffer from the typical drawbacks of wireless networks such as interference, time-varying channels, low reliability, limited transmission range, and so forth. Additionally, ad hoc networks have specific characteristics that make their deployment very challenging. Next, we describe the main ones:

1. Decentralization: nodes locally execute the algorithms and take all decisions by themselves:
2. Self-organization: nodes must be able to create, join, and manage an ad hoc network by their own means.
3. Limited network resources: the medium is shared between all devices in range.
4. Energy limitations: devices rely on battery.
5. Dynamism: nodes move, appear and disappear from the network.

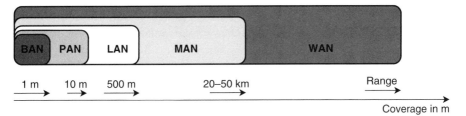

Figure 1.1. Classification of ad hoc networks in terms of the coverage area.

6. Heterogeneity: any kind of device with wireless capabilities may be able to join the network.
7. Scalability: nodes can join or leave the network at any time, therefore the number of nodes composing it is unpredictable.
8. Multihop: in order to communicate two remote nodes, devices have to also act as routers forwarding packets not intended for themselves.
9. Security: the lack of central authority, the changing topology, and the vulnerability of the channel makes difficult guaranteeing secure communications.

Chlamtac et al. [20] presented a classification of ad hoc networks in terms of the coverage of the devices (see Fig. 1.1). They can be differentiated into five different classes, explained below.

- Body area network (BAN) is a communication network (usually wireless) composed of small wearable nodes (earphones, microphones) that provides connectivity between those devices. It is also extended to small sensor nodes implanted in the human body that collect information about the patient's health and send it to an external unit. The range needed is just to cover the human body (i.e., 1–2 m).
- Personal area network (PAN) enables the communication of mobile devices carried by individuals, like smart phones, PDAs, and the like to other devices. The range varies with the technology used, from 10 to 100 m.
- Local area network (LAN) interconnects computer nodes with peripheral equipment at high data transfer in a predefined area such as an office, school, or laboratory. The communication range is restricted to a building or a set of buildings, between 100 and 500 m.
- Metropolitan area network (MAN) spans a city or a large campus. It usually interconnects different LANs. The size is variable, covering up to tens of kilometers.

- Wide area network (WAN) covers a large geographical area. It can relay data between different LANs or over long distances.

Both MAN and WAN still need much more work to become a reality in a near future. There are many challenges that are not solved yet like communication beyond line of sight, identification of devices, routing algorithms, and the like that keep researchers working on the topic [35, 38, 39, 68].

Apart from this classification, the ad hoc networking field has three well-defined research lines: (1) mobile ad hoc networks, (2) vehicular ad hoc networks, and (3) sensor networks. The first one is defined as an ad hoc network where devices do move and includes all personal devices like smart phones, PDAs, laptops, and gaming devices. When devices move at high speeds, without energy restrictions and the network is able to use road side units for communicating, we are talking about vehicular ad hoc networks. Finally, in sensor networks devices are generally meant to acquire data from the environment and report it to a central node or gateway. The next sections give a more detailed view of these three types of ad hoc networks.

1.1 MOBILE AD HOC NETWORKS

Mobile ad hoc networks, also called MANETs, are ad hoc networks where the devices that make up the network are mobile. Khan [43] extended the previously mentioned AlohaNet including repeaters, authentication, and coexistence with other possible systems in the same band. This new system was called the packet radio network, PRNET [43]. The PRNET project of the Defense Advanced Research Projects Agency, DARPA, started in 1973 and evolved through the years (1973–1987) to be a robust, reliable, operational experimental network. The MANETs were first defined in PRNET project. In Jubin and Tornow [41], a detailed description of PRNET is presented and in [40] PRNET is defined as a mobile ad hoc network.

Initially, MANETs were mainly developed for military applications, specially for creating communication networks on the battlefield. In the middle of 1991, when the first standard was defined (IEEE 802.11 [69]), and the first commercial radio technologies appeared, the great potential of ad hoc networks outside the military domain was envisioned. Apart from the military scenarios, all the previously mentioned applications for ad hoc networks (if we consider moving devices) are considered in this section. However, there are many applications like emergency services, multiuser gaming, e-commerce, information services, mobile office, that extend the cellular network.

Advances in the technology made possible Internet connection in portable devices. Mobile phones evolved to smart phones with large screens, cameras,

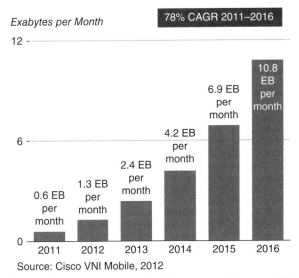

Figure 1.2. Cisco forecasts of mobile data traffic up to 2016.

GPS, bluetooth, high-speed data access, and a friendly operating system. At the end of 2013, the number of mobile devices will exceed the world's population, and by 2017 there will be 1.4 mobile devices per capita [52]. Moreover, as many people (not only industry) focused on developing applications for those smart phones, social networks such as Facebook or Twitter appeared. The former has, on average, 1.11 billion monthly active users as of March 2013 [64]. The latter has 140 million active users and 340 million Tweets a day [65] just after 6 years. No one could have predicted the amazing growth of social networking. Actually, those applications are not only used in computers but also in smart phones and tablets, increasing the mobile data traffic. It is expected that in 2016 the mobile data traffic will be more than eight times higher than in 2012, and only 0.3% of this traffic will be due to VoIP (voice over IP) [52]. Figure 1.2 shows the growth of mobile data, envisioning a 78% increase in the compound annual growth rate (CAGR) from 2011 to 2016.

With such numbers, the cellular network will be soon saturated. To alleviate this problem, part of the mobile data traffic can be delivered by a complementary network. This mechanism is known as *3G Offloading*. There are studies that present mobile ad hoc networks as this complementary network [14, 56].

Some of the main characteristics of mobile ad hoc networks that make their design challenging are mentioned below:

1. The lack of any infrastructure forces the node to perform network setup, management, self-healing, neighbor discovery, and the like.

2. Every node must have routing capabilities for communicating nodes out of range.

3. Energy constraints depend on batteries.

4. Network resource restrictions, as in wireless network, are shared (limited bandwidth, collisions, etc.).

5. Network partitioning is due to the limited transmission range and the mobility of devices:

6. Dynamic topology of the links is time varying because of the mobility of the nodes and appearance and disappearance of devices.

Although vehicular ad hoc networks and mobile sensor networks can be seen as a subclass of mobile ad hoc networks, the nodes composing the network are completely different. Therefore, the technologies used for each of the previously mentioned types of ad hoc networks are different. The main idea of mobile ad hoc networks is connecting any device in range (considering WLAN). The most common technology that gives service for computer communication in WLAN is Wi-Fi, which is already included in most of the commercial devices, making it the most suitable technology for mobile ad hoc networks.

Wi-Fi is a technology defined by the Wi-Fi Alliance [7] that allows wireless communication based on the IEEE 802.11 standards. The first IEEE 802.11 standard was published in 1997 [69], and there have been two updates, one in 2007 and another in 2012. It uses two frequency bands, 2.4 and 5 GHz. There exists a big variety of amendments to each of the standards that focus on different characteristics in wireless communication. Some examples are IEEE 802.11n, which allows MIMO antenna (multiple-input multiple-output), the IEEE 802.11s for mesh networking, and IEEE 802.11aa for video transport stream. For a complete view of the amendments and the time line, please refer to [69].

The most commonly used standards are IEEE 802.11b (1999) and IEEE802.11g (2003), which are amendments to the original standard IEEE 802.11-1997. They both work on the 2.4-GHz band, the latter being more recent with higher data rate but still fully compatible with IEEE 802.11b hardware. The IEEE 802.11n (2009) is an amendment to the IEEE 802.11-2007, which includes MIMO antenna, a significant increase in the throughput (from 54 to 600 Mbits/s), and operates in both frequency bands. These amendments are the most used versions of the IEEE 802.11 standard that provide wireless capabilities for everyday devices. Due to its reduced cost and its fast arrival on the market the IEEE 802.11b was widely adopted, making the adoption of IEEE 802.11g, which was fully compatible, very easy and fast.

1.2   VEHICULAR AD HOC NETWORKS

Vehicular ad hoc networks, hereinafter VANETs, are ad hoc networks where the devices making up the network are vehicles. In VANETs, apart from the nodes, there can also be base stations or fixed infrastructure called roadside units.

VANETs should not be confused with intelligent transportation systems (ITS). ITS cope with all kind of communications inside the vehicle, between cars or with the roadside unit, but are not limited to road transport. It also includes rail, water, and air transport. Thus, VANET is a component of ITS.

The idea of a network composed of base stations and vehicles is not new. The literature reveals that much effort has been applied to vehicular networks. Already in 1952, Friedberg discussed how to place a mobile antenna on a vehicle in order to communicate with the driver [29]. Researchers were not the only ones interested. So were companies. In 1966, General Motors Research Laboratory was already designing a real-time system for traffic safety. It was able to send voice messages alerting devices about road dangers ahead. Later, they were also considering systems that would not only make driving safer but more convenient and more enjoyable as well [33]. At that time, they were already proposing a two-way communication system, able to obtain road information but also enable drivers to ask for assistance. The system also provides (1) audio signs for receiving emergency messages and road conditions in the vehicle, (2) visual signs reproducing roadside traffic signs, and (3) navigation assistance of a preselected route. An extensive review of studies related to motorist information is presented in [50].

The PROMETHEUS Eureka program (1985–1993) was intended for developing an intelligent co-pilot that helps the driver but did not create an autonomous car. More than 60 participants from 5 different countries where involved and almost all the car manufactures. The project was divided into different subprograms: PRO-CAR, PRO-NET, and PRO-ROAD. The PRO-NET system depends on the communication links between vehicles [30]. In 1988, in the framework of the project they proposed vehicle-to-vehicle communication that would increase driving security [25]. In 1989, the Commission of the European Community launched the DRIVE program. The objectives were similar to the ones proposed in PROMETHEUS: improve road safety, traffic and transport conditions, and reduce environmental pollution; but while PROMETHEUS focuses on assisting the driver, DRIVE focuses on the infrastructure. A review of both projects and their differences can be found in [30].

Anwar et al. [16] proposed the use of packet radio networks for car-to-car communication in densely populated cities. They are considering mobile radio networks (MRN) where there are no central stations. Thus, they are actually talking about a mobile ad hoc network. They created a scenario with one- and two-way roads, traffic lights, buildings, collisions, and shadowing. In the same conference, Davoli et al. [27]. presented an architecture and a protocol for car-to-infrastructure communication using the packet radio network. But as mentioned in [34], the term VANET was first coined by Kenneth B. Laberteaux, who also conducted and promoted the first VANET workshop in 2004 as general co-chair [45].

Vehicular ad hoc networks can be considered as a subset of mobile ad hoc networks, but they have specific characteristics that distinguish them from typical mobile ad hoc networks and that make their design challenging. For example:

1. Constantly changing topology because devices move at very high speeds, typically varying from 0 to 180 km/h. The changing topology impacts network partitioning not only because of the high speeds of vehicles but also because when vehicles move from urban to rural areas the density of devices is lower.

2. Variable network density mostly depends on the time and the area. At rush hours the traffic is high and it is usually low in rural areas.

3. As a consequence of the high speed and the limited transmission range, the link availability is low (less than 1 minute), not only for devices moving in opposite directions but also cars driving in the same directions.

4. Unlike mobile or sensor ad hoc networks, vehicular ad hoc networks are not energy constrained.

5. Vehicles do not move at random, they move along lanes following routes. Additionally, a specific device might have predictable routes: Everyday, a driver goes from home to work and back again, at approximately the same time.

6. There exist two different operation modes: (1) car-to-car communication and (2) car-to-infrastructure communication.

In 1999, the U.S. Federal Communication Commission allocated 75 MHz of the dedicated short-range communication (DSRC) spectrum at 5.9 GHz to be used exclusively for vehicle-to-vehicle and infrastructure-to-vehicle communications [23]. DSRC technology allows high-speed communication between vehicles and the roadside or between vehicles that might be separated up to 1000 m. There exist differences in the frequency allocation between North America and Europe, but the intention is to be able to use the same antenna and transmitter/receiver. Different organizations like the

Institute of Electrical and Electronic Engineers (IEEE), International Standard Organization (ISO), or Car-to-Car Communication Consortium/GeoNet are working on developing an architecture for VANETs. There is no agreement between the different organizations on which of the different proposals is more convenient for vehicular networks. Thus, each of them is working on their own system: WAVE by IEEE, CALM by ISO, and C2CNet by C2C Communication Consortium. A general overview on the three schemes is given next.

1.2.1   Wireless Access in Vehicular Environment (WAVE)

The IEEE 1609 family of standards for wireless access in vehicular environments (WAVE) defines the architecture, communications model, management structure, security mechanisms and physical access for high-speed (up to 27 Mb/s) short-range (up to 1000 m) low-latency wireless communications in the vehicular environment. The primary architectural components defined by these standards are the on-board unit (OBU), road-side unit (RSU) and WAVE interface [55].

IEEE 1609 is composed of different standards tackling different layers that are already published, that is, IEEE1609.1 is the resource manager, IEEE 1609.2 copes with security services, IEEE 1609.3 with network services, and IEEE 1609.4 is for channel switching. However, part of this family of standards is still under development as IEEE 1609.0 the architecture, IEEE 1609.5 the communication manager, IEEE 1609.6 remote management service, IEEE 1609.11 for secure electronic payment, or IEEE 1609.12 identifier allocations, at the time of this writing.

In 2003, IEEE and American Society for Testing and Materials (ASTM) adopted a first version of the DSRC PHY [18], which was based on IEEE 802.11a. In 2004, in creating the 802.11p amendment within the IEEE 802.11 Working Group they agreed to add wireless access in vehicular environments (WAVE). The 802.11p [10] is built on its predecessor ASTM E2213, and it defines the required enhancements to IEEE 802.11 for supporting ITS applications.

Additionally, Society of Automotive Engineers (SAE) international standards J2735 [66] and SAE J2945.1 [57] (still under development) define a set of message formats for vehicular applications and the rules (like rate or power constraints), respectively. Those standards operate with applications using DSRC/WAVE, but they have been designed to potentially be also used with other wireless communication technologies.

Depending on the application requirements DSRC/WAVE can operate using the traditional internet protocols Internet Protocol Version 6 (IPv6),

User Datagram Protocol (UDP), and Transmission Control Protocol (TCP) defined by Internet Engineering Task Force (IETF), or using WAVE Short Messages Protocol (WSMP) defined in IEEE 1609.3. The non-IP WSMP aims at exchanging nonrouted data as safety messages.

The architecture proposed by IEEE has the IEEE 1609.x family as the core standard, the IEEE 802.11p at the physical and MAC layers, and the SAE J2735 and SAE J2945.1 at the top of the protocol stack. A detailed explanation of the architecture of the IEEE standard for DSRC can be found in [44].

1.2.2   Communication Access for Land Mobiles (CALM)

ISO TC204 WG16 is developing a family of international standards based on the CALM (communication access for land mobiles) concept. This family of standards specifies a common architecture, network protocols, and communication interface definitions for wired and wireless communications using various access technologies including cellular second generation, cellular third generation, satellite, infrared, 5-GHz microwave, 60-GHz millimeter-wave, and mobile wireless broadband. These and other access technologies that can be incorporated are designed to provide broadcast, unicast, and multicast communications between mobile stations, between mobile and fixed stations, and between fixed stations in the intelligent transport systems (ITS) sector [62].

The CALM standards are communication-centric that block out the application layer from the communication protocols. The idea behind it is that the CALM system will communicate using the most suitable communication technology depending on the application needs, the availability of the different technologies, the channel conditions, and the like. It is a heterogeneous system where devices have different interfaces and are able to support handover between the different technologies supported in CALM (cellular, infrared, DSRC, satellite, etc.). This is known as media-independent handover.

As of 2013, the set of CALM standards is still under development, but some research projects like COOPERS [4] or CVIS [8], already consider this technology. The CALM architecture (ISO 21217) is composed of six parts: *applications, management, security, facilities, networking, and transport*, and *access*. As it is based on a modification and an extension of the layered Open Systems Interconnection (OSI) model [72], there exists a correspondence between the OSI layers and some of the previously mentioned parts. The first two layers of the OSI model are included in access; layers three and four correspond with networking and transport; and facilities contain the remaining layers of the OSI model. For a more detailed explanation of the model refer to [63].

In CALM, the car is not only considered as one single device but more as a whole in-vehicle network with a variety of embedded and interconnected devices. The architecture must be able to cope with multiple technologies simultaneously and also with network mobility (NEMO). As vehicles move, the gateways to the Internet change, but the Internet connectivity to the in-vehicle network must be uninterrupted.

Similarly to WAVE, CALM operates using the IPv6 networking protocol, but for time-critical safety messages a specific non-IP protocol called FAST is used (ISO 29281). FAST supports vehicle–vehicle and vehicle–roadside communications with a very light header.

1.2.3   C2C Network

C2C Network (C2CNet) is a communication layer defined by the Car-2-Car Communication Consortium [3] specifically for car-to-car communication. As it was first defined in [24], the C2C Communication layers' architecture differentiates between three different type of applications: active safety, traffic efficiency, and infotainment. The first one relies on IEEE 802.11p and does not make use of the TCP/IP protocol. It uses a specific C2C network and C2C Transport for vehicular communications. The traffic efficiency applications can use both the IPv6 or the C2C Network over the conventional wireless LAN technologies based on IEEE 802.11 a/b/g/n. For the last kind of applications the TCP/IP (or UDP) will be used on top of other wireless technologies like General Packet Radio Service (GPRS) or Universal Mobile Telecommunications System (UMTS).

The C2C-CC system does not force all vehicles to be equipped with all the previously mentioned technologies, but at least the on-board unit must be able to communicate using the IEEE 802.11p radio technology for safety applications.

The C2C Network layer [54] is located between the network and the link layer. It supports geographical addressing and routing. The C2C header contains geographical locations. It does not use IP addresses, but IPv6 packets can be transmitted by encapsulating the IPv6 packet into a C2CNet packet (IPv4 will also be supported). That was defined in the GeoNet project [1] "IPv6 over C2CNet."

At the time of this writing, these three architectures are still under development. Therefore, the final architecture will possibly differ from the brief overview given here. Moreover, the final decision about which standard to adopt may depend on car manufactures and authorities considering various technical, business, and political aspects. A more detailed comparison between the three architectures is presented in [49].

1.3 SENSOR NETWORKS

Nowadays, sensor networks are widely used in practice for managing traffic lights, environmental conditions, system failures, security systems, and the like. But one of the main areas of sensor networks is in the field of medicine, and it is most probably one of the oldest sensor applications. Already in the early 1950s, doctors were using sensors for monitoring patients like electro-cardiographs, blood pressure recorders, electroencephalograph, and so forth. In 1956, Davis and Baldwin [26] proposed an intercommunication system for all members of the operating team, as well as for stimulating a patient during the surgical treatment of epilepsy. Moreover, they were exploring the possibility of a wireless system at that time.

Indeed, in 1957 Mackay and Jacobson [48] described a small unit (0.9 × 2.8 cm) that could be easily swallowed that was able to simultaneously trans-mit pressure and temperature signals for 2 weeks. A survey on the techniques available at that time can be found in [47].

The advances in microelectrical-mechanical systems (MEMS) technol-ogy made possible low-cost and small-size wireless sensor nodes. A sensor network is an ad hoc network composed of a large number of devices geo-graphically distributed, able to monitor different environmental or physical conditions (the data of interest). Each node usually gets the raw sensed data, processes it locally, and sends it to the node responsible for the data aggrega-tion, the sink or gateway (see Fig. 1.3). The user is able to access the gathered data from the gateway. There are many different configurations of sensor networks. It is possible to have a network with a single sink, where all the devices send the collected data to the sink and it uses the information locally. There could also be a gateway that connects the sink to other networks like the Internet, so that the user can access the data gathered (in this case, the gateway can also act as a sink). For scalability reasons, having more than one sink is desirable. Wireless sensor networks (WSN) can be programmed as self-organizing, according to different network topologies (star, linear, clus-tered, mesh, etc.) based on the specific application requirements. Akyildiz et al. [13] present an extensive survey on sensor networks.

Sensor networks have been widely used. Initially, they were mostly limited to military applications (surveillance, intrusion detection, targeting systems, etc.). Chong and Kumar [21] explained the history of sensor networks, the technology, and the challenges. An example of the early military use is the deployment of the seismic intrusion sensors in the Vietnam war around the camp as part of the intrusion warning system [46]. Nowadays, thanks to the reduction in cost and size, they are being applied in many different fields like in health for monitoring patients, for environmental measurements like temperature, pollution, pressure, or humidity, for monitoring disaster

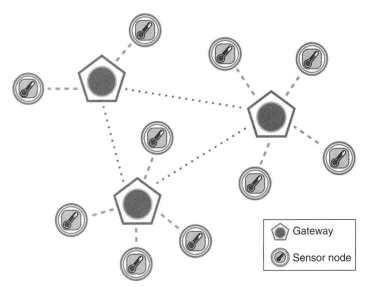

Figure 1.3. Example of a sensor network.

areas, in commercial for managing inventory, intelligent buildings, vehicle monitoring, animal monitoring, or machine monitoring.

The size of the node can vary depending on the application. Kahn et al. [42], propose a prototype called Smart Dust, so small that it could be suspended in the air for hours or even days (the volume is a few cubic millimeters). Regarding mobility, the nodes are typically fixed. However, in applications like data acquisition of twisters where the sensor nodes go inside the tornado, mobility is a key feature for capturing information.

Now, we focus on ad hoc WSNs and briefly explain them. In this kind of network (ad hoc networks in general), the network topology is not known a priori, thus, it must be constructed in real time. Moreover, due to new deployments of sensors or node failures, the topology must be updated periodically. In these networks, where nodes only communicate with neighbors, distributed algorithms are attractive because they are robust to topology changes. Chong and Kumar [21], claimed that decentralized algorithms are preferred to centralized ones (even if they can collect data from multiple sensor nodes) because the latter are less robust, less reliable, and have higher communication cost.

There are specific and challenging key features when designing a wireless sensor network that must be taken into account. Here, we mention some desired characteristics:

1. *Energy:* The tiny size and the constant sensing activity of the devices make energy consumption the critical factor in its design [28]. Some

decisions must be taken in order to balance the performance of the sensor network and the resource utilization. For example, gathering sensed data from a higher number of nodes will give more accurate results, but more communication resources are needed (i.e., energy).

2. *Low Latency:* Depending on the application, the data gathered can be already out of date in high latency networks. The delay the raw sensed data experiences from its acquisition until its utilization can be crucial depending on the application (e.g., patient monitoring).

3. *Scalability:* The number of nodes deployed in an area can vary from tens to thousands of sensors. Thus, algorithms used must be able to provide the desired performance regardless of the size of the network.

4. *Reliability:* Sensor nodes can fail due to the battery lifetime or because of extreme environmental conditions. Therefore, the algorithms designed must be resilient to failures and the network self-healing.

5. *Deployment:* Optimal distribution of the sensor over a spatial area is necessary.

There are some important differences between mobile ad hoc networks and sensor networks and also between their applications, which makes no straightforward reuse of algorithms and protocols of MANETs in sensor networks. The suitability of those algorithms must be checked before their actual implementation. We now mention some of those differences:

- In ad hoc networks the terminals are smart with high capacity, while in sensor they are simple, and the capacity rate in most of the applications is very low (few bytes).
- Unlike in ad hoc networks, in sensors not all the nodes act as routers.
- Although energy is considered a key feature, capacity is the most relevant characteristic that must be taken into consideration when designing an ad hoc network; while in sensor networks the energy is the most important restriction that must be always considered in their design [19].

In sensors, communications protocols must be designed that consider the energy restrictions. Indeed, the energy consumption needed for transmitting data is much bigger than the one needed for processing the data. However, the signal processing must not be neglected from the energy consumption as processing data sometimes can take much longer than transmitting the data and, therefore, consumes more than the transceiver in idle mode. Additionally, when the sleep mode is assumed in sensors, suitable synchronization is needed in order to have efficient communication between nodes.

As each sensor must sense, process, and communicate using a limited amount of energy, a cross-layer design that takes into consideration all these requirements (communication protocols, signal, and data processing) will provide some benefits.

Unlike MANETs or VANETs, sensors are being used in some real-world applications. Thus, there exist many different technologies for sensors depending on the necessities of the targeted application. Next, we introduce some of the most well-known technologies and standards that are available at the time of this writing.

1.3.1 IEEE 1451

The National Institute of Standards and Technology (NIST) [6] is developing a family of smart transducer interface standards IEEE 1451 *that describes a set of open, common, network-independent communication interfaces for connecting transducers (sensors or actuators) to microprocessors, instrumentation systems, and control/field networks. The key feature of these standards is the definition of Transducer Electronic Data Sheets (TEDS). TEDS is a memory device attached to the transducer, that stores transducer identification, calibration, correction data, measurement range, and manufacture-related information. The goal of 1451 is to allow the access of transducer data through a common set of interfaces whether the transducers are connected to systems or networks via a wired or wireless means* [51].

IEEE 1451 allows the sensors to have capabilities for self-identification, self-description, self-diagnosis, self-calibration, location awareness, time awareness, data processing, reasoning, data fusion, alert notification, standard-based data formats, and communication protocols [60]. It also provides plug-and-play capability. The definition of TEDS is the key feature that can be seen as an identification card that contains specific data of the transducer (including manufacturer information) allowing the sensor to connect to different networks.

1.3.2 IEEE 802.15.4

In 2003, the original standard of the IEEE for low-rate personal area networks (LR-PAN), IEEE 802.15.4, was approved. Unlike IEEE 1451, it only defines the two bottom layers of the OSI model considering very low power consumption, low complexity, and low cost. After this standard, the improved version was approved in 2006 (IEEE 802.15.4b), and in 2007 location capabilities were added in IEEE 802.15.4a. In order to make it compatible with the bands available in China and Japan, in 2009, 802.15.4c and 802.15.4d were approved. Recently, in 2011, IEEE 802.15.4 was extended, the ambiguities removed, and improvements included [70].

The network can have two different topologies: (1) star and (2) peer-to-peer. Moreover, two types of devices are defined: (1) full-function device (FFD) and (2) reduced-function device (RFD). The FFD has all network functionalities, while the RFD has low resources and is capable of very simple applications. There must exist at least one FFD for coordinating the network (PAN coordinator). In the star topology nodes can only communicate with the PAN coordinator, while in the peer-to-peer configuration any two nodes in range can connect, and they are able to self-organize, which is the basis for an ad hoc sensor network.

IEEE 802.15.4 serves as the low layers of many different specifications like ZigBee, 6LoWPAN, Wireless HART, ISA-SP100, and MiWi. We will now briefly consider some of these.

1.3.3 ZigBee

ZigBee is a standard-based network protocol created by the ZigBee Alliance [2]. It is based on the 802.15.4 standard and defines layer 3 and above in the OSI model. It was designed with for purpose of creating a network with low rate and low power capabilities that still covers a long area and that gives extra features like security. In ZigBee there are two possible access modes: beacon and nonbeacon. If the beaconing is not enabled, any node can transmit data whenever the channel is free. When beacons are enabled, the PAN coordinator assigns a time slot to every device for transmitting and sends beacon signals to synchronize all devices under its control.

Three different topologies are considered in ZigBee: (1) star, (2) cluster tree, and (3) mesh. The cluster tree topology is similar to the star, but there exists the possibility that other nodes rather than the PAN coordinator are able to communicate with each other. Unlike in the first two, in the mesh network any node can communicate with any other in range. Beaconing is not allowed in this latter topology.

The ZigBee Alliance offers two specification: ZigBee and ZigBee RF4CE. The former is intended for mesh networks offering all the features of ZigBee such as self-configuring, self-healing, and so forth. Additionally, two feature sets are available: ZigBee and ZigBee PRO (being low power consumption and a large network of thousands of devices). The latter aims at providing simple device-to-device topology, thus reducing the cost and the complexity. For a more detailed description of the ZigBee technology refer to [15, 31].

1.3.4 6LoWPAN

The idea of having all devices IP-enabled connected to the Internet and all the Internet services monitoring and controlling those devices is called Internet of Things and was first mentioned in 1999 [17]. It envisions trillions of nodes working under the Internet protocol IPv6. The problem arose when dealing with low power, low bandwidth, or battery-dependent devices, what is called the wireless embedded Internet.

The IPv6 [low-power wireless personal area networks (6LoWPAN)] working group of IETF defines a set of standards for adapting IPv6 to those resource-limited devices. In Shelby and Bormann [59], we find a formal definition: *6LoWPAN standards enable the efficient use of IPv6 over low-power, low-rate wireless networks on simple embedded devices through an adaptation layer and the optimization of related protocols.*

The IPv6 header is compressed and some functionalities are simplified, so that IPv6 packets can be transmitted over an IEEE 802.15.4 network. In this case, the topology considered is a mesh.

At the time of this writing several proposals were available. A more detailed explanation of them can be found in Yibo et al. [71].

1.3.5 Bluetooth

In 1994, engineers at Ericsson invented Bluetooth, founding the Bluetooth Special Interest Group (SIG) [61] in 1998 to expand and promote the concept. But it was not until 1999 when the first specification was published.

The main idea of Bluetooth is to enable wireless information transfer between electronic devices via short-range ad hoc radio connections in a wireless personal area network. It allowed the design of low-power, small-size, low-cost radios that can be embedded in existing portable devices. In [32] the Bluetooth radio system and its ad hoc capabilities are presented.

Bluetooth works in master–slave mode, where the master is able to communicate with up to seven devices at the same time. The ad hoc network formed by the master device and the slaves connected using Bluetooth technology make up a called a piconet.

From its creation, different versions of Bluetooth were released. At the time of writing this, the last published version is Bluetooth v4.0, which includes *classic* Bluetooth technology, Bluetooth low-energy technology, and Bluetooth high-speed technology, which can be used combined or separately [67].

In their early stages, although being similar technologies focusing on short-range wireless communication, Bluetooth and ZigBee were aiming at different objectives. ZigBee had lower power consumption and was able to support larger networks, while Bluetooth had higher bit rates, what clearly differentiated the application fields for each of them. While Bluetooth was used for mobile devices and peripherals, ZigBee focused on home automation and medical sensors. Lately, Bluetooth v4.0 includes Bluetooth low energy (BLE), aimed also at very low power applications.

1.3.6 Wireless Industrial Automation System

Both ISA100 or ISA-100.11a [9, 36] and WirelessHART [22] are specific for the process automation and manufacturing industries.

WirelessHART, the first specification for wireless field instruments, was released by the Highway Addressable Remote Transducer (HART) Communication Foundation (HCF) [5] in 2007.

ISA-100.11a was started by the International Society of Automation (ISA) [37] in 2008, and it was intended to provide reliable and secure wireless operation for noncritical monitoring, alerting, supervisory control, open-loop control, and closed-loop control applications.

There are many differences between the two standards. In WirelessHART, all field devices and adapters are routers capable of forwarding packets to and from other devices in the network, enabling a mesh network topology. In the case of ISA100.11a, a node can have router capabilities or not, which means that not all devices are able to allow a new node to join the network. On the one hand, in WirelessHART there are a few optional parameters making it less flexible than ISA100.11a, which has a complex specification with many parameters. On the other hand, the lack of flexibility makes easier the interoperability between different devices in WirelessHART. Additionally, as WirelessHART is an extension of the HART protocol, it is limited to this communication protocol. However, ISA100.11a is able to tunnel many different protocols, even supporting IPv6 using 6LoWPAN. For a more detailed comparison between both protocols refer to [53].

1.4 CONCLUSION

As previously mentioned in this chapter, the design and implementation of ad hoc networks is complex. There are many challenging aspects in ad hoc networks, some of them are specific for VANETs or sensors, but many others are common for any ad hoc network like changing topology, limited resources, network partitioned, energy constraints, scalability, and the like.

It was not mentioned before, but the design of algorithms for this kind of networks is based on simulations. Creating a real mobile ad hoc network for testing purposes is very unrealistic. For handling every device a person is needed (as devices do move), which makes it unlikely to be able to test a network with a high number of devices. Moreover, in order to reproduce the experiments, the same mobility patterns at exactly the same time as well as the same conditions must be given. Therefore, it is necessary to rely on simulations. The accuracy of the simulations directly impacts on the real performance of the designed protocol.

In this book, we try to overcome some of the problems of ad hoc networks that were mentioned above using metaheuristics. In Chapter 6, the optimization of the network resources used by a broadcasting algorithm is presented. The optimal configuration of an energy-efficient broadcast protocol restricting the communication latency is studied in Chapter 7. Chapter 8 reveals some hints for overcoming network partitioning. And finally, a mechanism for creating realistic simulations is explained in Chapter 9.

REFERENCES

1. *Geonet handbook.* GeoNet Deliverable D8.3. Available at `http://www.transport-research.info/Upload/Documents/201210/20121024_111737_62231_GeoNet-D.8.3-v1.0.pdf`. Accessed February 2014.
2. Zigbee Alliance. Available at `www.zigbee.org`. Accessed September 2012.
3. CAR 2 CAR Communication Consortium. Available at `http://www.car-to-car.org/`. Accessed July 2013.
4. COOPERS project (2006–2011). Available at `http://www.coopers-ip.eu/index.php?id=2`. Accessed July 2013.
5. HART Communication Foundation. Available at `http://www.hartcomm.org/hcf/aboutorg/aboutorg.html`. Accessed July 2013.
6. National Institute of Standards and Technology (NIST). Available at `http://www.nist.gov/`. Accessed July 2013.
7. Wi-Fi Alliance. Available at `http://www.wi-fi.org/`. Accessed July 2013.
8. CVIS project (2006–2010). Available at `http://www.cvisproject.org`. Accessed July 2013.
9. ISA 100.11a 2011 standard. Wireless systems for industrial automation: Process control and related applications, ISA-100, 2011.
10. IEEE 802.11p published standard. IEEE Standard for Information Technology—Local and metropolitan area networks—Specific requirements—Part 11: Wireless LAN medium access control (MAC) and physical layer (PHY) Specifications Amendment 6: Wireless Access in Vehicular Environments.

IEEE Std 802.11p-2010 (Amendment to IEEE Std 802.11-2007 as amended by IEEE Std 802.11k-2008, IEEE Std 802.11r-2008, IEEE Std 802.11y-2008, IEEE Std 802.11n-2009, and IEEE Std 802.11w-2009), pp. 1–51, 2010.

11. N. Abramson. The ALOHA system: Another alternative for computer communications. In *Proceedings of the November 17–19, 1970, Fall Joint Computer Conference*, pp. 281–285. ACM, New York, 1970.

12. N. Abramson. Development of the ALOHANET. *IEEE Transactions on Information Theory*, 31(2):119–123, 1985.

13. I. F. Akyildiz, W. Su, Y. Sankarasubramaniam, and E. Cayirci. A survey on sensor networks. *IEEE Communications Magazine*, 40(8):102–114, 2002.

14. L. Al-Kanj and Z. Dawy. Offloading wireless cellular networks via energy-constrained local ad hoc networks. In *IEEE Global Telecommunications Conference (GLOBECOM)*, pp. 1–6, 2011.

15. ZigBee Alliance. Specifications. Available at `http://www.zigbee.org/ Specifications.aspx`. Accessed July 2013.

16. T. Anwar, C. Jones, D. Schreib, and G. Strauch. Mobile PR-network in a densely populated urban environment. In *Proceedings of the Global Telecommunications Conference, 1990, and Exhibition. 'Communications: Connecting the Future' (GLOBECOM)*, pp. 1574–1578, 1990.

17. K. Ashton. That 'Internet of things' thing. *RFID Journal*, 22:97–114, 2009.

18. ASTM. ASTM E2213—03(2010) Standard specification for telecommunications and information exchange between roadside and vehicle systems—5 ghz band dedicated short range communications (DSRC) medium access control (MAC) and physical layer (PHY) specifications (2003). Available at `http:// www.astm.org/Standards/E2213.htm`. Accessed July 2013.

19. S. Basagni, M. Conti, S. Giordano, and I. Stojmenovic. *Mobile Ad Hoc Networking*. Wiley, San Francisco, 2004.

20. I. Chlamtac, M. Conti, and J.-N. Liu. Mobile ad hoc networking: Imperatives and challenges. *Ad Hoc Networks*, 1:13–64, 2003.

21. C-Y. Chong and S. P. Kumar. Sensor networks: Evolution, opportunities, and challenges. *Proceedings of the IEEE*, 91(8):1247–1256, 2003.

22. HART field communication protocol specification, revision 7.0, September 2007. Available at http://www.hartcomm.org. Accessed February 2014.

23. Federal Communications Commission. FCC News. Available at `http:// transition.fcc.gov/Bureaus/Engineering\_Technology/ News\_Releases/1999/nret9006.html` (1999). Accessed July 2013.

24. CAR 2 CAR communication consortium manifesto, version 1.1. Overview of the C2C-CC system, 2007. Available at http://elib.dlr.de/48380/1/C2C-CC_manifesto_v1.1.pdf. Accessed February 2014.

25. W. Dabbous and C. Huitema. PROMETHEUS: Vehicle to vehicle communications. Technical report, Research report. INRIA-Renault Collaboration, INRIA, France, 1988.

26. M. M. Davis and M. Baldwin. An intercommunication system for the surgical operating room. In *1956 IRE National Convention*, pp. 24–28. New York, 1956.

27. F. Davoli, A. Giordano, and S. Zappatore. Architecture and protocol design for a car-to-infrastructure packet radio network. In *Proceedings of the Global Telecommunications Conference, 1990, and Exhibition. "Communications: Connecting the Future" (GLOBECOM)*. IEEE, Vol. 3, pp. 1579–1585, 1990.

28. V. Dyo and C. Mascolo. Adaptive distributed indexing for spatial queries in sensor networks. In *Proceedings of the 16th International Workshop on Databases and Expert Systems Applications*, pp. 1103–1107, 2005.

29. M. R. Friedberg. Mobile antennas for vehicular communications. *Transactions of the IRE Professional Group on Vehicular Communications*, 1(1):100–104, 1952.

30. W. J. Gillan. PROMETHEUS and DRIVE: Their implications for traffic managers. In *Proceedings of the Vehicle Navigation and Information Systems Conference, 1989. Conference Record*, pp. 237–243, 1989.

31. D. Gislason, Ed. *Zigbee Wireless Networking*. Elsevier, 2008.

32. J. C. Haartsen. The Bluetooth radio system. *IEEE Personal Communications*, 7(1):28–36, 2000.

33. E. A. Hanysz, C. E. Quinn, J. E. Stevens, and W. G. Trabold. DAIR—A new concept in highway communications for added safety and driving convenience. In *Proceedings of the 17th IEEE Vehicular Technology Conference*, Vol. 17, pp. 108–120, 1966.

34. H. Hartenstein and K. Laberteaux, Ed. *VANET Vehicular Applications and Inter-Networking Technologies*. Wiley, Hoboken, 2009.

35. J.-P. Hubaux, J.-Y. Le Boudec, S. Giordano, and M. Hamdi. The Terminode project: Towards mobile ad-hoc WANs. In *Proceedings of the IEEE International Workshop on Mobile Multimedia Communications*, pp. 124–128. San Diego, 1999.

36. International Society of Automation. ISA100 wireless standard. Available at `http://www.isa100wci.org/`. Accessed July 2013.

37. ISA. International Society of Automation. Available at `http://www.isa.org/`. Accessed July 2013.

38. J. G. Jetcheva, Y.-C. Hu, S. PalChaudhuri, A. K. Saha, and D. B. Johnson. Design and evaluation of a metropolitan area multitier wireless ad hoc network architecture. In *Proceedings of the IEEE Workshop on Mobile Computing Systems and Applications*, pp. 32–43, 2003.

39. E. E. Johnson, T. Zibin, M. Balakrishnan, Z. Huiyan, and S. Sreepuram. Routing in HF ad-hoc WANs. In *Proceedings of the IEEE Military Communications Conference (MILCOM)*, Vol. 2, pp. 1040–1046, 2004.

40. D. B. Johnsort. Routing in ad hoc networks of mobile hosts. In *Proceedings of the First Workshop on Mobile Computing Systems and Applications*, pp. 158–163, 1994.

41. J. Jubin and J. D. Tornow. The DARPA Packet Radio Network Protocols. *Proceedings of the IEEE*, 75:21–32, 1987.

42. J. M. Kahn, R. H. Katz, and K. S. J. Pister. Next century challenges: Mobile networking for "Smart Dust." In *Proceedings of the 5th Annual ACM/IEEE International Conference on Mobile Computing and Networking*, pp. 271–278. ACM, New York, 1999.

43. R. Kahn. The organization of computer resources into a packet radio network. *IEEE Transactions on Communications*, 25:177–186, 1977.

44. J. B. Kenney. Dedicated short-range communications (DSRC) standards in the United States. *Proceedings of the IEEE*, 99(7):1162–1182, 2011.

45. K. P. Laberteaux, R. Sengupta, C.-N. Chuah, and D. Jiang, Eds. *Proceedings of the First International Workshop on Vehicular Ad Hoc Networks, Philadelphia, PA, USA*. ACM, New York, 2004.

46. J. R. Lundien and H. Nikodem. A mathematical model for predicting microseismic signals in terrain materials. Technical Report M-73-4. U.S. Army Engineer Waterways Experiment Station, 1973.

47. R. S. Mackay. Radio telemetering from within the human body. *IRE Transactions on Medical Electronics*, ME-6(2):100–105, 1959.

48. R. S. Mackay and B. Jacobson. Endoradiosonde. *Nature*, 179:1239–1940, 1957.

49. S. A. Mohammad, A. Rasheed, and A. Qayyum. VANET architectures and protocol stacks: A survey. In T. Strang, C. R. Garcia, A. Festag, A. Vinel, and R. Mehmood, Eds., *Proceedings of the Third International Conference on Communication Technologies for Vehicles*, Nets4Cars/Nets4Trains'11, pp. 95–105. Springer-Verlag, Berlin, 2011.

50. J. M. Mounce. Human factors requirements for real-time motorist information displays. Technical Report DOT-11-8505. Texas Transportation Institute, Texas A&M University, College Station, Texas, 1978.

51. National Institute of Standards and Technology (NIST). IEEE 1451 family of standards. Available at `http://www.nist.gov/el/isd/ieee/ieee1451.cfm`. Accessed July 2013.

52. Visual networking index. Cisco forecast. Available at `http://www.cisco.com/en/US/solutions/collateral/ns341/ns525/ns537/ns705/ns827/white\paper\c11-520862.html`. Accessed July 2013.

53. S. Petersen and S. Carlsen. WirelessHart versus ISA100.11a: The format war hits the factory floor. *IEEE Industrial Electronics Magazine*, 5:23–34, 2011.

54. Geonet Project. D 1.2 final geonet architecture design, 2010.

55. Research and Innovative Technology Administration (Rita). Intelligent Transportation Systems. IEEE 1609—Family of Standards for Wireless Access in Vehicular Environments (WAVE) (Sept. 2009). Available at `http://www.standards.its.dot.gov/fact_sheet.asp?f=80`. Accessed July 2013.

56. N. Ristanovic, J-Y. Le Boudec, A. Chaintreau, and V. Erramilli. Energy efficient offloading of 3G networks. In *Proceedings of the Eighth IEEE International Conference on Mobile Ad-Hoc and Sensor Systems (MASS)*, pp. 202–211, 2011.

57. DSRC Committee. SAE Draft Std. J2945.1, Revision 2.2, SAE International. Draft DSRC minimum performance requirements—Basic safety messages for vehicle safety applications, 2011.

58. M. Schwartz and N. Abramson. The AlohaNet—Surfing for wireless data [history of communications]. *IEEE Communications Magazine*, 47(12): 21–25, 2009.

59. Z. Shelby and C. Bormann. *6LoWPAN: The Wireless Embedded Internet.* Wiley, Hoboken, 2009.

60. E. Y. Song and K. Lee. Understanding IEEE 1451—Networked smart transducer interface standard—What is a smart transducer? *IEEE Instrumentation Measurement Magazine*, 11(2):11–17, 2008.

61. Special Interest Group (SIG). Bluetooth. Available at `https://www.bluetooth.org/apps/content/`. Accessed July 2013.

62. ITS Standards. CALM Standards for ITS (Nov. 2009). Available at `http://its-standards.info/Feeds/21217Intro.html`. Accessed July 2013.

63. ITS Standards. Communications in Cooperative Intelligent Transport Systems—CALM for C-ITS. Available at `http://calm.its-standards.info/`. Accessed July 2013.

64. Facebook statistics. Available at `http://newsroom.fb.com/content/default.aspx?NewsAreaId=22`. Accessed July 2013.

65. Twitter statistics. Available at `http://blog.twitter.com/2012/03/twitter-turns-six.html`. Accessed July 2013.

66. SAE Std. J2735. SAE International. Dedicated short-range communications (DSRC) message set dictionaty (2009). Available at `http://standards.sae.org/j2735_200911`. Accessed July 2013.

67. Bluetooth v4.0. Core specification. Available at `http://developer.bluetooth.org/KnowledgeCenter/TechnologyOverview/Pages/v4.aspx`. Accessed July 2013.

68. C. Wewetzer, M. Caliskan, and A. Luebke. The feasibility of a search engine for metropolitan vehicular ad-hoc networks. In *Proceedings of the IEEE Globecom Workshops*, pp. 1–8, 2007.

69. IEEE 802.11 Working Group. IEEE 802.11 timelines (1991). Available at `http://www.ieee802.org/11/Reports/802.11_Timelines.htm`. Accessed July 2013.

70. IEEE 802.15 Working Group. 802.15.4-2011—IEEE standard for local and metropolitan area networks—Part 15.4: Low-Rate wireless personal area networks (LR-WPANss), 2011.

71. C. Yibo, K-M. Hou, H. Zhou, H-L. Shi, X. Liu, X. Diao, H. Ding, J-J. Li, and C. de Vaulx. 6LoWPAN Stacks: A survey. In *Proceedings of the 7th International Conference on Wireless Communications, Networking and Mobile Computing (WiCOM)*, pp. 1–4, 2011.

72. H. Zimmermann. OSI reference model. *IEEE Transactions on Communications*, 28(4):425, 1980.

2

INTRODUCTION TO EVOLUTIONARY ALGORITHMS

Different approaches exist in optimization. As presented in Fig. 2.1, those methods can be classified into two main classes: exact and approximate. Exact methods ensure finding the optimal solution to the problem but are non-polynomial (NP) time algorithms for NP-complete problems. When tackling real-world optimization problems like in mobile ad hoc networks, their complexity and high computational demand are such that exact methods are not adapted. We therefore focus on the class of approximate methods, and more precisely evolutionary algorithms (EAs), which are population-based metaheuristics able to obtain acceptable solutions in reasonable time. However, based on the famous "no free lunch theorem" [37], none of these algorithms will outperform all the others on all classes of problems. In this book, we thus propose to use and analyze the performance of several EAs on different problems from the mobile ad hoc networks domain.

This chapter is organized as follows. Section 2.1 provides some introduction of basic optimization concepts. Section 2.2 then proposes a brief

Evolutionary Algorithms for Mobile Ad Hoc Networks, First Edition. Bernabé Dorronsoro, Patricia Ruiz, Grégoire Danoy, Yoann Pigné, and Pascal Bouvry.
© 2014 John Wiley & Sons, Inc. Published 2014 by John Wiley & Sons, Inc.

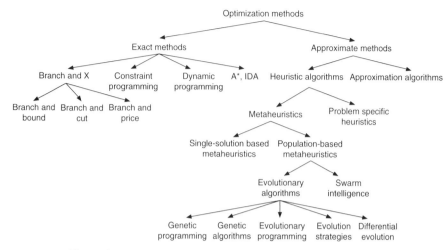

Figure 2.1. Optimization methods taxonomy (adapted from [34]).

introduction to EAs. In Section 2.3, a detailed description of the main components of EAs is given. The different types of EAs used in the experimental chapters of this book are presented according to their population structure, starting with panmictic EAs in section 2.4 and followed by structured population EAs in Section 2.5. Multi-objective optimization (i.e., the optimization of multiple conflicting objectives) basic concepts and techniques are described in Section 2.6. Finally Section 2.7 concludes this introductory chapter on EAs.

2.1   OPTIMIZATION BASICS

This section proposes elementary notions and formal definitions of some basic optimization concepts. First of all, a global optimization problem can be defined as follows:

Definition 2 (Optimization Problem) *An optimization problem consists in finding the best elements s^* from the set of solutions to the problem (aka. the search space) S, according to some quality criteria $F = \{f_1, f_2, \dots, f_n\}$.*

Each quality criterion, also named objective function, assigns a real value to each solution $s \in S$, indicating its quality, and is defined as

$$f : S \to \mathbb{R}. \tag{2.1}$$

Considering the case where a single criterion f if optimized, also referred to as single-objective optimization, the objective is to find a global optimum element s^*, minimum or maximum depending on the problem. The global optimum can be formulated as follows:

Definition 3 (Global Optimum) *Assuming a minimization problem, a solution $s^* \in S$ is a global optimum of an objective function f if*

$$f(s^*) \leq f(s) \; \forall s \in S. \tag{2.2}$$

It is worth noting that even in single-objective optimization several optimal solutions might exist.

When dealing with metaheuristics, a definition of the closeness of solutions, referred to as neighborhood, is necessary to move from one solution to another in the search space. The choice of this neighborhood structure will influence the performance of the algorithm.

Definition 4 (Neighborhood) *A neighborhood function $N : S \rightarrow 2^S$ defines for each solution $s \in S$ the set of neighbors $N(s) \in S$.*

A solution $s' \in S$ is said to be in the neighborhood of s if it belongs to $N(s)$.

For hard optimization problems like the ones tackled in this book, a solution might be optimal only in its neighborhood or in some predefined neighborhood but not the global optimum, that is, in the complete search space. Optimization algorithms might thus get trapped in so-called local optimum, defined as:

Definition 5 (Local Optimum) *A solution $s \in S$ is a local optimum, for a given neighborhood function N, if it is better than all its neighbors:*

$$f(s) \leq f(s') \; \forall s' \in N(s). \tag{2.3}$$

The difference between local and global optimum is illustrated in Fig. 2.2.

2.2 EVOLUTIONARY ALGORITHMS

Since the middle of the 20th century and the emergence of computers, the idea of mimicking some of the nature's mechanisms to create artificial intelligence (AI) has attracted many researchers to computer science. Indeed, many fields of research have emerged following these principles. Among them, "evolutionary algorithms" (EAs) propose to use nature-inspired evolving strategies for solving complex problems. More precisely, EAs are based

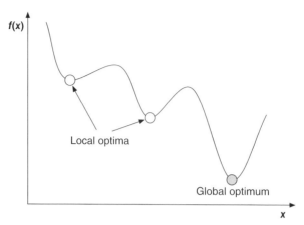

Figure 2.2. Local vs. global optimum.

on the Darwinian theory of evolution [8], which describes the capacity of biological systems to modify their genetic material to adapt to a changing environment and ensure their survival.

Evolutionary Algorithms are iterative heuristics that evolve a set of candidate solutions, represented as individuals that are grouped in a population. Pseudocode 2.1 presents an EA. Initial solutions are typically generated at random (line 2) and their quality, referred to as fitness, is evaluated using some objective function (line 3). This population of solutions is then iteratively evolved by the EA using different genetic operators such as the selection operator to choose parent individuals (line 5) followed by genetic variation operators (line 6) like the recombination (also named crossover) and mutation operators. These stochastic variation operators produce new solutions, that is, offsprings, which are in turn evaluated (line 7). The new population is then composed of a subset of the parent and offspring individuals selected with some replacement strategy (line 8). This iterative process is called generation and stops after some termination condition is met (e.g., predefined number of iterations). The best individual found is finally returned by the algorithm (line 9). An illustration of the EA functioning is provided in Fig. 2.3.

Different EAs following this template have been proposed and further developed in the last decades (see Fig. 2.1). These include evolution strategies (ES) first proposed by Rechenberg [29] and Schwefel [31], evolutionary programming (EP) introduced by Fogel [17], and genetic algorithm (GA) developed by Holland [22], among others. Genetic programming (GP) was then created in the 1980s by Cramer [7] and Koza [23], and differential evolution (DE) at the end of the 1990s by Storn and Price [32]. These EAs differ by the solution encoding used and the number and order of genetic

Pseudocode 2.1   Evolutionary Algorithm

```
 1: //Algorithm parameters in 'EA'
 2: InitializePopulation(EA.pop);
 3: Evaluation(EA.pop);
 4: while ! StopCondition() do
 5:     EA.Pop' ← ParentsSelection(EA.Pop);
 6:     EA.Pop' ← ApplyVariationOperators(EA.Pop');
 7:     Evaluation(EA.Pop');
 8:     EA.Pop ← SelectNewPopulation(EA.Pop,EA.Pop');
 9:     Return best solution
10: end while
```

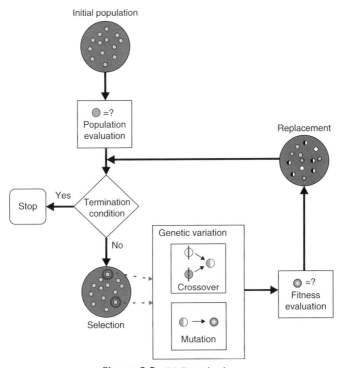

Figure 2.3. EA Functioning.

operators applied (lines 4 and 5 of Pseudocode 2.1). For instance, a GA uses a sequence composed of selection–crossover–mutation while ES use selection and mutation.

Since their introduction, EAs have been successfully applied to many optimization problems, from continuous test functions to real-world combinatorial problems.

2.3   BASIC COMPONENTS OF EVOLUTIONARY ALGORITHMS

Different components are specific to EAs and shared between all the existing variants previously mentioned. These include solution representation, selection strategy, and variation operators. Such components have to be carefully defined in order to efficiently apply EAs. The following subsections provide some detailed information on these components.

2.3.1   Representation

One of the first and fundamental steps when using an evolutionary algorithm is to define the encoding of solutions to the problem. Indeed, it has been shown that representation has a drastic influence on the algorithm's performance, both in terms of its convergence and solution quality [30]. This is also linked to the fact that genetic operators are dependent on the chosen encoding. In biological terms, the encoding is defined as the *genotype*, while the *phenotype* defines the solution itself. Many different representations have been proposed in the literature, from simple linear ones as binary encoding or permutation to complex nonlinear ones like trees. Specific encodings can also be of variable lengths or use a different phenotype to genotype mappings (e.g., one solution is represented by many encodings).

2.3.2   Fitness Function

In evolutionary computation, the fitness function $f(x)$ represents the objective of the problem. It is used to assign a value to an individual, that is, it measures the quality of the genotype in the phenotype space. It permits sorting the solutions in the population based on their performance, which is later used in the selection and replacement processes. The fitness function is problem dependent, and its definition is crucial as it is responsible for guiding the search to good solutions.

2.3.3   Selection

The selection operator is the first genetic operator involved in the EA process. It stochastically chooses individuals to be included in the mating pool. As already mentioned, it is a fitness-dependent strategy that drives the search to better solutions. In brief, the best individuals have a higher chance of being selected; however, to keep diversity in the population and prevent premature convergence to local optima, the worst individuals should still be possibly chosen. Many different selection operators exist. We here list a few prominent ones:

- Roulette wheel selection: Simplest selection scheme, also called stochastic sampling with replacement. The chance of a chromosome to get selected is proportional to its fitness, that is, it is equal to its fitness divided by the total population fitness. One disadvantage is that fittest individuals will be assigned a high probability and thus might lead to premature convergence of the algorithm.
- Tournament selection: The tournament operator selects m individuals at random and inserts the best individual among the m in the mating pool. The value of m is usually comprised between 1 and 5, and the process has to be repeated N times for a population of size N. A variant called soft tournament exists in which the winner is accepted with some predefined probability.
- Rank selection: The rank selection operator assigns a rank to each individual in the population depending on its fitness, ranging from 1 for the worst individual to $N-1$ for the best individual. The selection probability is then linearly assigned based on the individuals' rank value.

2.3.4 Crossover

The crossover operation, also named recombination, produces an offspring by mixing the genetic material of two or more parent individuals with some probability p_c (typically between 0.6 and 1). The objective is to combine the genes of both parents in order to produce better offspring. Crossover mostly depends on the representation used, and a large body of work has been spent on proposing novel operators. We here focus on the most known ones and illustrate them on binary representation (of individuals of size 10).

- One-point crossover: One-point crossover is also referred to as single-point crossover (SPX). One position is selected uniformly at random within the chromosome length, and the genes of the two parents are exchanged at this point to create two offsprings. Figure 2.4 shows an example of a one-point crossover recombining two binary chromosomes, the crossover point being represented by the vertical line between the fourth and fifth genes.
- Two-point crossover: Two-point crossover (DPX) is one instantiation of n-point crossover where $n=2$. Two positions are selected uniformly at random to exchange the genetic material of the parents and produce two offsprings. Figure 2.5 shows an example of a two-point crossover

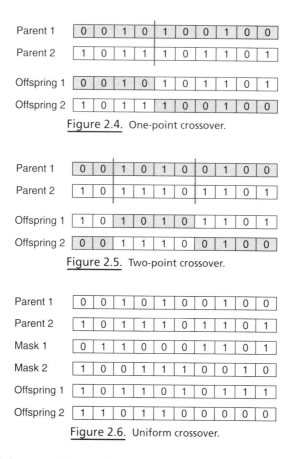

Figure 2.4. One-point crossover.

Figure 2.5. Two-point crossover.

Figure 2.6. Uniform crossover.

recombining two binary chromosomes, the two crossover points being represented by the two vertical lines.

- Uniform crossover: Uniform crossover (UX) [33] does not assume any specific crossing point(s), but instead each gene of the offspring is randomly chosen from one of the parents. Both parents thus equally contribute to the offsprings generation. Figure 2.6 illustrates an example of the uniform crossover for binary individuals of size 10. For each gene position, offspring 1 is composed of gene of parent 1 if the mask 1 value is 1 or from parent 2 if mask gene value is 0. Usually offspring 2 is created using the inverse mask.

2.3.5 Mutation

The mutation operator is used to introduce some small changes in the individual in order to prevent converging prematurely to local optima. It typically

Figure 2.7. Bit-flip mutation.

modifies each gene of the individual with some constant low probability p_m, usually between 0.001 and 0.01 (but it can also be dependent on the solution vector size, for example, p_m=1/chromosome length). If a binary encoding is used, as shown in Fig. 2.7, mutation can be defined as a change of a 1 into a 0 and vice versa, which is known as bit-flip mutation.

2.3.6 Replacement

Once an offspring individual is obtained after genetic variation and evaluated using the fitness function, it is inserted in the fixed-size population using some replacement strategy. Two main strategies exist: the generational replacement in which all parents are replaced by the offsprings in every generation and the steady-state replacement where only one parent is replaced by one offspring (e.g., replace worst) in every generation.

Using μ and λ to represent, respectively, the number of parents and the number of offsprings, the generational strategy is named (μ, λ) with $\mu = \lambda$ and the steady-state $(\mu + \lambda)$ with $\lambda = 1$.

2.3.7 Elitism

Elitism consists in copying the current best individual (or set of best individuals) directly in the offspring population. It permits ensuring that the best fitness (or average, depending on the level of elitism) can only improve from one generation to another. However, it can also induce some premature convergence if diversity is lost too fast.

2.3.8 Stopping Criteria

Since EAs are iterative algorithms, the typical stopping criterion, also referred to as termination condition, is a fixed number of iterations, that is, number of generations or fitness evaluations. Another criterion can be to stop the EA after some predefined amount of time. Finally, some more complex criteria might also be used, such as stopping if the population diversity is below some threshold or if there is no improvement of the best individual for some predefined number of iterations.

2.4   PANMICTIC EVOLUTIONARY ALGORITHMS

Panmictic evolutionary algorithms are chronologically the first EAs and also the simplest ones. In such EAs, individuals are grouped into a single structureless population, also referred to as panmixia. Individuals can thus mate with any other individual in the population. In this section, we will describe two panmictic EAs used in the experimental chapters, the generational EA and the steady-state EA.

2.4.1   Generational EA

The generational EA (genEA), also referred as "standard evolutionary algorithm," is the most known EA [22]. As mentioned in Section 2.3.6, its generational property comes from the way new individuals, that is, offsprings, are inserted in the population (cf. line 8 of Pseudocode 2.1). During the breeding loop, the offsprings obtained after selection and variation operations (crossover and/or mutation) are inserted in an auxiliary population that will become the current population once full (possibly using some elitist criterion), that is, it is a (μ, λ)-EA, with $\mu = \lambda$.

2.4.2   Steady-State EA

As previously mentioned, the steady-state evolutionary algorithm (ssEA) [36] differs from the generational model in the way individuals are inserted in the population. Contrary to the genEA, which uses an auxiliary population filled with the generated offsprings, in the ssEA, the offspring is directly inserted back in the population using some replacement strategy, for instance "replace worst individual." The population is thus updated asynchronously while it is synchronous in the generational EA [it is a $(\mu+1)$-EA].

2.5   EVOLUTIONARY ALGORITHMS WITH STRUCTURED POPULATIONS

One main issue in EAs is their premature convergence. Indeed, panmictic EAs can rapidly converge to local optima and thus never reach the global optimum. This is mainly due to a too fast propagation of "good" individuals in the population, which prevents the algorithm from visiting new regions of the search space. Indeed, good individuals can rapidly overtake the population since they can mate with any other individual in such structureless populations.

Several solutions have been proposed to overcome these drawbacks, one of them being EAs with structured populations. Two main models have been developed in the last decades, a fine-grained model and a coarse-grained model. The former structures the population at the individual level (individuals can only interact with some neighboring individuals), while the latter splits the population into interacting subpopulations that evolve in parallel.

The following two sections provide details on a fine-grained model, the cellular evolutionary algorithm (cEA), and a coarse-grained model, the cooperative coevolutionary evolutionary algorithm (CCEA).

2.5.1 Cellular EAs

Cellular evolutionary algorithms [2] still consider a single population, but as opposed to the panmictic EAs, it is a structured one. Individuals are typically placed on a 2-D toroidal mesh and can only mate with individuals belonging to their neighborhood. The population topology thus introduces "isolation by distance," that is, the further two individuals are from each other, the longer it will take them to receive mutual information. The information is then slowly propagated on the population grid thanks to the overlapping neighborhoods, which ensures a better diversity preservation than panmictic EAs. The diffusion speed can be controlled by the neighborhood radius. Indeed, the bigger the overlap, the faster the information will spread in the population [3].

Examples of neighborhoods are presented in Fig. 2.8 in increasing radius size order: linear 5, compact 9, and diamond 13 (from left to right). Some overlapping neighborhoods are illustrated as dashed line shapes and dashed line center individual.

Cellular EAs, thus, bring additional parameters that have been vastly studied, such as the influence of neighborhood size and shape [12], the population ratio (width/height), and the dynamic adaptation of the ratio [4]. However, the algorithm presented in [13] uses adaptive mechanisms for both of them, removing these two parameters from the cellular GA (CGA) configuration.

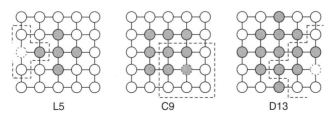

L5   C9   D13

Figure 2.8. Examples of cellular EA neighborhoods (from left to right): linear 5, compact 9, and diamond 13.

Cellular EAs have proven to perform well on a very large set of complex problems ranging from the well-known vehicle routing problem (VRP) [1] or satisfiability problem (SAT) [18], to bioinformatics problems like the DNA fragment assembly [11].

2.5.2 Cooperative Coevolutionary EAs

In order to deal with complex problems or problems with no explicit fitness function, researchers referred again to natural processes through the exploitation of the coevolutionary paradigm. The so-called coevolutionary algorithms (CEAs) [24] consider the evolution of different species evolving subsets of solutions and that interaction mutually influences their evolution. The concept of coevolution also dates from Darwin's *Origin of Species* even if it is often attributed to Ehrlich and Raven's study on butterflies and host plants [14].

Instead of evolving a population of similar individuals representing a global solution as in classical EAs, CEAs consider the coevolution of subpopulations of individuals representing different species. Each subpopulation typically runs a genetic algorithm. The specificity of coevolution comes from the fact that the fitness of an individual is dependent on its interaction with other individual(s). These interactions can be either positive or negative according to their influence on the population. Negative interactions mean that the success of one species implies the failure of other species; this is competitive coevolution. Positive interactions mean that the success of one species is conditioned to the success of other species; this is cooperative coevolution.

In this book only the cooperative model will be considered and more precisely the CCEA from Potter and De Jong [26], which is the most prominent one. Since its introduction in 1994, this cooperative coevolutionary framework has been used to solve many problems, for example, learning [27, 28], function optimization [25], and real-world optimization [15] problems.

In the CCEA, each decision variable of the global solution vector is evolved in parallel in a separate subpopulation using an EA (originally a GA). In order to evaluate complete solutions on the global problem, all subpopulations cooperate by exchanging representatives of their respective species (subpopulations). However, subpopulations do not interbreed, which means that representatives are not inserted in the destination subpopulation, contrary to other coarse-grained models like the island model [5]. The fitness of a partial solution is then equal to the fitness of the obtained assembled individual (i.e., received representatives combined with current partial solution). This credit assignment method stimulates cooperation between

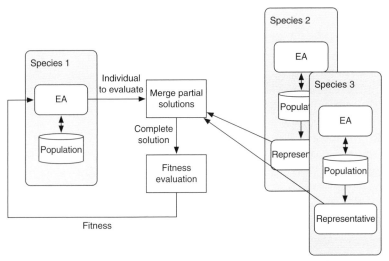

Figure 2.9. Cooperative coevolutionary EA from the perspective of species number one [26].

species as it measures to which extent a partial solution cooperates in solving the problem.

Figure 2.9 presents the general architecture of Potter's cooperative coevolutionary framework and the way each evolutionary algorithm computes the fitness of its individuals by combining them with selected representatives from all the other species.

2.6 MULTI-OBJECTIVE EVOLUTIONARY ALGORITHMS

The previous sections focused on the optimization of problems with one objective, also referred to as single-objective optimization. However, most of real-world problems (e.g., in finance, industry, bioinformatics, etc.) are inherently multi-objective problems (MOPs), involving several conflicting objectives. For instance, a car manufacturer would like to minimize its vehicles fuel consumption while maximizing their performance.

The main difference when optimizing multiple conflicting objectives comes from the fact that a single optimal solution for all objectives cannot be found. Consequently, the optimal solution is a set of so-called Pareto optimal solutions (or Pareto optimal set), which cannot be improved on one objective without decreasing their quality on one or more other objective(s).

The target in multi-objective optimization is to help decision makers (DMs) in finding the Pareto solution that best fits their requirements. This interaction with the DM is called multicriteria decision making (MCDM)

and can intervene a priori, using the DM problem knowledge to assign pref-
erences on the objectives before the optimization, be *interactive* with the DM
feedback provided to the algorithm at runtime on the found Pareto solutions,
or a posteriori where the DM chooses its preferred solutions from the final
Pareto optimal set. MCDM is a different field of research and will not be
further discussed in this book. The interested reader may refer to [35] for
additional information.

Multi-objective optimization has thus become an important research
domain in the last decades in which algorithms must be developed to tackle
ever increasing problem sizes in reasonable time. Such constraints stimulated
the usage and development of many multi-objective metaheuristics, including a large amount of multi-objective EAs [6, 10], which aim at finding the
best possible approximation of the Pareto optimal set. New metrics have to be
used to assess the quality of the obtained solutions (i.e., fronts), both in terms
of their convergence (i.e., distance to the optimal Pareto front) and diversity, to avoid their nonuniform distribution and thus potentially miss some
parts of the information. A detailed description of the metrics used for the
multi-objective problems tackled in this book is provided in Chapter 5.

2.6.1 Basic Concepts in Multi-Objective Optimization

This section presents definitions of basic concepts in multi-objective optimization. More precisely, the concepts of *multi-objective problem* (MOP),
dominance, *Pareto optimal set*, and *Pareto front* are defined. In the following,
we assume, without loss of generality, the minimization of all the objectives.
A general multi-objective optimization problem can therefore be formally
defined as follows:

Definition 6 (MOP) *Find a vector* $\mathbf{x}^* = \left[x_1^*, x_2^*, \ldots, x_n^*\right]$ *that satisfies the*
m inequality constraints $g_i(\mathbf{x}) \geq 0, i = 1, 2, \ldots, m$, *the p equality con-*
straints $h_i(\mathbf{x}) = 0, i = 1, 2, \ldots, p$, *and minimizes the vector function* $\mathbf{f}(\mathbf{x}) =$
$[f_1(\mathbf{x}), f_2(\mathbf{x}), \ldots, f_k(\mathbf{x})]$, *where* $\mathbf{x} = [x_1, x_2, \ldots, x_n]$ *is the vector of decision*
variables.

The set of all values satisfying the constraints given by the MOP defines
the *feasible region* Ω of the problem, and any point $\mathbf{x} \in \Omega$ is a *feasible*
solution.

As previously mentioned, in multi-objective optimization, it is not trivial
to decide whether one solution is better than another one or not, because it
could be better for several objectives but worse for some other ones. Therefore, we say that a solution *dominates* another if it is better or equal for every

objective and strictly better for at least one of them. Two solutions are said to be *nondominated* if neither dominates the other. We mathematically define the concept of *dominance* as:

Definition 7 (Dominance) *A vector* $\mathbf{u} = (u_1, \ldots, u_k)$ *is said to dominate* $\mathbf{v} = (v_1, \ldots, v_k)$ *(denoted by* $\mathbf{u} \preccurlyeq \mathbf{v}$*) if and only if* $\mathbf{u}$ *is partially less than* $\mathbf{v}$*, that is,* $\forall i \in \{1, \ldots, k\},\ u_i \leq v_i \wedge \exists i \in \{1, \ldots, k\} : u_i < v_i$.

The goal of multi-objective optimization is to find the set of nondominated solutions to the problem, called the Pareto optimal set, and mathematically defined as:

Definition 8 (Pareto Optimal Set) *For a given MOP* $\mathbf{f}(\mathbf{x})$*, the Pareto optimal set is defined as* $\mathcal{P}^* = \{\mathbf{x}^* \in \Omega | \neg \exists \mathbf{x}' \in \Omega, \mathbf{f}(\mathbf{x}') \preccurlyeq \mathbf{f}(\mathbf{x}^*)\}$.

Finally, the projection of the Pareto optimal set in the objectives domain is called the Pareto front:

Definition 9 (Pareto Front) *For a given MOP* $\mathbf{f}(\mathbf{x})$ *and its Pareto optimal set* $\mathcal{P}^*$*, the Pareto front is defined as* $\mathcal{PF}^* = \{\mathbf{f}(\mathbf{x}), \mathbf{x} \in \mathcal{P}^*\}$.

Figure 2.10 presents an example of Pareto front in the biobjective case.

Because the exact (or optimal) Pareto front might contain a large number of solutions, a good multi-objective algorithm should look for a Pareto front with a limited number of solutions, and it should be as close as possible to the optimal Pareto front. Additionally, these solutions should be uniformly

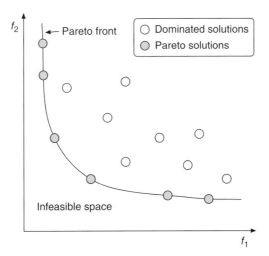

Figure 2.10. Example of Pareto front in the biobjective case.

spread along the Pareto front; otherwise information would be lost for the decision maker.

We briefly classify the main existing techniques to solve MOPs. We first may distinguish between *hierarchical* or *simultaneous* approaches.

2.6.2 Hierarchical Multi-Objective Problem Optimization

Hierarchical multi-objective problem optimization, also called *lexicographic ordering* in the specialized literature [16], relies on an ordering of the different criteria. The problem is then transformed into a set of monoobjective problems, starting from the highest priority objective, providing thus a single solution to the problem. The next objectives are then optimized in the given priority order without worsening the value of the higher priority ones. Lexicographic optimization can be formalized as follows:

$$\min\ f_i(\mathbf{x})$$
$$\text{s.t.}\ \ f_j(\mathbf{x}) \le f_j(x_j^*),\quad i = 1,\dots,k,\quad j = 1, 2,\dots,i-1,\quad \text{if } i > 1 \quad (2.4)$$

with i the position of the considered function in the preference order, and $f_j(\mathbf{x}_j^*)$ the optimum found for the *jth* objective in the *jth* iteration. A simple illustration of the lexicographic ordering functioning in a biobjective case is provided in Fig. 2.11 (left-hand side). Empty circles represent solutions that are first optimizing f_1, the objective with highest priority. Once f_1 has been optimized, the algorithm optimizes the second objective, f_2. The black circle represents the solution provided by the algorithm.

The main drawback of this technique is that a predefined ordering of objectives is required. This is not always easy, and may bias the search and, therefore, the obtained result and the performance of the algorithm.

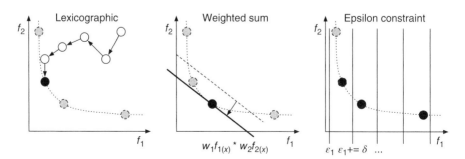

Figure 2.11. Example of multi-objective techniques (from left to right): lexicographic ordering, weighted sum, and ϵ-constraint.

2.6.3 Simultaneous Multi-Objective Problem Optimization

The alternative to lexicographic ordering is to optimize the criteria at the same time. Several approaches have been proposed, the main ones being (1) function aggregation, (2) ϵ constraint, and (3) Pareto dominance.

In the *function aggregation technique* [19], also referred to as secularization technique, the multicriteria problem is transformed into a single-objective one by aggregating the criteria into one single weighted function:

$$f(\mathbf{x}) = \sum_{i=1}^{k} w_i f_i(\mathbf{x}), \qquad \mathbf{x} \in \Omega. \tag{2.5}$$

This method is commonly used in the literature because of its easy implementation, but it still provides a single solution and does not work in concave regions of the Pareto front, regardless of the weights used [9]. Additionally, knowledge on the problem is required a priori since the solution found by the algorithm is biased by the weights used in the function aggregation. Figure 2.11 (middle) presents an example of the function aggregation technique for a biobjective case, that is, the unique solution found with specific weights (w_1, w_2).

The ϵ-*constraint technique* [21] is based on the optimization of one of the objectives, defined as the primary one, while considering the other objectives as constraints bound by some allowable levels ϵ_j:

$$\min f_i(\mathbf{x}) \text{ s.t. } f_j(\mathbf{x}) \le \epsilon_j, \qquad \mathbf{x} \in \Omega. \tag{2.6}$$

The problem is thus reduced to a type of single-objective problem f_i constrained by some upper bound ϵ_j on the other objectives. This bound is iteratively increased by some predefined constant δ. In practice, it will be difficult to set accurate values for the constraints, that is, to set δ that will still allow finding feasible solutions. Indeed since a single solution can be found in the defined interval, it is necessary to choose a δ small enough to find solutions but not too small to prevent wasting iterations in empty regions of the objective space. Figure 2.11 (right-hand side) illustrates the ϵ constraint functioning with a specific δ value that permits one to find three out of the four Pareto solutions, represented as black circles.

In the *Pareto dominance technique*, all the criteria are tackled as independent functions, and the algorithm is optimizing all of them at the same time. Originally introduced by Goldberg [20], it uses the concept of *dominance* presented in Section 2.6.1. Several different dominance-based ranking schemes exist, the three main ones being: (1) *dominance rank*, which returns the number of solutions that dominate the considered solution, (2)

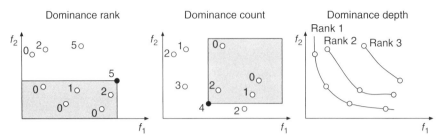

Figure 2.12. Example of dominance-based ranking techniques (from left to right): dominance rank, dominance count, and dominance depth.

dominance count is based on the number of solutions dominated by the considered solution, and (3) *dominance depth* relies on a division of the population of solutions in different dominance levels (i.e., nonoverlapping fronts), a solution being assigned the depth of the front to which it belongs. Examples of these three dominance-based ranking techniques are illustrated on a simple biobjective case in Fig. 2.12. In the dominance rank case (left-hand side), the gray cube emphasizes the five solutions that dominate the black circle solution, respectively, the four solutions that are dominated by the black circle solution in the dominance count case (middle). The right-hand side represents the three ranks obtained with the dominance depth technique.

In contrast to the previously mentioned methods, the output of this technique is a set of nondominated solutions, and not only one single solution. The objective of metaheuristics based on the Pareto dominance technique is to look for the best approximation of the front, both in terms of convergence (i.e., distance to the optimal front) and diversity (i.e., best solution spread). The accuracy of the Pareto front approximation is measured using some quality indicators that are further described in Chapter 5.

Three out of the four mobile ad hoc network problems tackled in this book are multi-objective. In Chapters 6 and 7, respectively, dealing with broadcasting protocol and energy management optimization, a Pareto dominance-based approach is used. Chapter 8 focused on topology management optimization considers a function aggregation technique.

2.7 CONCLUSION

This introductory chapter on evolutionary algorithms has provided the basic background required to understand EAs origins, concept, and functioning. Two types of EAs, panmictic and structured populations EAs, which are applied and compared on the different mobile ad hoc optimization problems in the next chapters, have been detailed.

Information has been provided on the type of optimization algorithms applied and compared to the four different mobile ad hoc optimization problems, that is, panmictic and structured populations EAs for single- and multi-objective optimization.

More precisely, multi-objective EAs using the Pareto dominance technique are used in Chapters 6 and 7 for, respectively, optimizing the performance of a broadcasting algorithm and of the adaptive enhanced distance-based broadcasting algorithm. The third problem considering the optimization of small-world properties of a vehicular network using backbone-connected devices is tackled using single-objective EAs with a function aggregation technique. Finally, the last problem focusing on the optimization of the realism of a vehicular mobility model is achieved with single-objective EAs.

REFERENCES

1. E. Alba and B. Dorronsoro. Solving the vehicle routing problem by using cellular genetic algorithms. In J. Gottlieb and G. Raidl, Ed., *Evolutionary Computation in Combinatorial Optimization*, Vol. 3004 of *Lecture Notes in Computer Science*, pp. 11–20. Springer, Berlin and Heidelberg, 2004.

2. E. Alba and B. Dorronsoro. *Cellular Genetic Algorithms*. Vol. 2 of Operations Research/Computer Science Interfaces. Springer-Verlag, Heidelberg, 2008.

3. E. Alba, B. Dorronsoro, M. Giacobini, and M. Tomassini. In Decentralized cellular evolutionary algorithms. *Handbook of Bioinspired Algorithms and Applications*, Chapter 7, pp. 103–120. CRC Press, Boca Raton, FL, 2006.

4. E. Alba and J. M. Troya. Cellular evolutionary algorithms: Evaluating the influence of ratio. In M. Schoenauer, K. Deb, G. Rudolph, X. Yao, E. Lutton, J. J. Merelo and H.-P. Schwefel, Eds., *Proceedings of the Parallel Problem Solving from Nature (PPSN VI)*, pp. 29–38. Springer-Verlag, London, 2000.

5. E. Cantú-Paz. *Efficient and Accurate Parallel Genetic Algorithms*, Vol. 1 of *Book Series on Genetic Algorithms and Evolutionary Computation*, 2nd ed. Kluwer Academic, Norwell, MA, 2000.

6. C. A. Coello Coello, G. L. Lamont, and D. A. van Veldhuizen. *Evolutionary Algorithms for Solving Multi-Objective Problems. Genetic and Evolutionary Computation*, 2nd ed. Springer, Berlin and Heidelberg, 2007.

7. N. L. Cramer. A representation for the adaptive generation of simple sequential programs. In J. J. Grefenstette, Ed., *Proceedings of an International Conference on Genetic Algorithms and Their Applications, Carnegie-Mellon University, July 24-26, 1985*, Lawrence Erlbaum Associates, Hillsdale, 1985.

8. C. Darwin. *The Origin of Species by Means of Natural Selection: Or, The Preservation of Favored Races in the Struggle for Life*. London, 1859.

9. I. Das and J. E. Dennis. A closer look at drawbacks of minimizing weighted sums of objectives for pareto set generation in multicriteria optimization problems. *Structural and Multidisciplinary Optimization*, 14(1):63–69, 1997.

10. K. Deb. *Multi-Objective Optimization Using Evolutionary Algorithms*. Wiley Interscience Series in Systems and Optimization. Wiley, Chichester, 2001.

11. B. Dorronsoro, E. Alba, G. Luque, and P. Bouvry. A self-adaptive cellular memetic algorithm for the dna fragment assembly problem. In J. Wang, Ed., *Proceedings of the IEEE Congress on Evolutionary Computation (CEC)*, pp. 2651–2658, June 2008.

12. B. Dorronsoro and P. Bouvry. Adaptive neighborhoods for cellular genetic algorithms. In *Proceedings of the IEEE International Symposium on Parallel and Distributed Processing Workshops and Phd Forum (IPDPSW)*, pp. 388–394, 2011.

13. B. Dorronsoro and P. Bouvry. Cellular genetic algorithms without additional parameters. *Journal of Supercomputing*, 63(3):816–835, 2013.

14. P. R. Ehrlich and P. H. Raven. Butterflies and plants: A study in coevolution. *Evolution*, 18(4):586–608, 1964.

15. R. Eriksson and B. Olsson. Cooperative coevolution in inventory control optimisation. In *Proceedings of the Third International Conference on Artificial Neural Networks and Genetic Algorithms*, University of East Anglia, Norwich, UK. Springer-Vienna, 1998.

16. P. C. Fishburn. Lexicographic orders, utilities and decision rules: A survey. *Management Science*, 20:1442–1471, 1974.

17. F. G. Fogel. Toward inductive inference automata. In M. Popplewell, Ed., *International Federation for Information Processing Congress (IFIP)*, pp. 395–400, 1962.

18. G. Folino, C. Pizzuti, and G. Spezzano. Parallel hybrid method for sat that couples genetic algorithms and local search. *IEEE Transactions on Evolutionary Computation*, 5(4):323–334, August 2001.

19. S. Gass and T. L. Saaty. The computational algorithm for the parametric objective function. *Naval Research Logistics Quarterly*, 2:39, 1955.

20. D. E. Goldberg. *Genetic Algorithms in Search, Optimization and Machine Learning*, 1st ed. Addison-Wesley Longman, Boston, MA, 1989.

21. Y. Y. Haimes, L. S. Lasdon, and D. A. Wismer. On a bicriterion formulation of the problems of integrated system identification and system optimization. *IEEE Transactions on Systems, Man and Cybernetics*, SMC-1(3):296–297, 1971.

22. J. H. Holland. *Adaptation in Natural and Artificial Systems: An Introductory Analysis with Applications to Biology, Control, and Artificial Intelligence*. University of Michigan Press, Ann Arbor, MI, 1975.

23. J. R. Koza. *Genetic Programming: On the Programming of Computers by Means of Natural Selection*. MIT Press, Cambridge, MA, 1992.

24. J. Paredis. Coevolutionary life-time learning. In H.-M. Voigt, W. Ebeling, I. Rechenberg, and H.-S. Schwefel, Eds., *Proceedings of the Parallel Problem Solving from Nature–PPSN IV*, pp. 72–80. Springer, Berlin, 1996.

25. M. A. Potter. The design and analysis of a computational model of cooperative coevolution. PhD thesis, George Mason University, Fairfax, Virginia, 1997.

26. M. A. Potter and K. De Jong. A cooperative coevolutionary approach to function optimization. In Y. Davidor, H.-P. Schwefel and R. Männer, Eds., *Proceedings of the Parallel Problem Solving from Nature (PPSN III)*, pp. 249–257. Springer, Berlin, 1994.

27. M. A. Potter and K. A. De Jong. The coevolution of antibodies for concept learning. In A. E. Eiben, T. Bäck, M. Schoenauer, and H.-P. Schwefel, Eds., *Proceedings of the Parallel Problem Solving from Nature (PPSN V)*, pp. 530–539. London, Springer-Verlag, 1998.

28. M. A. Potter and K. A. De Jong. Cooperative coevolution: An architecture for evolving coadapted subcomponents. *Evolutionary Computation*, 8(1): 1–29, 2000.

29. I. Rechenberg. Cybernetic solution path of an experimental problem. Technical Report. Royal Air Force Establishment, 1965.

30. F. Rothlauf. *Representations for Genetic and Evolutionary Algorithms*, Vol. 104 of *Studies in Fuzziness and Soft Computing*. Springer, Heidelberg, 2002.

31. H. P. Schwefel. *Kybernetische Evolution als Strategie der experimentellen Forschung in der Strömungstechnik*. Diplomarbeit, Technische Universität Berlin, Hermann Föttinger—Institut für Strömungstechnik, März, 1965.

32. R. Storn and K. Price. Differential evolution – a simple and efficient heuristic for global optimization over continuous spaces. *Journal of Global Optimization*, 11:341–359, 1997.

33. G. Syswerda. Uniform crossover in genetic algorithms. In J. D. Schaffer, Ed., *Proceedings of the Third International Conference on Genetic Algorithms*, pp. 2–9. Morgan Kaufmann, San Francisco, CA, 1989.

34. E. G. Talbi. *Metaheuristics: From Design to Implementation*. Wiley, Hoboken, 2009.

35. E. Triantaphyllou. *Multi-Criteria Decision Making Methods: A Comparative Study (Applied Optimization, Vol. 44)*. Springer, 2000.

36. D. Whitley and J. Kauth. GENITOR: A different genetic algorithm. In *Proceedings of the Rocky Mountain Conference on Artificial Intelligence*, pp. 118–130, 1988.

37. D. H. Wolpert and W. G. Macready. No free lunch theorems for optimization. *IEEE Transactions on Evolutionary Computation*, 1(1):67–82, 1997.

3

SURVEY ON OPTIMIZATION PROBLEMS FOR MOBILE AD HOC NETWORKS

As mentioned in Chapter 1, communication networks have highly impacted present-day society. Thirty years ago, no one could envision the incredible success and the participation of mobile phones and their successors (PDAs, tablets, smartphones, etc.) in our everyday life. To mirror this ubiquity, the next-generation networks are envisioned to provide information and communication services between any device at any time.

Technology in networking is evolving faster than information systems; tiny devices are already provided with communication capabilities. But the existing communication systems are not appropriate or efficient for such heterogeneous networks. Self-organization mechanisms able to handle heterogeneity, the dynamic nature, resource constraints, scalability, failures, and the like are needed.

It is possible to find similarities when analyzing biological systems: self-organization, recovering from failures, collaborative behavior, minimization resources, finding stability, and so forth. Most of these systems achieved this

Evolutionary Algorithms for Mobile Ad Hoc Networks, First Edition. Bernabé Dorronsoro, Patricia Ruiz, Grégoire Danoy, Yoann Pigné, and Pascal Bouvry.
© 2014 John Wiley & Sons, Inc. Published 2014 by John Wiley & Sons, Inc.

behavior after evolving for millions years. Thus, many researchers are developing algorithms inspired by nature in order to efficiently tackle different problems. For example, they have been widely applied for network design and optimization in the literature [28].

In this chapter, we give an overview of the most relevant works that apply metaheuristics to address some of the problems we can find in ad hoc networks. We focus on the most relevant challenges, which are listed next.

Energy Efficiency. Nodes depend on battery life, therefore, reducing the energy consumption will increase the network lifetime. There are different approaches for reducing the energy consumption of a node: decreasing the transmission power, turning devices into sleep mode, reducing the number of communications or the number of forwarded messages, and the like.

Broadcast. A node sends a message to all nodes in the network. As there is no central structure, guaranteeing full coverage is not possible. Therefore, the main goal is to cover as many nodes as possible relying on multihop forwarding. The problem is that, if all nodes resend all received packets, it leads to the congestion of the network. That is known as the *broadcast storm problem* [82]. Additionally, in terms of the energy consumption, it is not efficient that a node resends all the received messages, as one of the main consuming operation is communication.

Routing. A node sends a packet to a destination. As there is no central station or infrastructure in the network, if the destination is not within the source range, intermediate nodes must act as routers and forward the packet. The length of the route found directly impacts on energy consumption and network resources, as well as the maintenance of the routes, route failures, and so forth.

Network Connectivity. Devices do move, and the channel varies in time, so that distant nodes might not be always connected. Maintaining connectivity within the whole network so that there is always a path between any two nodes provides more robustness and resilience to failures.

Clustering. Nodes are grouped into clusters, and each cluster has a cluster head responsible for the main operations. This approach reduces the network overhead, increasing the system capacity.

Node Deployment. In sensor network it is important to minimize the number of nodes needed for covering a concrete area and maximizing at the same time the network lifetime. An efficient node allocation is crucial for the efficiency of the network.

Selfish Behavior. Due to the lack of infrastructure, multihop communication is needed for the proper operation of the network. However, nodes are battery limited, and acting as routers will only decrease their capabilities with no reward. Selfish nodes are not motivated to collaborate in the forwarding process and drop all packets that are not intended for themselves.

Security. Malicious nodes can perturb the network by compromising its integrity or the availability of a resource. Intrusion detection systems are used to prevent those attacks.

Quality of Service. Ad hoc networks usually face adverse conditions such as fading, interferences, packet losses, abrupt bandwidth changes, and so forth. Therefore, providing Quality of Service (QoS) is challenging.

3.1   TAXONOMY OF THE OPTIMIZATION PROCESS

This chapter presents some of the most relevant works that use nature-inspired algorithms for solving some of the above-mentioned challenges in ad hoc networking. We classify them in terms of execution mode, information needed, and platform executing the algorithm.

3.1.1   Online and Offline Techniques

The literature reveals two different approaches when applying metaheuristics for solving problems in mobile ad hoc networks: online and offline techniques. As explained in [12, 119], the main difference between them lies on the moment when the optimization algorithm is applied.

Online metaheuristics approaches are used for correcting behaviors or making decisions during runtime, trying to find the best next step. They can be implemented either in the (constrained) network node(s) or in a central unit, but usually require intensive computation. However, the second option contradicts ad hoc networks essence.

Offline metaheuristics approaches are executed beforehand. The main goal is to find the best possible configuration, settings, decisions, and the like that will be later used during runtime. The algorithm stops after performing a pre-defined number of generations or when the optimal value is found (in case it is known). The quality of the solutions found is usually tested by simulation, thus, it directly depends on the modeling of the system. However, there is a compromise between the accuracy of the model and the optimization time. These offline metaheuristic approaches are useful when the system does not need to adapt to changes during runtime.

3.1.2 Using Global or Local Knowledge

Considering the information used during the optimization process, it is possible to differentiate between algorithms that use information about the whole network or just local information gathered in the vicinity of the nodes.

It is said that algorithms use *global knowledge* when information on the complete network is required. Depending on the targeted problem, this approach can be irrelevant as it is not realistic for nodes to access information about all devices in a network that is spontaneously created without any infrastructure.

However, when the optimization algorithm only requires local information, or information that can be gathered by itself, it is said to use *local knowledge*. This local information does not only concern the node itself but also information from neighboring nodes obtained by exchanging beacons, messages, or just by eavesdropping the channel.

It is not conceivable to design an online optimization process running on a decentralized MANET where global knowledge such as the position of nodes is required. However, offline optimization is useful, for instance, in the case of node placement optimization for the deployment of a static sensor network, as it is straightforward to use the knowledge of the whole area in the optimization process. Therefore, the use of global knowledge does not seem appropriate for online techniques in the optimization of mobile ad hoc networks, while it might make sense for offline algorithms.

3.1.3 Centralized and Decentralized Systems

A *centralized system* is considered when a central unit optimizes the whole system using global knowledge, or the different network nodes optimize locally a part of the problem but send the information to the central unit (or decision maker), which will decide in terms of the information gathered from all the nodes. It requires significant coordination between the components as well as communication overhead and delays. Additionally, the whole system depends on the central unit for the proper functioning, therefore, a failure on this unit implies the failure of the complete system.

On the contrary, when each node locally executes an optimization algorithm and, according to the results obtained, the node modifies its own behavior, it is called a *decentralized system*.

In MANETs, the use of centralized systems at runtime is not realistic as the existence of the central unit is contrary to the essence of ad hoc networks.

3.2 STATE OF THE ART

Next, we are reviewing the literature in bio-inspired algorithms applied to solve problems in ad hoc networks. We briefly present some of the most relevant works and classify them according to the taxonomy presented above, and also in terms of the challenges tackled and the techniques used for solving them.

3.2.1 Topology Management

Considering that nodes are able to change their transmission power, topology control is about deciding the transmission range that provides a desired property to the network (e.g., connectivity). The main goals of topology control are to reduce nodes' energy consumption and increase the capacity and extend the lifetime of the network. For a more detailed explanation, please refer to [94]. Different techniques have been applied for achieving those objectives, like turning devices into sleep mode, power allocation, or node deployment. Next, we are reviewing some works addressing these challenges.

3.2.1.1 Sleep Mode. In sensor networks, in order to save energy and extend the lifetime of nodes, and thus the network lifetime, there are some approaches that consider turning off some nodes for a period of time. There always exist two different sets of nodes, a set that is active and gathering the data and a set of sleeping nodes. Efficient synchronization and scheduling is needed when using this technique.

Finding the minimal set of active sensors that covers a targeted area while maintaining the rest in sleeping mode is the NP-complete problem addressed in [56]. The multi-objective genetic algorithm Non-dominated Sorting Genetic Algorithm-II (NSGA-II) is used in order to maximize the coverage (the targeted area) and minimize the cost, that is, the number of nodes. They use an offline and centralized approach that requires global knowledge.

Ferentinos and Tsiligiridis [30, 31] authors used a genetic and a memetic algorithm, respectively, for optimizing seven different objectives in an aggregative function. The main goal is the minimization of some energy-related parameters and the maximization of sensing points' uniformity, subject to some connectivity constraints and the spatial density requirement.

Decisions about the set of active nodes, the role of cluster heads or the transmission range of the active nodes are given by the algorithms. They are implemented repeatedly over different network configurations, providing then a dynamic sequence of operation modes. They run offline in a centralized way using global knowledge.

An ant colony optimization-based method, mc-ACO, is used in [120] for prolonging the network lifetime by dividing sensors in two layers. The first layer is the activated set of nodes, and the second layer is the successor set, which are in sleep mode until an active sensor runs out of battery. A genetic algorithm is proposed in [50] for the same problem, which focuses on finding the maximal number of disjoint cover sets. Both algorithms were compared in [120] and the results show which mc-ACO performs better for the studied cases. The two approaches are centralized and offline using global knowledge.

In [40], a routing protocol based on ant colonies for MANETs is presented. One of the main characteristics is that nodes turn to sleep mode when the value of the pheromone reaches a predefined threshold. When the node is in sleep mode, it only processes packets that are destined to it. This routing protocol based on ants runs online, is decentralized, and uses only local knowledge.

3.2.1.2 *Power Allocation.* The most straightforward approach for reducing the energy consumption of a device is reducing the transmission power. However, this cannot be done without considering the impact on other aspects of the network, such as its connectivity.

It is usually assumed that networks are homogeneous, where all nodes use the same transmission range, the same energy consumption, and the same battery life. But it could also be possible to consider that nodes can adjust their transmission power according to their neighbor's location, so that the network is still connected but the node can save energy.

We will next present some works that try to find the best possible assignments for the transmission ranges using bioinspired algorithms.

An improved adaptive particle swarm optimization (PSO) algorithm for solving the joint opportunistic power and rate allocation in static wireless ad hoc networks, in which all links share the same frequency band, is proposed in [42]. The goal is to find a configuration that maximizes the sum of all source utilities while minimizing the total power consumption for all links. It is an offline and centralized algorithm that uses global knowledge.

Both linear programming and genetic algorithms are used in [114] to decide the transmission range of the nodes in static networks, so that the overall energy consumption is optimized, subject to some QoS constraints. It is an offline and centralized technique that uses global knowledge.

A reversed engineered approach is used in [85]. First, near-optimal networks using a GA are created, local features of those networks are discovered, and then local adaptive rules are obtained. Once all the nodes have been deployed and have selected an operating radius based on the heuristic, the local rules are applied to the nodes so that a heterogeneous network characterized by low short paths and congestion is obtained. The GA is executed offline, centralized, and has global knowledge (nodes are assumed to know their global position).

Differential evolution and PSO algorithms are used in [121, 122], respectively, to optimize the power allocation for parallel interference cancellation in wireless code division multiple-access (CDMA) system. CDMA is not specific to ad hoc networks, but it is an access channel method suitable for them. The maximum number of users can be increased using the technique proposed instead of the uniform power distribution. It is an offline and centralized optimization that uses global knowledge.

A memetic algorithm is used in [64] for tackling the minimum energy network connectivity problem in wireless sensor networks. It uses a genetic algorithm with a problem-specific light-weighted local search that looks for strongly connected networks (they propose a repair method to apply to nonstrongly connected networks), with the minimum overall energy consumption. The targeted networks are static and node positions are known. It runs offline on the sink of the sensor network, which distributes the solution to the sensors using either multihop broadcasting or direct communicating broadcasting. Therefore, it is an offline and centralized approach that uses global knowledge.

Some authors are considering the joint problem of node location and transmission range assignment at the same time. A multi-objective evolutionary algorithm based on decomposition (MOEA/D) is proposed in [65] to solve the deployment and power assignment problem in static WSN by maximizing the coverage and lifetime of the network. They propose problem-specific evolutionary operators that adapt to the requirements of the specific subproblems into which the original problem is decomposed. It first obtains the Pareto front and Pareto set and then choose the best network topology depending on the scenario. The same algorithm is applied to the k-connected deployment and power assignment problem in [63] for optimizing the network coverage and lifetime, while maintaining a connectivity constraint in small-scale dense WSN. A hybridization of the same MOEA/D with a problem-specific local search is presented in [62]. All works propose centralized and offline approaches that use global knowledge.

Nowadays, most devices have more than one communication interface, therefore, using a combination of the available interfaces for extending the connectivity of the network has been already addressed in the literature. In [21, 26], the authors focus on the network connectivity and propose the use of bypass links through hybrid networks to optimize it. Different GAs (coevolutionary, cellular, panmictic) were used to find the most appropriate devices to connect in order to maximize connectivity (high clustering coefficient and low characteristic path length) and to minimize the number of bypass links used (aggregated function). Later, in [27], the same concept was used for vehicular ad hoc networks. Some nodes were selected for connecting to a distant device using other kinds of technology. All the approaches are centralized and offline using global knowledge.

3.2.1.3 Node Deployment.

One of the first steps in the design of wireless sensor networks is to arrange the location of nodes to maximize the coverage of a targeted area. An efficient deployment of sensor nodes is crucial for covering the targeted area while at the same time maintaining the connectivity, reducing the communication cost, and improving the resource management for extending the network lifetime.

A genetic algorithm is presented in [43] for the topological design of ad hoc networks with static and mobile nodes for collaborative transport applications. ns-2 is used as fitness function. They try to find the best node's position and speed to maximize the communication distances. The optimization process is centralized, offline, and requires global knowledge.

In many sensor networks, nodes can be differentiated into sensors and actuators. The latter should collect and process the data from the sensors nodes, among other functionalities. In [67], a genetic algorithm is used to find the location and the minimum number of actors that cover all the sensors. This approach is centralized and offline, using global knowledge.

A new multi-objective optimization algorithm MOEA/DFD for node deployment in wireless sensor networks is presented in [96]. It looks for the optimal arrangement that maximizes the area of coverage and the network lifetime, minimizes the energy consumption, and the number of deployed sensor nodes while maintaining connectivity between each sensor and the sink node for proper data transmission. It introduces the concept of fuzzy Pareto dominance for comparing solutions. It is compared to a wide number of other state-of-the-art algorithms, outperforming all of them. It is an offline and centralized approach that uses global knowledge.

A multi-objective PSO is presented in [83] that tries to optimize both coverage and lifetime of the network, while considering connectivity as a constraint. The algorithm outperforms NSGA-II in terms of the three considered metrics: (1) the size of dominance space, (2) the set coverage metric, and (3) the nonuniformity of the Pareto front. Additionally, a fuzzy-based mechanism is used to find out the best compromised solutions. Another PSO for node deployment in sensor networks is presented in [7]. Both approaches are centralized, offline, and use global knowledge.

We should also consider the possibility of an autonomous distribution of the nodes of the targeted area when nodes are mobile. In [74], the problem of the optimal sensor deployment in WSN is addressed with a glowworm swarm optimization algorithm. The goal is to enhance the global coverage in a self-organized way (sensors are able to move). Nodes emit luciferin and its intensity depends on the distance to its neighboring nodes. Sensors are attacked and move to neighbors with higher intensity. This method was proposed for unknown deployment environment, and/or dynamically changing ones. The bioinspired distributed algorithm is run online. It needs global knowledge as nodes calculate the distance with neighbors.

A distributed and scalable genetic algorithm that also uses traditional and evolutionary game theory for self-spreading autonomous nodes uniformly over a dynamic area is proposed in [70]. Initially, nodes are placed in a small section simulating a common entry, and the goal is to completely cover the targeted area with a uniform node distribution. Once the location of nodes conform a stable topology, there is no incentive to change the location in the future. It is a decentralized approach that runs online, using local knowledge.

Different GAs are studied and compared to hill climbing and random walk in order to obtain a uniform distribution of nodes over a geographical area in [107]. Each node contains a mobile agent running a GA, which decides the next direction and speed of the node. It is an online and distributed approach that uses local knowledge.

The literature reveals that PSO algorithms have been extensively used in wireless sensor networks for determining the position of the minimum number of nodes that provides the coverage, connectivity, and energy desired [68]. A couple of the works mentioned in [68] also consider the mobility of the sensors. In both cases [73, 110], the optimization criterion is to maximize the coverage using a centralized approach with global knowledge. Li et al. [73] consider a PSO and borrow the crossover and mutation operator from a GA, while [110] combines a coevolutionary algorithm with the PSO.

Dengiz et al. [24] use a PSO algorithm for connectivity management in MANETs by defining some agents that move around to improve the network. They propose to optimize the movements and locations of these agents. The connectivity is measured using a maximum flow formulation. It is a centralized and online approach that requires global knowledge.

3.2.2 Broadcasting Algorithms

Broadcast is a communication protocol that consist of sending one message to all other nodes composing the network. It is one of the most important low-level operation as many other applications and even other protocols rely on this service. In mobile ad hoc networks, guaranteeing full coverage is not possible due to the network partitions, collisions, mobility, varying channel, and so forth. Additionally, as mentioned in the introduction of the chapter, it is associated with the broadcast storm problem [82], thus, many works are focusing on efficiently addressing this problem.

In [37], an ant colony algorithm (ACO) was used to minimize the total energy consumption and the lifetime of a protocol for energy efficient Broadcasting in wireless sensor networks based on Ant colony system Optimization Algorithm (BAOA). Ge et al. [37] consider a stationary multihop wireless network where the location of every node is known so that each sensor is able to estimate the distance to any node. This distance is the weight of the corresponding edge. The path of each ant is stored in a tabu list, and the pheromone on every path is updated in terms of the number of ants that traversed it. The goal is to find a path where source and destination are the same node and that passes through all other nodes in the network. It is an online and decentralized approach that uses global knowledge.

The minimum energy broadcast (MEB) is a NP-hard problem [14]. It is defined as finding the tree rooted at the source node that minimizes the total energy used to cover all nodes in the network. Different optimization techniques have been applied to solve this problem in static wireless ad hoc networks. PSO [49], GAs [113], Ant Colony Optimization (ACO) [45, 46], evolutionary local search [111], Iterated Local Search (ILS) [58], or hybrid GAs [100] are some examples. In all cases, the approaches are centralized, offline, and use global knowledge.

In [2], the authors use the Elitist Simulated Binary Evolutionary Algorithm (ESBEA), a multi-objective genetic algorithm that applies binary mechanisms to real numbers. It optimizes the performance of a probabilistic broadcast strategy for every node according to their local network density for an efficient broadcast in vehicular ad hoc networks. Four objectives are defined, focusing on the minimization of the channel utilization and the broadcasting time. The ns-2 simulator is used to evaluate the fitness function. Abdou et al. [2] do not provide enough details of the simulation procedure, thus, there is no information about working with local or global knowledge, but the approach is centralized and offline.

GrAnt, a greedy ACO (ACO with a greedy transition rule) is proposed in [108] for finding the most promising forwarders from a node's social connectivity in delay-tolerant networks. The algorithm calculates the degree centrality, the betweenness utility, and the social proximity using global knowledge (the total number of nodes in the network) for characterizing the connectivity of nodes. It outperforms two state-of-the-art protocols: PROPHET and Epidemic in the studied scenarios. It is an online and decentralized approach that uses global knowledge.

Another NP-hard problem it is possible to find in the literature is the minimum power symmetric connectivity. It is defined as finding a spanning tree that minimizes the energy used to connect all nodes of the wireless network using bidirectional links. Wolf et al. [112] proposed an iterated local search that outperforms the state of the art. A genetic algorithm is used in [113] for finding the minimum power broadcast problem in wireless ad hoc networks. It outperforms the well-known Broadcast Incremental Power (BIP) algorithm. These two approaches are also centralized, offline, and use global knowledge.

3.2.3   Routing Protocols

In ad hoc networks, a packet that is sent from a source node to an intended destination that is not in range must be relayed by intermediary nodes to be delivered. This is known as multihop communication. Routing algorithms are in charge of finding a reliable route between any source and destination. The lack of central infrastructure, the changing topology, the limited resources, and the decentralized nature of ad hoc networks make routing a challenging service.

There are mainly two different approaches in routing algorithms: (1) proactive and (2) reactive. The former approach periodically exchanges topology information, thus maintaining routing tables that are available immediately. The drawback of this approach is the cost of maintaining such routing tables, specially if the topology is highly changeable. The reactive strategy only establishes a route when it is needed. Some hybrid approaches have also been proposed with characteristics from both reactive and proactive strategies. A survey on routing algorithms can be found in [13].

As it is a challenging problem in ad hoc networking, the literature reveals many works trying to efficiently route a packet to the destination by means of bioinspired algorithms. There is a big community proposing routing protocols based on ant colony optimization algorithms. The reason is that it can be executed online with local knowledge, making it directly applicable to real ad hoc networks. There are different surveys on ant-based routing algorithms; some of them can be found in [54, 57, 86, 99, 101]. An extensive survey for swarm intelligence-based routing protocols in sensor networks is presented in [92].

Next, we briefly mention some of the most relevant routing protocols in the literature that are based on ants. Ant-AODV is proposed in [79]. It combines AODV with a distributed topology discovery mechanism based on ants, providing low end-to-end delay. The Ad hoc Network Routing Based on Ants (ANRBA) is another ant-based algorithm that selects the routing paths based on the node status and the network link [33]. It is shown to outperform AODV in MANETs. The Ant Routing Algorithm for Mobile Ad-hoc networks (ARAMA) [53] is also an ACO for MANETs that pursues fare resource usage across the network. FACO [38] presents a fuzzy ACO that uses fuzzy logic to take decisions according to several considered routing parameters. A routing algorithm, called Distributed Ant Routing (DAR) for critical connectivity based in ants in presented in [87]. DAR outperforms AODV in terms of signaling load and convergence time. Two novel routing algorithms for data networks with dynamic topology based on ants are proposed in [103]. Robust routing is achieved in [32] using routing history. A distributed and autonomic ant-based algorithm for efficient routing to maximize the WSN lifetime is proposed in [22]. It uses information on battery life to update routing tables. Yet other ant-based routing algorithms are the self-organised Emergent Ad hoc Routing Algorithm (EARA) [76], Mobile Ants Based Routing (MABR) [44], and Adaptive swarm-based distributed routing (Adaptive-SDR) [59].

HOPNET is presented in [109], a hybrid routing algorithm for MANETs based on ACO and zone routing framework of bordercasting (ZRP). It is compared versus AODV and AdHocNet (not based on zone routing framework), showing a better performance both for low and high mobility and a remarkably higher scalability. AntHocNet is presented in [15], a hybrid ACO-based routing algorithm for MANETs that combines proactive and reactive behavior. The hybridization of dynamic MANET on-demand (DYMO) protocol with ACO to design MAR-DYMO (mobility-aware ant colony optimization routing DYMO) as a routing protocol for Vehicular Ad Hoc Networks (VANETs) is proposed in [19]. It was validated against other protocols (AODV and DYMO) on an idealistic urban scenario. A combination of ACO and zone-based hierarchical link state (ZBHLS) protocol is proposed in [4].

There are some works dealing with swarm intelligence based on bees. For instance, BeeSensor and BeeAdHoc [29, 93] are bee-inspired power-aware routing protocols that outperform other state-of-the-art routing protocols. The Nature Inspired Scalable Routing (NISR) protocol [39] is a scalable routing protocol combining both ant and bee intelligence. Bees are in charge of finding new routes to the destination and their quality, while ants are in charge of updating the pheromone path. They are all online approaches that use local knowledge.

In the literature, we can find other metaheuristics for the routing problem in ad hoc networks. All these approaches are centralized and offline techniques that use global knowledge for optimizing the protocol. A genetic algorithm is proposed in [9] for routing in MANETs with different QoS considerations (delay time, transmission success rate, and communication cost). They consider a multi-objective problem that is solved using the multidivision group model that evolves solutions in the domains of the different objectives separately. There are some limitations on the network changes: They can only occur after some period of stability.

Another GA is used in ad hoc underwater acoustic networks in [102]. It maximizes the network lifetime. Each node sends a table to the master node (sink) with the ID and the required power level of every neighbor. The master node gives all this information to the GA, which computes the optimal routes. The final optimized routing tree is sent to the nodes.

In [118], both NSGA-II and MODE (multi-objective differential evolution) algorithms are applied for finding optimal routes in fully connected ad hoc networks. Yetgin et al. [118] focus on minimizing two objectives: energy consumed and end-to-end delay. It is assumed global knowledge so that the source node can evaluate the cost of each potential route to the destination. Results showed that MODE finds solutions closer to the true Pareto front than NSGA-II and also converges faster.

Different approaches of genetic algorithms are studied in [115] for finding the shortest path in mobile ad hoc networks. Several immigrants and/or memory schemes are integrated into the GAs. It adds individuals to an already evolved population and memory schemes to reuse stored useful information from previous generations (best individuals in this case). In this work, two approaches are tackled: (1) the elite from the previous generation is used for creating the immigrants, and (2) apart from the elite, additional random individuals are created and introduced in the population. Both immigrant and memory schemes enhance the performance of GAs for finding the shortest path in MANETs.

3.2.3.1 Multipath Routing. Due to the mobility of the nodes and the variability of the quality of the shared medium, the path obtained by routing algorithms between a source and a destination can usually fail. Multipath routing consists in finding several routes from source to destination, so that the routing service is more robust, providing reliability of data transmission, load balance (congested nodes), energy conservation (for nodes that are routing most of the packets), QoS, and so forth. For a more detailed explanation, please refer to [81].

Next, we collect some of the most relevant works focusing on multipath routing in ad hoc networks.

Similarly to the previously mentioned routing algorithms, many works use ant-colony-inspired algorithms to find multiple paths between a source and a destination. They are all online, decentralized, and using local knowledge. A multipath dynamic source routing algorithm (MP-DSR) is hybridized in [5] with ACO for better performance. An efficient energy aware multi-path routing protocol based on ant colony optimization is presented in [80]. The authors validate their protocol versus Energy-Aware Ant-Based Routing (EAAR) AODV, AntHocNet, and Minimum-Maximum Battery Cost Routing (MMBCR). A Probabilistic Emergent Routing Algorithm (PERA) based on ACO that finds several paths that are used as backup of the best ones is presented in [8]. Another ant-based routing protocol, Ant-Colony-Based Routing Algorithm (ARA) is proposed in [41]. It is a reactive protocol that broadcasts ants on demand, thus reducing the overhead. Its performance is compared to AODV and DSR. Liu and Feng [75] proposed Ant Based Multi-cast Routing (AMR), an on-demand routing protocol that combines swarm intelligence and node-disjoint multipath routing for achieving robustness. It is compared to DSR and Ant-based Distributed Routing Algorithm (ADRA), outperforming both of them in terms of the packet delivery ratio, end-to-end delay, and routing load.

A novel swarm intelligence algorithm, based on the behavior of termites, is proposed in [88] for dynamic routing in MANETs, to minimize the load of nodes using alternative paths. An optimized version of the protocol was recently proposed and validated versus AODV in [48]. As well as ant colony optimization algorithms, Opt-Termite is also an online and decentralized technique that uses local knowledge.

Genetic algorithms have also been applied to the multipath routing problem. In [69], a new hybrid protocol, Genetic Zone Routing Protocol (GZRP) that uses both proactive and reactive behavior for finding routes is presented. It is an extension of the zone routing protocol (ZRP), and it uses a genetic algorithm for providing a set of alternative routes to the destination. This approach is centralized, offline, and requires global knowledge.

3.2.3.2 Multicast Routing.

It is an important network service, consisting of the optimal delivery of information from a source node to a number of destinations or a group. In [10], a complete review of the state of the art is given, as well as a taxonomy of the different kinds of protocols. It is an NP-complete problem, and its scalability becomes a very important issue when increasing the network size.

The use of a GA to solve the dynamic QoS multicast problem in MANETs is proposed in [16]. The GA quickly adapts to the tracked topology changes and adapts the solutions accordingly, producing high-quality ones. Another GA for multicast routing was presented in [18]. Both are centralized and offline approaches requiring global knowledge.

This problem has also been addressed in vehicular ad hoc networks too. Bitam and Mellouk [11] present a multicast routing protocol with QoS considerations. The protocol implements an EA (BLA–bees life algorithm) that assumes global knowledge to look for the optimal multicast tree for every node. They work on a static network and it is centralized and offline.

A decentralized multicast routing algorithm that uses local knowledge online is proposed in [51]. The protocol adapts to the topology variations and satisfying some multimedia QoS requirements using PSO in the devices. The packets priority schedule at every node is also considered and optimized with the PSO. Thus, every device executes two PSOs using local information, one for the multicast and the other one for the schedule.

Multicast routing has been extensively addressed by means of the spanning tree. All the approaches found are centralized, offline, and using global knowledge. Both [116] and [117] construct a multicast tree for dealing with multicast routing. Both use a genetic algorithm for obtaining near-optimal routes on demand. The second approach adds QoS by considering multiple constraints. Another approach that uses a GA for optimizing the spanning tree is proposed in [6]. A hybrid discrete PSO presented in [1] also looks for the multicast tree. An aggregate function is used to optimize the packet delivery ratio (PDR), network routing load (NRL), and end-to-end delay (E2ED). Another multi-objective approach was presented in [20] that guarantees some QoS.

3.2.4   Clustering Approaches

Clustering lies in arranging the network into groups, introducing some hierarchy into the network, so that some nodes have a special role (usually known as cluster heads), controlling the neighboring devices. It offers advantages such as making routing tables more stable, higher-layer protocols more scalable, extending the network lifetime, and the like. However, the way nodes are grouped or the selection of the cluster heads is not trivial. Indeed, clustering is an NP-complete problem. Next, we review some works using metaheuristics to solve this problem.

A genetic algorithm is proposed in [60] for finding an optimized clustering for energy-efficient routing in static WSN and, therefore, extend network lifetime, its stability period, its throughput (number of packets sent from cluster heads to sink nodes), and the total energy left in the network. The obtained protocol is compared to Low Energy Adaptive Clustering Hierarchy (LEACH), Stable Election Protocol (SEP), and Hierarchical Cluster-Based routing (HCR), another GA for clustering [52], clearly outperforming all of them. It is a centralized, offline approach that uses global knowledge.

Another genetic algorithm is used in [84] for finding the optimal cluster configuration in a sensor network. Additionally, a protocol for maximizing the network lifetime is presented and an upper bound is obtained. This approach runs offline in a centralized manner and uses global knowledge.

Liu et al. [77] proposed a modified version of the LEACH protocol using Chaos-PSO. Chaotic motion is included in the traditional PSO in order to avoid getting into local optima. Unlike LEACH, the proposed algorithm considers the residual energy of the nodes and the distance of the cluster head to the sink. It is an online approach that uses global knowledge. Another online approach is found in [61] that uses a reduced complexity GA for obtaining the optimal number of clusters and cluster heads in a sensor network using global knowledge.

There are some works dealing with clustering in mobile ad hoc networks. For example, [17] proposes a number of GAs for the dynamic load balanced clustering problem in MANETs, that is, to find a clustering such that the size of all clusters is balanced. They use static topologies in which some nodes appear/disappear at every change (so nodes do not move), and the frequency of topology changes is given by the GA (i.e., every 20 generations). It is a centralized and offline algorithm with global knowledge.

In [106], a GA is used to optimize the number of clusters in a mobile ad hoc network. It first uses the weighted clustering algorithm (WCA) as initial information in order to evolve to a better configuration. It is a centralized and offline technique that uses global knowledge. A similar work was later presented in [55] using a decentralized PSO. In this work, the number of nodes depending on a cluster head is restricted in order to ensure efficient access to the shared medium. Nodes are divided into groups and four nodes of each group run the PSO. These are offline techniques that make use of global knowledge.

3.2.5   Protocol Optimization

Due to the unpredictable and changing topology of mobile ad hoc networks, communication protocols usually rely on some parameters that adapt their behavior to the current circumstances. The performance of the protocol is highly sensitive to small changes in the set of those configuration parameters. Therefore, fine tuning them for optimally configuring a communication protocol is a complex and critical task. Additionally, due to the drawbacks present in MANETs there is not a single goal to be satisfied but several like network resources, QoS, energy used, and so forth.

Some researchers are using metaheuristics for finding the optimal configuration of the parameters conforming a specific protocol. Next, we consider some of the most relevant works on this topic.

A multi-objective approach to find optimal configurations of the Delayed Flooding with Cumulative Neighbourhood (DFCN) broadcasting protocol accounting for network use, coverage, and time is proposed in [3]. It uses a custom simulator (*madhoc* [47]) for evaluating the fitness function over a set of different networks. It is a centralized and offline approach that uses local knowledge. Different optimization algorithms have been applied to solve this broadcast algorithm using different hybridizations. For example, in [34] a multi-objective particle swarm optimization (MOPSO) combined with evolution strategy with the Non-dominated Sorting Genetic Algorithm-II (NSGA-II), referred to as ESN is used. In [72], a team evolutionary algorithm uses three algorithms of the state of the art for configuring the DFCN broadcast algorithm. The three algorithms that cooperate are Strength Pareto Evolutionary Algorithm (SPEA). Strength Pareto Evolutionary Algorithm 2 (SPEA2) and NSGA-II. A different approach is used in [71], where a hybrid algorithm that combines a parallel island-based scheme with a hyperheuristic approach is proposed.

Several evolutionary algorithms are used for optimizing the parameters of the Optimized Link State Routing (OLSR) protocol for vehicular ad hoc networks in [36, 104, 105]. They consider different objectives in a weighted fitness function. In both [36, 104], PSO, GA, DE, and Simulated Annealing (SA) are applied for finding the best configuration parameters, while in [105] a parallel genetic algorithm that tries to reduce the power consumption is used. All the proposed techniques are offline, centralized, and use local knowledge.

The optimal configuration of the AODV routing protocol is optimized in [35]. Different optimization algorithms are used: PSO, DE, GA, ES, and SA for finding all the configuration parameters in a specific VANET scenario in terms of the packet delivery ratio, the normalized routing load, and the average end-to-end delay of a data packet.

Finding the optimal configuration set of the Enhanced Distance Based Broadcasting Algorithm (EDB) using a multi-objective evolutionary algorithm that focuses on maximizing the coverage while reducing the network resources and the broadcast time was proposed in [90]. The quality of the solution is evaluated on different networks using ns3. In [89], an adaptive energy efficient dissemination algorithm is optimized in order to find the most scalable configuration. Both approaches are centralized and offline using local knowledge.

3.2.6   Modeling the Mobility of Nodes

Creating test beds for mobile ad hoc networks is not only costly but also very difficult. Reproducible experiments are needed for designing and testing protocols, as well as large-scale networks for studying the scalability. For small static networks, a test bed could be feasible, but not for large-scale mobile ad hoc networks.

Because of all the previously mentioned difficulties, most of the existing works in the literature rely on simulation. Therefore, the accuracy of the simulation is crucial for obtaining the real behavior of the algorithm studied. As will be mentioned in Chapter 4, the realism of the simulator chosen for the experiments is very important. There are many signal propagation models already implemented, however, modeling the mobility is still flawed.

In vehicular ad hoc networks, devices move at high speeds, on roads, one after the other. Addressing real mobility patterns has been tackled by [98]. It uses real data obtained from counters on the road (number of cars) and information about the most attractive places in Luxembourg for accomplishing a realistic traffic simulator. A genetic algorithm is used to improve the accuracy of the mobility model obtained. This technique is offline, centralized, and uses local knowledge.

Traffic routing is addressed in [66] by means of a modified ACO, where ants stop being attracted by the edges that would be most probably chosen by the other ants. Vehicles are prevented from choosing potential congested roads, thus alleviating traffic jams. It uses an online technique that requires a priori knowledge.

3.2.7   Selfish Behaviors

Most of the nodes in ad hoc networks run on batteries, therefore, acting as a router and relying messages to other nodes is battery consuming. Thus, dropping all the messages that are not intended for the node itself and saving energy is tempting. This is known as selfish behavior, and it is a real threat in ad hoc networks where cooperation between nodes for forwarding packets on behalf of others is crucial. Some researchers are solving this problem by equipping nodes with a reputation management system, where each node of the network is rated in terms of its own experience and reputation data from other nodes.

In [97], a genetic algorithm is used for finding good strategies in network cooperation. Nodes that do not cooperate are not able to use the network for their own purposes. The proposed strategy obtained with the GA enforces a high level of cooperation between nodes. It is a centralized and offline technique that uses local knowledge.

A service-based negotiation mechanism is presented in [25] to encourage node cooperation in ad hoc networks. The model uses a GA for generating the offer or counteroffer considering the opponent's offer for obtaining a quick agreement. The algorithm is run online in every negotiation agent, using local knowledge.

3.2.8 Security Issues

In mobile ad hoc networks, the lack of central authority, the changing topology, and the vulnerability of the channel makes difficult guaranteeing secured communications. The deployment of security mechanisms is needed.

In [95], genetic programming and grammatical evolution is used for evolving intrusion detection programs in MANETs. It uses evolutionary computation techniques for evolving intrusion detection rules of two types of known attacks in routing algorithms. The rules obtained will be executed online and locally. As intrusion detection systems are resource consuming, a multi-objective algorithm, SPEA2, is used for obtaining optimal trade-off between intrusion detection and power consumption. It minimizes the energy consumption while maximizes the coverage and exposure of the sensor nodes. Both are centralized and offline approaches that use global knowledge.

Localizing the intruder (malicious node) in wireless ad hoc networks is achieved using anchor points in [23]. A node detecting an intrusion triggers the localization estimation algorithm, and sends messages to calculate the distance. The anchor points use a GA for locating the intruder given the signal strength inputs. It is a centralized and online approach that uses global knowledge.

3.2.9 Other Applications

A lossy compression algorithm for sensor networks is presented in [78]. As sensors are battery limited and radio communication is, generally, power consuming, the goal is to reduce the data transmitted as much as possible. There is always a trade-off between the compression rate and the information loss. For that, the well-known multi-objective evolutionary algorithm, NSGA-II, is used to obtain a set of optimal solutions with different trade-offs among the information entropy, the complexity, and the signal-to-noise ratio (SNR). Therefore, the user can decide the most suitable combination depending on the application. It is an offline and centralized approach that uses global knowledge.

In MANETs, packet losses are not due only to congestion as it used to be in wired networks. A middleware that allows an adaptive behavior of the application layer according to the network conditions while still maintaining QoS in adverse situations is presented in [91]. It uses a genetic algorithm for finding the best values of the parameters that conform the middleware, as the best moment to trigger the adaptation process. It is a centralized approach that runs offline using global knowledge.

3.3 CONCLUSION

In this chapter, we have presented an overview of the most relevant existing literature that uses bioinspired algorithms to solve optimization problems in ad hoc networks. We classified them in terms of the who, when, and how the optimization process occurred. The *who* means whether the optimization algorithm runs in a central unit that gives a global output, that is, centralized, or in a decentralized fashion where each node locally executes an optimization algorithm.

The *when* refers to the moment the optimization algorithm is executed. It can be executed during the runtime (online), thus being able to modify the behavior of the node, or offline and a priori in order to find the best possible configuration or behavior before hands.

The *how* implies the knowledge required for an efficient optimization. If the algorithm requires global information about the network, that is, global knowledge, it only uses the information locally available at the node.

In Fig. 3.1, a classification of the works that were previously described is shown. As we can see, we could not find any work that executes the optimization algorithm offline in a decentralized manner. That is normal as there is no

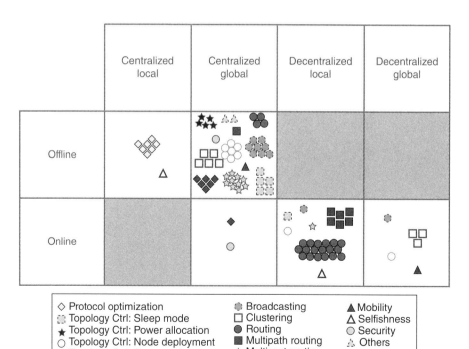

Figure 3.1. Classification of the described works.

need of decentralization if the algorithm is not run locally on every node. We did not find either any algorithm that is executed online, but using a central unit with local knowledge, as it makes no sense to use a central unit that only uses local information.

From the figure, we can see that most of the works are based on a centralized and offline approach that uses global knowledge. However, most of the works dealing with routing or multipath routing are using a decentralized and online technique that uses local knowledge (generally, ACO). Regarding the optimization of protocols, they all follow the same approach by optimizing offline in a central structure but using local knowledge, as usually the network is not known, and indeed, the topology is changing.

REFERENCES

1. R. F. Abdel-Kader. Hybrid discrete PSO with GA operators for efficient QoS-multicast routing. *Ain Shams Engineering Journal*, 2(1):21–31, 2011.

2. W. Abdou, A. Henriet, C. Bloch, D. Dhoutaut, D. Charlet, and F. Spies. Using an evolutionary algorithm to optimize the broadcasting methods in mobile ad hoc networks. *Journal of Network and Computer Applications*, 34(6):1794–1804, November 2011.

3. E. Alba, B. Dorronsoro, F. Luna, A. J. Nebro, P. Bouvry, and L. Hogie. A cellular multi-objective genetic algorithm for optimal broadcasting strategy in metropolitan MANETs. *Computer Communications*, 30(4):685–697, 2007.

4. S. Asadinia, M. K. Rafsanjani, and A. B. Saeid. A novel routing algorithm based-on ant colony in mobile ad hoc networks. In *Proceedings of the 3rd IEEE International Conference on Ubi-media Computing (U-Media)*, pp. 77–82, 2010.

5. E. K. Asl, M. Damanafshan, M. Abbaspour, M. Noorhosseini, and K. Shekoufandeh. EMP-DSR: An enhanced multi-path dynamic source routing algorithm for MANETs based on ant colony optimization. In *Proceedings of the Third Asia International Conference on Modelling Simulation (AMS)*, pp. 692–697, 2009.

6. N. M. Asraf, R. N. Ainon, and P. K. Keong. QoS parameter optimization using multi-objective genetic algorithm in MANETs. In *Proceedings of the Fourth Asia International Conference on Mathematical/Analytical Modelling and Computer Simulation (AMS)*, pp. 138–143, 2010.

7. N. A. A. Aziz, A. W. Mohemmed, and M. Zhang. Particle swarm optimization for coverage maximization and energy conservation in wireless sensor networks. In *Applications of Evolutionary Computation*, Vol. 6025 of *Lecture Notes in Computer Science*, pp. 51–60. Springer, Heidelberg, 2010.

8. J. S. Baras and H. Mehta. A probabilistic emergent routing algorithm for mobile ad hoc networks. In *Proceedings of the International Symposium on Modeling and Optimization in Mobile AdHoc and Wireless Networks (WiOpt)*, pp. 1–10, 2003.

9. A. Barolli, E. Spaho, F. Xhafa, L. Barolli, and M. Takizawa. Application of GA and multi-objective optimization for QoS routing in ad-hoc networks. In *Proceedings of the 14th International Conference on Network-Based Information Systems (NBiS)*, pp. 50–59, 2011.

10. R. C. Biradar and S. S. Manvi. Review of multicast routing mechanisms in mobile ad hoc networks. *Journal of Network and Computer Applications*, 35(1):221–239, 2012.

11. S. Bitam and A. Mellouk. Bee life-based multi constraints multicast routing optimization for vehicular ad hoc networks. *Journal of Network and Computer Applications*, 36(3):981–991, 2013.

12. P. P. Bonissone, R. Subbu, N. Eklund, and T. R. Kiehl. Evolutionary algorithms + domain knowledge = real-world evolutionary computation. *IEEE Transactions on Evolutionary Computation*, 10(3):256–280, 2006.

13. A. Boukerche, B. Turgut, N. Aydin, M. Z. Ahmad, L. Bölöni, and D. Turgut. Routing protocols in ad hoc networks: A survey. *Computer Networks*, 55(13):3032–3080, 2011.

14. M. Cagalj, J. P. Hubaux, and C. Enz. Minimum-energy broadcast in all-wireless networks: NP-hardness and distribution issues. In *Proceedings of the 8th Annual International Conference on Mobile Computing and Networking (MobiCom)*, pp. 172–182. ACM, New York, 2002.

15. G. Di Caro, F. Ducatelle, and L. M. Gambardella. AntHocNet: An adaptive nature-inspired algorithm for routing in mobile ad hoc networks. *European Transactions on Telecommunications*, 16:443–455, 2005.

16. H. Cheng and S. Yang. Genetic algorithms with immigrants schemes for dynamic multicast problems in mobile ad hoc networks. *Engineering Applications of Artificial Intelligence*, 23(5):806–819, 2010.

17. H. Cheng, S. Yang, and J. Cao. Dynamic genetic algorithms for the dynamic load balanced clustering problem in mobile ad hoc networks. *Expert Systems with Applications*, 40(4):1381–1392, 2013.

18. T.-C. Chiang, C.-H. Liu, and Y.-M. Huang. A near-optimal multicast scheme for mobile ad hoc networks using a hybrid genetic algorithm. *Expert Systems with Applications*, 33(3):734–742, 2007.

19. S. L. O. B. Correia, J. Celestino, and O. Cherkaoui. Mobility-aware ant colony optimization routing for vehicular ad hoc networks. In *Proceedings of the IEEE Wireless Communications and Networking Conference (WCNC)*, pp. 1125–1130. IEEE, 2011.

20. X. Cui, C. Lin, and Y. Wei. A multiobjective model for QoS multicast routing based on genetic algorithm. In *Proceedings of the International Conference on Computer Networks and Mobile Computing (ICCNMC)*, pp. 49–53, 2003.

21. G. Danoy, P. Bouvry, and L. Hogie. Coevolutionary genetic algorithms for ad hoc injection networks design optimization. In *Proceedings of the IEEE Congress on Evolutionary Computation (CEC)*, pp. 4273–4280. IEEE, 2007.

22. M. F. De Castro, L. B. Ribeiro, and C. H. S. Oliveira. An autonomic bio-inspired algorithm for wireless sensor network self-organization and efficient routing. *Journal of Network and Computer Applications*, 35(6):2003–2015, November 2012.

23. C. J. Debono and E. Sammut. Location estimation of an intruder in wireless ad hoc networks. In *Proceedings of the 14th IEEE Mediterranean Electrotechnical Conference (MELECON)*, pp. 158–162. IEEE, 2008.

24. O. Dengiz, A. Konak, and A. E. Smith. Connectivity management in mobile ad hoc networks using particle swarm optimization. *Ad Hoc Networks*, 9(7): 1312–1326, 2011.

25. Z. Dongmei, Z. Qu, Y. Yang, and X. Feng. A service negotiation mechanism in mobile ad hoc network. In *Proceedings of the 7th International Conference on Wireless Communications, Networking and Mobile Computing (WiCOM)*, pp. 1–4. IEEE, 2011.

26. B. Dorronsoro, G. Danoy, P. Bouvry, and E. Alba. Evaluation of different optimization techniques in the design of ad hoc injection networks. In *Proceedings of the International Conference High Performance Computing & Simulation (HPCS), in Conjunction with The 22nd European Conference on Modeling and Simulation (ECMS)*, pp. 290–296, 2008.

27. B. Dorronsoro, P. Ruiz, G. Danoy, P. Bouvry, and L. Tardón. Towards connectivity improvement in VANETs using bypass links. In *Proceedings of the IEEE Congress on Evolutionary Computation (CEC)*, pp. 2201–2208, 2009.

28. F. Dressler and O. B. Akan. A survey on bio-inspired networking. *Computer Networks*, 54(6):881–900, 2010.

29. M. Farooq. *Bee-Inspired Protocol Engineering: From Nature to Networks*. Natural Computing Series, Springer, Heidelberg, 2008.

30. K. P. Ferentinos and T. A. Tsiligiridis. Adaptive design optimization of wireless sensor networks using genetic algorithms. *Computer Networks*, 51(4): 1031–1051, 2007.

31. K. P. Ferentinos and T. A. Tsiligiridis. A memetic algorithm for optimal dynamic design of wireless sensor networks. *Computer Communications*, 33(2):250–258, 2010.

32. K. Fujita, A. Saito, and T. Matsui. An adaptive ant-based routing algorithm used routing history in dynamic networks. In *Proceedings of the 4th Asia-Pacific Conference on Simulated Evolution And Learning (SEAL)*, pp. 46–50, 2002.

33. S. Gai-Ping, G. Hai-Wen, W. Dezhi, and W. Jiang-Hua. A dynamic ant colony optimization algorithm for the ad hoc network routing. In *Proceedings of the Fourth International Conference on Genetic and Evolutionary Computing (ICGEC)*, pp. 358–361. IEEE Computer Society, Washington, D.C., 2010.

34. S. García, C. Luque, A. Cervantes, and I. Galván. Multiobjective algorithms hybridization to optimize broadcasting parameters in mobile ad-hoc networks. In *Proceedings of the 10th International Work-Conference on Artificial Neural Networks Part I: Bio-Inspired Systems: Computational and Ambient Intelligence*, Vol. 5517 of Lecture Notes in Computer Science, pp. 728–735, 2009.

35. J. García-Nieto and E. Alba. Automatic parameter tuning with metaheuristics of the AODV routing protocol for vehicular ad-hoc networks. In *Applications of Evolutionary Computation*, Vol. 6025 of Lecture Notes in Computer Science, pp. 21–30, 2010.

36. J. García-Nieto, J. Toutouh, and E. Alba. Automatic tuning of communication protocols for vehicular ad hoc networks using metaheuristics. *Engineering Applications of Artificial Intelligence*, 23(5):795–805, 2010.

37. F. Ge, Y. Wang, Q. Wang, and J. Kang. Energy efficient broadcasting based on ant colony system optimization algorithm in wireless sensor networks. In *Proceedings of the Third International Conference on Natural Computation (ICNC)*, Vol. 4, pp. 129–133, 2007.

38. M. M. Goswami, R. V. Dharaskar, and V. M. Thakare. Fuzzy ant colony based routing protocol for mobile ad hoc network. In *Proceedings of the International Conference on Computer Engineering and Technology (ICCET)*, Vol. 2, pp. 438–444, 2009.

39. S. J. Gudakahriz, S. Jamali, and E. Zeinali. NISR: A nature inspired scalable routing protocol for mobile ad hoc networks. *International Journal of Computer Science Engineering and Technology*, 1(4):180–184, 2011.

40. M. Günes, M. Kähmer, and I. Bouazizi. Ant-routing-algorithm (ARA) for mobile multi-hop ad-hoc networks—New features and results. In *Proceedings of the 2nd Mediterranean Workshop on Ad-Hoc Networks (Med-Hoc-Net)*, pp. 9–20, 2003.

41. M. Günes, U. Sorges, and I. Bouazizi. ARA—The ant-colony based routing algorithm for MANETs. In *Proceedings of the International Conference on Parallel Processing Workshops*, pp. 79–85, 2002.

42. S. Guo, C. Dang, and X. Liao. Joint opportunistic power and rate allocation for wireless ad hoc networks: An adaptive particle swarm optimization approach. *Journal of Network and Computer Applications*, 34(4):1353–1365, 2011.

43. D. Gutiérrez-Reina, S. L. Toral Marín, P. Johnson, and F. Barrero. An evolutionary computation approach for designing mobile ad hoc networks. *Expert Systems with Applications*, 39(8):6838–6845, 2012.

44. M. Heissenbüttel and T. Braun. Ants-based routing in large scale mobile ad hoc networks. In *Kommunikation in verteilten Systemen (KiVS)*, pp. 91–99, 2003.

45. H. Hernández and C. Blum. Ant colony optimization for multicasting in static wireless ad-hoc networks. *Swarm Intelligence*, 3:125–148, 2009.

46. H. Hernández and C. Blum. Minimum energy broadcasting in wireless sensor networks: An ant colony optimization approach for a realistic antenna model. *Applied Soft Computing*, 11(8):5684–5694, 2011.

47. L. Hogie. The madhoc simulator. Technical Report. Le Havre University, 2005.

48. P. K. G. Hoolimath, M. Kiran, and G. R. M. Reddy. Optimized termite: A bio-inspired routing algorithm for MANET's. In *Proceedings of the International Conference on Signal Processing and Communications (SPCOM)*, pp. 1–5, 2012.

49. P.-C. Hsiao, T.-C. Chiang, and L.-C. Fu. Particle swarm optimization for the minimum energy broadcast problem in wireless ad-hoc networks. In *Proceedings of the IEEE Congress on Evolutionary Computation (CEC)*, pp. 1–8, 2012.

50. X.-M. Hu, J. Zhang, Y. Yu, H. S.-H. Chung, Y.-L. Li, Y.-H. Shi, and X.-N. Luo. Hybrid genetic algorithm using a forward encoding scheme for lifetime maximization of wireless sensor networks. *IEEE Transactions on Evolutionary Computation*, 14(5):766–781, 2010.

51. C.-J. Huang, Y.-T. Chuang, and K.-W. Hu. Using particle swarm optimization for QoS in ad-hoc multicast. *Engineering Applications of Artificial Intelligence*, 22(8):1188–1193, 2009.

52. S. Hussain, A. W. Matin, and O. Islam. Genetic algorithm for hierarchical wireless sensor networks. *Journal of Networks*, 2(7):87–97, 2007.

53. O. H. Hussein, T. N. Saadawi, and J. L. Myung. Probability routing algorithm for mobile ad hoc networks' resources management. *IEEE Journal on Selected Areas in Communications*, 23(12):2248–2259, 2005.

54. S. S. Iyengar, H.-C. Wu, N. Balakrishnan, and S. Y. Chang. Biologically inspired cooperative routing for wireless mobile sensor networks. *IEEE Systems Journal*, 1(1):29–37, 2007.

55. C. Ji, Y. Zhang, S. Gao, P. Yuan, and Z. Li. Particle swarm optimization for mobile ad hoc networks clustering. In *Proceedings of the IEEE International Conference on Networking, Sensing and Control*, Vol. 1, pp. 372–375, 2004.

56. J. Jia, J. Chen, G. Chang, J. Li, and Y. Jia. Coverage optimization based on improved NSGA-II in wireless sensor network. In *Proceedings of the IEEE International Conference on Integration Technology*, pp. 614–618, 2007.

57. B. Kalaavathi, S. Madhavi, S. VijayaRagavan, and K. Duraiswamy. Review of ant based routing protocols for MANET. In *Proceedings of the International Conference on Computing, Communication and Networking (ICCCN)*, pp. 1–9, 2008.

58. I. Kang and R. Poovendran. Iterated local optimization for minimum energy broadcast. In *International Symposium on Modeling and Optimization in Mobile, Ad Hoc, and Wireless Networks (WIOPT)*, pp. 332–341, 2005.

59. I. Kassabalidis, M. A. El-Sharkawi, R. J. Marks, P. Arabshahi, and A. A. Gray. Adaptive-SDR: Adaptive swarm-based distributed routing. In *Proceedings of the International Joint Conference on Neural Networks (IJCNN)*, Vol. 1, pp. 351–354. IEEE, 2002.

60. E. A. Khalil and B. A. Attea. Energy-aware evolutionary routing protocol for dynamic clustering of wireless sensor networks. *Swarm and Evolutionary Computation*, 1(4):195–203, 2011.

61. R. Khanna, L. Huaping, and C. Hsiao-Hwa. Self-organization of sensor networks using genetic algorithms. In *Proceedings of the IEEE International Conference on Communications (ICC)*, Vol. 8, pp. 3377–3382, 2006.

62. A. Konstantinidis and K. Yang. Multi-objective energy-efficient dense deployment in wireless sensor networks using a hybrid problem-specific MOEA/D. *Applied Soft Computing*, 11(6):4117–4134, 2011.

63. A. Konstantinidis and K. Yang. Multi-objective k-connected deployment and power assignment in WSNs using a problem-specific constrained evolutionary algorithm based on decomposition. *Computer Communications*, 34(1):83–98, 2011.

64. A. Konstantinidis, K. Yang, H.-H. Chen, and Q. Zhang. Energy-aware topology control for wireless sensor networks using memetic algorithms. *Computer Communications*, 30(14/15):2753–2764, 2007.

65. A. Konstantinidis, K. Yang, Q. Zhang, and D. Zeinalipour-Yazti. A multi-objective evolutionary algorithm for the deployment and power assignment problem in wireless sensor networks. *Computer Networks*, 54(6):960–976, 2010.

66. P. Kromer, J. Martinovic, M. Radecky, R. Tomis, and V. Snasel. Ant colony inspired algorithm for adaptive traffic routing. In *Proceedings of the Third World Congress on Nature and Biologically Inspired Computing (NaBIC)*, pp. 329–334. IEEE, 2011.

67. R. Kulandaivel, S. Periyanayagi, and S. Susikalac. Performance comparison of WSN & WSAN using genetic algorithm. *Procedia Engineering*, 30:107–112, 2012.

68. R. V. Kulkarni and G. K. Venayagamoorthy. Particle swarm optimization in wireless-sensor networks: A brief survey. *IEEE Transactions on Systems, Man, and Cybernetics, Part C: Applications and Reviews*, 41(2):262–267, 2011.

69. P. S. Kumar and S. Ramachandram. The performance evaluation of genetic zone routing protocol for MANETs. In *Proceedings of the IEEE Region 10 Conference (TENCON)*, pp. 1–6. IEEE, 2008.

70. J. Kusyk, C. S. Sahin, M. U. Uyar, E. Urrea, and S. Gundry. Self-organization of nodes in mobile ad hoc networks using evolutionary games and genetic algorithms. *Journal of Advanced Research*, 2:253–264, 2011.

71. C. León, G. Miranda, and C. Segura. Optimizing the configuration of a broadcast protocol through parallel cooperation of multi-objective evolutionary algorithms. In *Proceedings of the 2nd International Conference on Advanced Engineering Computing and Applications in Sciences*, pp. 135–140, 2008.

72. C. León, G. Miranda, and C. Segura. Optimizing the broadcast in MANETs using a team of evolutionary algorithms. In *Proceedings of the 6th International Conference on Large-Scale Scientific Computing*, Vol. 4818 of *Lecture Notes in Computer Science*, pp. 569–576. Springer-Verlag, Heidelberg, 2009.

73. J. Li, K. Li, and W. Zhu. Improving sensing coverage of wireless sensor networks by employing mobile robots. In *Proceedings of the IEEE International Conference on Robotics and Biomimetics (ROBIO)*, pp. 899–903, 2007.

74. W.-H. Liao, Y. Kao, and Y.-S. Li. A sensor deployment approach using glowworm swarm optimization algorithm in wireless sensor networks. *Expert Systems with Applications*, 38(10):12180–12188, 2011.

75. L. Liu and G. Feng. Swarm intelligence based node-disjoint multi-path routing protocol for mobile ad hoc networks. In *Fifth International Conference on Information, Communications and Signal Processing*, pp. 598–602, 2005.

76. Z. Liu, M. Z. Kwiatkowska, and C. Constantinou. A swarm intelligence routing algorithm for MANETs. In *Communications, Internet, and Information Technology*, pp. 484–489, 2004.

77. Z. Liu, Z. Liu, and L. Wen. A modified LEACH protocol for wireless sensor networks. In *Proceedings of the Fourth International Workshop on Advanced Computational Intelligence (IWACI)*, pp. 766–769, 2011.

78. F. Marcelloni and M. Vecchio. Enabling energy-efficient and lossy-aware data compression in wireless sensor networks by multi-objective evolutionary optimization. *Information Sciences*, 180(10):1924–1941, 2010.

79. S. Marwaha, C. K. Tham, and D. Srinivasan. Mobile agents based routing protocol for mobile ad hoc networks. In *Proceedings of the IEEE Global Telecommunications Conference (GLOBECOM)*, Vol. 1, pp. 163–167, 2002.

80. S. Misra, S. K. Dhurandher, M. S. Obaidat, P. Gupta, K. Verma, and P. Narula. An ant swarm-inspired energy-aware routing protocol for wireless ad-hoc networks. *Journal of Systems and Software*, 83(11):2188–2199, 2010.

81. S. Mueller, R. Tsang, and D. Ghosal. Multipath routing in mobile ad hoc networks: Issues and challenges. In *Performance Tools and Applications to Networked Systems*, Vol. 2965 of *Lecture Notes in Computer Science*, pp. 209–234. Springer-Verlag, Heidelberg, 2004.

82. S.-Y. Ni, Y.-C. Tseng, Y.-S. Chen, and J.-P. Sheu. The broadcast storm problem in a mobile ad hoc network. In *Proceedings of the ACM/IEEE International Conference on Mobile Computing and Networking*, pp. 151–162, 1999.

83. P. M. Pradhan and G. Panda. Connectivity constrained wireless sensor deployment using multiobjective evolutionary algorithms and fuzzy decision making. *Ad Hoc Networks*, 10(6):1134–1145, 2012.

84. M. Qin and R. Zimmermann. Studying upper bounds on sensor network lifetime by genetic clustering. In V. K. Prasanna, S. S. Iyengar, P. G. Spirakis and M. Welsh, Eds., *Distributed Computing in Sensor Systems*, Vol. 3560 of *Lecture Notes in Computer Science*, pp. 408–408. Springer, Heidelberg, 2005.

85. P. Ranganathan, A. Ranganathan, K. Berman, and A. Minai. Discovering adaptive heuristics for ad-hoc sensor networks by mining evolved optimal configurations. In *Proceedings of the IEEE Congress on Evolutionary Computation (CEC)*, pp. 3064–3070, 2006.

86. F. De Rango and A. Socievole. Meta-heuristics techniques and swarm intelligence in mobile ad hoc networks. In *Mobile Ad Hoc Networks: Applications*, pp. 245–264. InTech, 2011.

87. L. Rosati, M. Berioli, and G. Reali. On ant routing algorithms in ad hoc networks with critical connectivity. *Ad Hoc Networks*, 6(6):827–859, 2008.

88. M. Roth and S. Wicker. Termite: ad-hoc networking with stigmergy. In *Proceedings of the IEEE Global Telecommunications Conference (GLOBECOM)*, Vol. 5, pp. 2937–2941, 2003.

89. P. Ruiz, B. Dorronsoro, and P. Bouvry. Finding scalable configurations for AEDB broadcasting protocol using multi-objective evolutionary algorithms. *Cluster Computing*, 16(3): 527–544, 2013.

90. P. Ruiz, B. Dorronsoro, G. Valentini, F. Pinel, and P. Bouvry. Optimisation of the enhanced distance based broadcasting protocol for MANETs. *Journal of Supercomputing*, 62(3):1213–1240, 2012.

91. P. M. Ruiz and A. F. Gomez-Skarmeta. Using genetic algorithms to optimize the behaviour of adaptive multimedia applications in wireless and mobile scenarios. In *Proceedings of the IEEE Wireless Communications and Networking Conference (WCNC)*, Vol. 3, pp. 2064–2068, 2003.

92. M. Saleem, G. A. Di Caro, and M. Farooq. Swarm intelligence based routing protocol for wireless sensor networks: Survey and future directions. *Information Sciences*, 181(20):4597–4624, 2011.

93. M. Saleem, I. Ullah, and M. Farooq. BeeSensor: An energy-efficient and scalable routing protocol for wireless sensor networks. *Information Sciences*, 200:38–56, 2012.

94. P. Santi. *Topology Control in Wireless Ad Hoc and Sensor Networks*. Wiley, Hoboken, 2005.

95. S. Sen and J. A. Clark. Evolutionary computation techniques for intrusion detection in mobile ad hoc networks. *Computer Networks*, 55(15):3441–3457, 2011.

96. S. Sengupta, S. Das, M. D. Nasir, and B. K. Panigrahi. Multi-objective node deployment in WSNs: In search of an optimal trade-off among coverage, lifetime, energy consumption, and connectivity. *Engineering Applications of Artificial Intelligence*, 26(1):405–416, 2013.

97. M. Seredynski, P. Bouvry, and M. A. Klopotek. Evolution of strategy driven behavior in ad hoc networks using a genetic algorithm. In *Proceedings of the IEEE International Parallel and Distributed Processing Symposium (IPDPS)*, pp. 1–8, 2007.

98. M. Seredynski, G. Danoy, M. Tabatabaei, P. Bouvry, and Y. Pigné. Generation of realistic mobility for VANETs using genetic algorithms. In *Proceedings of the IEEE Congress on Evolutionary Computation (CEC)*, pp. 1–8, 2012.

99. H. Shokrani and S. Jabbehdari. A survey of ant-based routing algorithms for mobile ad-hoc networks. In *Proceedings of the International Conference on Signal Processing Systems*, pp. 323–329, 2009.

100. A. Singh and W. N. Bhukya. A hybrid genetic algorithm for the minimum energy broadcast problem in wireless ad hoc networks. *Applied Soft Computing*, 11(1):667–674, 2011.

101. G. Singh, N. Kumar, and A. Kumar Verma. Ant colony algorithms in MANETs: A review. *Journal of Network and Computer Applications*, 35(6):1964–1972, 2012.

102. E. M. Sözer, M. Stojanovic, and J. G. Proakis. Initialization and routing optimization for ad-hoc underwater acoustic networks. In *Proceedings of Opnetwork*, 2000.

103. D. Subramanian, P. Druschel, and J. Chen. Ants and reinforcement learning: A case study in routing in dynamic networks. In *Proceedings of the Fifteenth International Joint Conference on Artificial intelligence (IJCAI)*, Vol. 2, pp. 832–838. Morgan Kaufmann, 1997.

104. J. Toutouh, J. García-Nieto, and E. Alba. Intelligent OLSR routing protocol optimization for VANETs. *IEEE Transactions on Vehicular Technology*, 61(4):1884–1894, 2012.

105. J. Toutouh, S. Nesmachnow, and E. Alba. Fast energy-aware OLSR routing in VANETs by means of a parallel evolutionary algorithm. *Cluster Computing*, 16(3):435–450, 2013.

106. D. Turgut, S. K. Das, R. Elmasri, and B. Turgut. Optimizing clustering algorithm in mobile ad hoc networks using genetic algorithmic approach. In *Proceedings of the IEEE Global Telecommunications Conference (GLOBECOM)*, Vol. 1, pp. 62–66, 2002.

107. E. Urrea, C. S. Şahin, I. Hökelek, M. I. Uyar, M. Conner, G. Bertoli, and C. Pizzo. Bio-inspired topology control for knowledge sharing mobile agents. *Ad Hoc Networks*, 7(4):677–689, 2009.

108. A. C. K. Vendramin, A. Munaretto, M. R. Delgado, and A. C. Viana. GrAnt: Inferring best forwarders from complex networks' dynamics through a greedy ant colony optimization. *Computer Networks*, 56(3):997–1015, 2012.

109. J. Wang, E. Osagie, P. Thulasiraman, and R. K. Thulasiram. HOPNET: A hybrid ant colony optimization routing algorithm for mobile ad hoc network. *Ad Hoc Networks*, 7(4):690–705, 2009.

110. X. Wang, S. Wang, and J.-J. Ma. An improved co-evolutionary particle swarm optimization for wireless sensor networks with dynamic deployment. *Sensors*, 7(3):354–370, 2007.

111. S. Wolf and P. Merz. Evolutionary local search for the minimum energy broadcast problem. In *Evolutionary Computation in Combinatorial Optimization*, Vol. 4972 of *Lecture Notes in Computer Science*, pp. 61–72. Springer, Heidelberg, 2008.

112. S. Wolf and P. Merz. Iterated local search for minimum power symmetric connectivity in wireless networks. In *Evolutionary Computation in Combinatorial Optimization*, Vol. 5482 of *Lecture Notes in Computer Science*, pp. 192–203. Springer, Heidelberg, 2009.

113. X. Wu, X. Wang, and R. Liu. Solving minimum power broadcast problem in wireless ad-hoc networks using genetic algorithm. In *Proceedings of the Communication Networks and Services Research Conference (CNSR)*, pp. 203–207, IEEE Computer Society, 2008.

114. K. K. Yadu, A. Tiwari, and O. G. Kakde. Optimization based topology control for wireless ad hoc networks to meet QoS requirements. In *IEEE Symposium on Reliable Distributed Systems*, pp. 30–36, 2010.

115. S. Yang, H. Cheng, and F. Wang. Genetic algorithms with immigrants and memory schemes for dynamic shortest path routing problems in mobile ad hoc networks. *IEEE Transactions on Systems, Man, and Cybernetics, Part C: Applications and Reviews*, 40(1):52–63, 2010.

116. Y-S. Yen, Y-K. Chan, H-C. Chao, and J. H. Park. A genetic algorithm for energy-efficient based multicast routing on MANETs. *Computer Communications*, 31(4):858–869, 2008.

117. Y-S. Yen, H-C. Chao, R-S. Chang, and A. Vasilakos. Flooding-limited and multi-constrained QoS multicast routing based on the genetic algorithm for MANETs. *Mathematical and Computer Modelling*, 53(11–12):2238–2250, 2011.

118. H. Yetgin, K. T. K. Cheung, and L. Hanzo. Multi-objective routing optimization using evolutionary algorithms. In *IEEE Wireless Communications and Networking Conference (WCNC)*, pp. 3030–3034, 2012.

119. P. Zanchetta, M. Sumner, F. Cupertino, M. Marinelli, and E. Mininno. On-line and off-line control design in power electronics and drives using genetic algorithms. In *IEEE Industry Applications Conference*, Vol. 2, pp. 864–871, 2004.

120. J. Zhong and J. Zhang. Energy-efficient local wake-up scheduling in wireless sensor networks. In *Proceedings of the IEEE Congress on Evolutionary Computation (CEC)*, pp. 2280–2284, 2011.

121. K. Zielinski, P. Weitkemper, R. Laur, and K.-D. Kammeyer. Parameter study for differential evolution using a power allocation problem including interference cancellation. In *Proceedings of the IEEE Congress on Evolutionary Computation (CEC)*, pp. 1857–1864, 2006.

122. K. Zielinski, P. Weitkemper, R. Laur, and K.-D. Kammeyer. Optimization of power allocation for interference cancellation with particle swarm optimization. *IEEE Transactions on Evolutionary Computation*, 13(1):128–150, 2009.

4

MOBILE NETWORKS SIMULATION

An overview of mobile ad hoc networks was presented in Chapter 1, which classifies them as MANETs, VANETs, and sensor networks. These networks, as well as classical networks, require communication services like data routing. Yet, routing protocols designed for classical networks are revealed to be useless in infrastructure-less communication systems. Mobile ad hoc networks need dedicated algorithms taking into account different constraints such as the overhead of transmitted data [58], the quality of the communication links [37], or the geographical motion of the stations [48].

Mobile networks are, by nature, distributed over a rather large environment. They usually constitute an uncontrolled setup where devices are managed by their owners. This makes very difficult the design, validation, and optimization of protocols for such networks. Consequently, researchers need to rely on different mechanisms for evaluating, validating, and optimizing any protocols designed for these networks. The existing mechanisms are creating testbeds, or simulations.

Evolutionary Algorithms for Mobile Ad Hoc Networks, First Edition. Bernabé Dorronsoro, Patricia Ruiz, Grégoire Danoy, Yoann Pigné, and Pascal Bouvry.
© 2014 John Wiley & Sons, Inc. Published 2014 by John Wiley & Sons, Inc.

Testbeds are experimental networks that allow researchers to run experiments in real devices. However, they present many drawbacks that usually prevent researchers from using them. Among these drawbacks, we can highlight the high cost related to their creation, the difficulty of monitoring them, the small number of nodes involved, the limited mobility of devices, the lack of reproducibility, and the like. Additionally, the few testbeds that are available for research purposes (like the C-VET test bed [31]) do not scale well.

The obvious solution that ensures low cost and scalability is simulation. Mobile network simulation requires simulating both wireless communication and mobility. Then, the question of the accuracy of simulation compared to real-life networks is raised. In a wireless network, the simulation of some components is straightforward. Indeed, high layers of the Open Systems Interconnection (OSI) stack are easily simulated or emulated because they are already computer programs. However, the physical layer is a key and complicated issue for simulation, as wireless communication depends on signal propagation, which is a hard physical phenomenon to model. Existing models are bounded to a trade-off between accuracy and computation time.

Regarding the simulation of the mobility of devices, different mobility models must be considered according to our needs, as devices carried by people do not have the same mobility patterns as cars moving on a road, for instance. For providing efficient and realistic models, some mobility simulators require real data as input.

This chapter gives a general overview of simulation techniques and tools available to achieve mobile network simulation. As we will see, tools vary with the kind of network we wish to simulate. The chapter is organized as follows. Section 4.1 provides an overview of the signal propagation issues and admitted models. In Section 4.2, network simulators are reviewed, while the the state of the art of mobility simulators is presented in Section 4.3. Finally, some conclusions are given in Section 4.4.

4.1 SIGNAL PROPAGATION MODELING

This section gives a general overview of the problem of modeling signal propagation. Not intended to be exhaustive, this introduction is targeting a reader who is not yet used to mobile network simulation problems. Researchers who are not familiar with this research field will find enough information to get the general trends and issues dealing with signal propagation when trying to do mobile wireless simulation. For a broader and more in-depth overview of the subject, the reader may refer to Chapter 2 of [68].

Signal propagation depends on many factors. The power and characteristics of transmitters and receivers, particularly the dimension of antennas, play an important role. Communication protocols, depending on the frequency range they operate, are highly influenced by the environment. Finally, the environment itself will be the main actor in the signal transmission. All these factors are ruled by a set of physical phenomena presented next.

4.1.1 Physical Phenomena

The main phenomena that alter signal propagation can be listed as follows.

Path Loss. Also called path attenuation, this phenomenon illustrates the reduction of power density of the electromagnetic wave in space. On an open area, without any other effect that could alter the signal, this attenuation is proportional to the square of the distance from the transmitter. Figure 4.1 illustrates this density decay as the wave sphere propagates into space.

Reflection. This is the most common phenomenon met, after path loss, in signal propagation. When the signal finds an obstacle of a different medium, it then changes its direction to continue in the same medium, with an angle that is opposed to the normal (right angle of the incident surface). The obstacle can be the ground (which is still present in open areas), buildings, walls, ceilings, and the like. Figure 4.2 shows the phenomenon with part of signal f_0 being reflected to signal f_1. From the receiver point of view, in an open area, reflection is a strong component that is added to the original signal coming from the direct line of sight (LOS).

Refraction. This phenomenon occurs when the signal wave reaches another medium with an angle different than 90° or 0°. The signal crosses

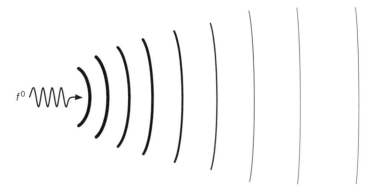

Figure 4.1. Signal attenuation (or path loss) phenomenon.

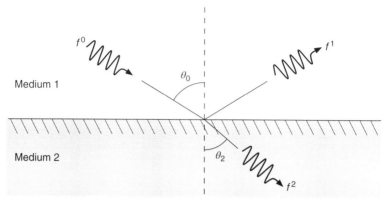

Figure 4.2. Signal reflection and refraction phenomena.

the new medium with a different angle than its incidence angle because of the variation in density or impedance between the two media. Figure 4.2 shows the refraction of a signal with incident angle θ_0 and refraction angle θ_2 in a denser medium. Refraction is indeed a physical phenomenon that impacts radio waves, but it mostly happens between atmospheric layers and thus concerns longer wavelength signals than the ones used in mobile networking. Indeed, low frequencies (between 30 and 3000 kHz) are guided between Earth and the ionosphere. Higher frequency bands like television signals [VHF (30–300 MHz)] can benefit from tropospheric ducting (refraction). Frequencies dealing with wireless networking are thus too high and have too limited ranges for this kind of phenomenon to occur.

Diffraction. When reaching the edge of an obstacle, the signal has a tendency to spread anew from this edge as if it were the origin of the signal. The consequence from an observer's point of view is a variation in the incident angle, which results in the creation of multiple paths from one sender to one receiver. Contrary to refraction, diffraction is met at various scales. At larger scales, the edge of a hill blocking a direct LOS between a transmitter and a receiver may redirect part of the signal to the latter. At a lower scale, the edge of a building in a urban environment may also bend the original signal. Figure 4.3 shows how a signal f^0 bends when reaching an obstacle. A possible secondary signal f^3 with a different angle arises from this edge.

Doppler Effect. This phenomenon is inherent to the movement of transmitters and receivers. The mobility or actually the variation of distance between transmitter and receiver is responsible for a shift in the frequency of the original signal. As Fig. 4.4 illustrates, the perceived frequency will be higher when the distance between a transmitter and a receiver is reducing and lower in the opposite case.

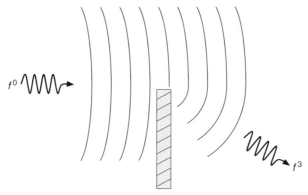

Figure 4.3. Signal diffraction phenomenon.

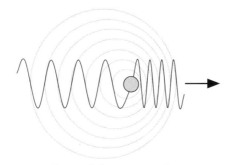

Figure 4.4. Doppler effect.

Scattering. Scattering is the effect produced by objects disturbing and bending the signal's original trajectory. Therefore, the phenomenon depends on the frequency of the signal. The effect appears when an object's diameter is significantly smaller than the wavelength. In the range of frequencies we are interested (wavelengths between 5 and 12 cm), insects, fog, clouds, or even rain or snow can play a role, even though rain also produces refraction. In terms of modeling, it is impossible to produce an analytical model for such phenomenon, so it is considered with stochastic approaches.

Absorption. It is a comparable effect with scattering but at a sub-molecular scale where electromagnetic energy is caught by electrons and transformed into other forms of energy like heat. Again, this phenomenon, if ever modeled in a simulator will refer to stochastic processes.

Multipath. It is not per se a physical phenomenon but rather a resultant observation from the effect of other phenomena, especially reflection and diffraction. Indeed, crowded environments like urban areas, with building and other massive objects obstructing the signal, produce reflection and

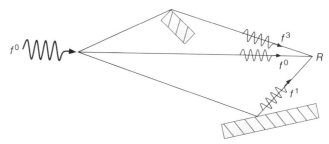

Figure 4.5. Multipath effect in signal transmission.

diffraction. Figure 4.5 shows a possible set of paths taken by an initial signal f^0. The receiver R will sense a mixture of subsignals from the direct LOS f^0, a reflected component f^1 (from a large obstacle at the bottom of the figure), and a diffracted signal f^3 against the edge of the upper obstacle.

Fading. Like multipath, fading is more a resultant observation of physical phenomena than a phenomenon itself. Fading illustrates the overall alteration that an original signal may have suffered from a transmitter to a receiver. The alteration occurs in terms of power density reduction but also in delay or in frequency shifts. Fading can be the result of all the aforementioned phenomena. Consequently, models that try to figure out fading are usually based on stochastic approaches. Four kinds of fading are usually identified:

- *Flat fading* happens with random and weak obstruction in open areas with an LOS. It is preferably modeled with a normal random variable.
- *Selective fading.* When the bandwidth of the transmitted signal is broader than the usable bandwidth of the physical channel, then a frequency-dependent fading occurs. Bands of frequencies of a signal will not be equally affected. Selective fading is observed as a slow and repetitive disturbance with nulls (phase oppositions that cancel the signal) and a stronger attenuation on some frequencies. This problem is lessened with the use of modulation schemes that ensure a diversity of frequencies are used to mitigate the effect.
- *Slow fading* illustrates attenuations and frequency shifts provoked by large objects (buildings, hills, etc.). This kind of obstruction is also called *shadowing*. It has a constant effect on the signal or at least it changes in time at a lower scale than the operation time (e.g., the time needed to receive a complete packet). Lognormal random variables are most frequently used to model slow fading.
- *Fast fading* models physical phenomena that end up modifying the signal with a strong and fast variation over time. The scale of the signal may

vary during the operation time and is in the order of the wavelength of the signal. It is the result of multipath interference. Multipath fast fading can be destructive or constructive for the signal and is usually good for the final reception since higher values of the signal enhance the reception, while short duration nulls can be ignored thanks to correction codes. Fast fading is modeled with a Rayleigh distribution for builtup urban environments with a non-LOS (NLOS) signal [64]. A Nakagami distribution [55] with parameter $m = 1$ can also be used. Actually, Rayleigh is a special case of Nakagami distribution where $m = 1$. When an LOS dominates the signal, a Rician distribution is used [23]. Depending on its parameters, a Weibull distribution can also be used [32].

4.1.2 Signal Propagation Models

In theory, the electromagnetic radiation created by a transmitter can be fully qualified and computed at the receiver. Considering the environment is completely known as well as all the physical effects (reflection, diffraction, Doppler effect, attenuation, etc.), an exact resolution of the received signal can be provided. However, this is not an easy task. The technologies we are interested in operate in different ranges of frequencies. For example, cellular networks vary between 0.9, 1.9, or 5.8 GHz; Wi-Fi around 2.4 GHz, or 5.9 GHz for WAVE. Thus, wavelengths in these signals range from 5 to 33 cm. This means that an accurate computation of multipath would require the knowledge of the environment at the scale of a few centimeters, making too complex the exact computation of electromagnetic fields of large areas. Therefore, we rely on models that do some approximations and simplify this computation.

A considerable number of models have been proposed for approximating the signal transmission. Several categories can be established depending on the type of model (analytic or stochastic), on the frequency at which they operate (microwaves or low frequencies), or on the nature of the transmission between transmitter and receiver (LOS or NLOS). Next, a brief survey of the most common models that can fit (frequencies and environments) into the mobile networking is presented.

Free Space. The simplest and most popular model for computing signal propagation only considers the effect of the distance d between a transmitter and a receiver. The free-space path loss model computes the attenuation of the received signal at distance d considering LOS. No other phenomenon is considered, only the amplitude of the signal is affected. The computed loss is proportional to the square of the distance between transmitter and receiver and also proportional to the square of the frequency. This path loss (PL) is given by the formula

$$PL = \left(\frac{4\pi df}{c}\right)^2,$$ (4.1)

with d the distance in meters, f the frequency of the signal in hertz, and c the speed of light in meters per second. This formula can also be expressed in decibels (dB):

$$PL = 20 \log_{10}(d) + 20 \log_{10}(f) + 20 \log_{10}\left(\frac{4\pi}{c}\right).$$ (4.2)

The Friis equation is a more accurate model that takes into account the antennas' characteristics. The attenuation is expressed in terms of input power at the receiver's antenna P_r in comparison to the output power at the transmitter antenna P_t. The power received at reception is thus

$$P_r = P_t G_t G_r \left(\frac{\lambda}{4\pi d}\right),$$ (4.3)

where G_t and G_r are, respectively, the gain of the transmitting and receiving antennas, λ is the wavelength of the signal in meters, and d the distance in meters between the two antennas. To sum up, the free-space path loss model is an analytical model for outdoor, LOS, and long-distance signals.

Two-Ray Ground. This model is similar to the free-space model but adds a second component to the LOS that represents the reflection on the ground. For that, the height of both the transmitter h_t and the receiver h_r are considered in the computation. The received power will thus be calculated as

$$P_r = P_t G_t G_r \left(\frac{h_t^2 h_r^2}{d^4}\right),$$ (4.4)

with all parameters identical to those in Equation (4.3). In this one, the power of the signal decreases with the fourth power of the distance d while the free-space model follows the square of that distance. In addition, it does not take into consideration the influence of the frequency of the original signal. The two-ray ground path loss model is considered to be a better approximation than the free-space model for long distances. Like the free-space path loss model, the two-ray ground model is an analytical formula dedicated to LOS, open outdoor areas.

Okumura and Followers. The original model [56] is not specifically appropriated to the range of frequencies in which we are interested in this book since it is dedicated to the 150 to 1920 MHz band. However, the model is usually extrapolated up to 3 GHz, allowing the inclusion of Wi-Fi bands. It is dedicated to the signal attenuation met in urban areas. This model has been constructed based on real measurements in the city of Tokyo. The real data served to create curves of signal attenuation depending on distances. This model computes a median path loss L composed of:

- A classical free-space attenuation
- The value of attenuation given by the computed curves from real data
- Some predefined factors that characterize the environment (obstacles, water surfaces, etc.)

Based on the measurements carried out in the Okumura model, the Hata model was developed [41]. It proposes a larger set of environments, that is, open, suburban, and urban areas. The urban model integrates frequency shifts, reflections, and scattering effects. In addition, the COST 231 project [4] also proposed a more accurate model using real measures from the Okumura model.

The Okumura model and its followers are based on both empirical data and analytical formulas. They focus on various outdoor environments and consider a number of physical phenomena. They are widely used in the field of cellular communication. Unfortunately, they are difficult to adapt to Wi-Fi or WAVE.

ITU Recommendations. The International Telecommunication Union (ITU) is the United Nations specialized agency for information and communication technologies. This organization provides recommendations on the use of such technologies for indoor and outdoor use. In [44], the organization advertises guidance for indoor signal propagation on a wide range of frequency bands. Based on real measurements, statistical propagation models are proposed. Common physical phenomena are investigated and specific problems like frequency reuse between floors are tackled.

Log-Distance. Rappaport [60], proposes a statistical general approach to take into account general fading phenomena, as well as various environmental factors. The model estimates the received signal in terms of a reference distance d_0 from the transmitter. It also includes a statistical estimation of the various frequency shifts and power loss with appropriate random variables.

The general formula computing the path loss PL expressed in decibels is:

$$PL = P_t - P_r = PL_0 + 10\gamma \ \log_{10} \frac{d}{d_0} + X, \tag{4.5}$$

where

   P_t = transmission power

   P_r = reception power

   d = distance between transmitter and receiver

   d_0 = reference distance between transmitter and a reference point

   PL_0 = path loss in decibels of the reference point, which can be computed
          with an analytical formula such as the free-space model shown in
          equation (4.2)

   γ = path loss exponent

   X = random variable that takes into account unpredictable fading

Variable X varies according to the kind of fading that occurs. If only flat fading is considered, a Gaussian variable with 0 mean is used to reflect small LOS variations. When slow fading provoked by shadowing of high buildings is considered, a lognormal random variable is used with a variance σ expressing the attenuation in decibels. Finally, when fast fading is important, the result of multipath propagation is modeled with a Rayleigh distribution [64] in urban environments with NLOS signals or with a Nakagami distribution [55] with parameter $m = 1$. If the LOS dominates in the signal, a Rician distribution [23] is used. A Weibull distribution can also be used for indoor fast fading [32].

There are mainly two parameters in this model. First, the path loss exponent γ and, second, the variance σ of the random variable. Recommendations are given for those parameters depending on the environment (urban, suburban, indoor, office, store, etc.).

The log-distance path loss model is probably the most used one in mobile networks simulation because it fits well for both outdoor and indoor environments with more or less crowded areas where one can expect MANETs or VANETs. The statistical approach is heavily dependent on parametric data obtained from real experiments like the ones carried out by the ITU.

Kun 2.6 GHz. Based on the ITU recommendations and on real outdoor experiments, Kun et al. [50] came out with a path loss model for urban areas in the range of frequencies used by 802.11b/g Wi-Fi. The model computes the path loss in decibels such as

$$PL = 36 + 26 \ \log_{10} d, \tag{4.6}$$

with d being the distance between transmitter and receiver.

4.2   STATE OF THE ART OF NETWORK SIMULATORS

The literature reveals the existence of several network simulators. In this section, a brief explanation of the most commonly used ones is presented, pointing out the features that differentiate one from another.

The main requirement for a network simulator is the accuracy of the simulated traffic data, in comparison to the real traffic generated in identical conditions. Thus, simulators can be validated with real network data. As we mentioned before, one of the main difficulties to overcome in a simulation is the emulation of an accurate physical layer. Ideally, simulators should implement different wireless technologies. They should also be easy to extend to fit any specific need. They may also allow interactions with other tools such as mobility simulators.

Providing an exhaustive list of all available network simulators is out of the scope of this book. The existing network simulators cover a wide area. For instance, GNS3 [7], PacketTracer [16], and NETSim [10] are three very good simulators when considering the simulation of wired router networks and especially Cisco devices. But, we here focus on simulators for wireless communication (and especially the Wi-Fi family) and devices mobility.

The number of available simulators for wireless mobile networks has seen a huge growth during the first decade of this century. Several research labs have developed their own simulator, resulting in either open-source projects or a commercial product. Nowadays, the number of network simulation projects tend to settle down to a reduced set of well admitted tools.

4.2.1   Simulators

Next, a list of simulation software tools that are or have been relevant to the community of mobile network simulation is given.

CNET. From the University of Western Australia, the CNET project [2] is a event-based simulator. It is available for several UNIX architectures and provides a visualization tool that has great educational interest. The main characteristic of the project is its fast learning curve, since the user rapidly understands how to create topologies and other mobility scenarios.

However, CNET suffers from a poor physical layer modeling (only free-space path loss is implemented) and also has too few protocols implemented. Moreover, the computational model is not scalable. For these reasons, CNET is not adapted for research purposes, and it is not widely used for mobile network simulation. But as mentioned before, it is still a good teaching tool.

OMNeT++. Objective Modular Network Test-bed in C++ (OMNeT++) is a component-based, modular simulation framework [69] available at [14]. The project proposes an academic public license that is close to the GNU (GNU's Not UNIX) public License, but restricts the use to noncommercial activities. A commercial version of the simulator, available at [13], offers technical assistance and extra features. It is basically an event-driven library and a framework, written in C++. The distribution of the core is provided by means of Message Passing Interface (MPI) primitives so that all simulations can be run on a grid.

A strong emphasis is put on the modularity of the architecture. In order to ease the code inheritance, the development guidelines emphasize the use of virtual member function in the C++ code. The intermodule communication model is based on the message passing paradigm, which prevents interdependence between modules, facilitating the development and adaptation of models to contributors.

This modularity has encouraged the development of a number of successful modules, also called frameworks:

- The *INET-framework* is the first efficient framework implementing wireless protocols.
- An attempt for simulating VANETs using INET-framework was reported in [54].
- *INETMANET* brings mobile ad hoc network modeling to the INET-Framework.
- *MiXiM* is a framework specially designed for static and mobile wireless networks (sensors networks, MANETs, and VANETs). MiXiM offers detailed signal propagation models in terms of power decay, frequency shift, and delay [72]. The so-called *AnalogueModel* class reference gives access to the classical models previously presented. Moreover MiXiM offers the possibility to the user to define its own propagation model based on statistical characteristics in a three-dimensional space (frequency, time, and distance).
- The *Veins* project [65] is a complete intervehicular communication simulator that brings both realistic communication with the full implementation of IEEE 802.11p and IEEE 1609.4 DSRC/WAVE models into MiXiM [35, 36] and realistic vehicular mobility thanks to a bidirectional interaction with the vehicular mobility simulator Simulation of Urban Mobility (SUMO) [27].

OPNET. OPNET Technologies, Inc. (formally MIL 3, Inc.) [15] is a software company created in 1986 whose first product was OPNET Modeler, a software tool, developed in C++, dedicated to network simulation. It then diversified its activities with specialized services for providers, network planning, or network equipment. One of its activities is a university program. This program is a license agreement that offers free access to the OPNET suite. It gives academia access to the network simulator and to other modules like the OPNET Modeler Wireless Suite, which includes a wide range of wireless protocols.

The architecture is said to be fully scalable with a parallel kernel and it supports simulation distribution on a grid. The core simulator relies on discrete event simulation but also on a hybrid mode that combines an analytical and a discrete model. This mode relies on the modeling of a background traffic and a specific traffic. Specific traffic is detailed at packet level while the background traffic only gives an overview of the inherent load and interference. This last mode is faster but less accurate than the pure discrete event model.

While at the time of this writing there exists support for WLAN 802.11a, b, e, g, and n, no implementation of 802.11p or any VANET-related protocol is available in OPNET. Dealing with vehicular mobility, the authors in [46] claim to have linked OPNET to the SUMO vehicular traffic simulator (described in Section 4.3).

ns-2. Since 1989, the ns (network simulator) family is a series of discrete event simulators aimed at simulating network protocols. It is very popular and probably the most used in academia. ns-2 [11] received a wide support and most of the state-of-the-art protocols were implemented, if not designed, in it. Signal propagation modeling is also well supported.

The core of ns-2 has its modules written in C++. The configuration of scenarios relies on an object-oriented version of Tool Command Language (Tcl). Both languages are needed for testing new algorithms, but only OTcl for simulating a protocol that is already implemented in ns-2.

There are, however, some drawbacks in the architecture of the project. First, the modular architecture is hardly respected and makes some modules strongly interdependent. The architecture forces any developer willing to produce a new module to include it in the building process of the core. No precise integration process of these modules exists. This problem ends up in various forks of the project, and sometimes it is very difficult for an end user to have two different modules working together with the same ns-2 core.

Because of the several flaws of ns-2, discussions in the ns mailing list in 2005 proposed starting over with a new code base for a third version of the popular simulator. This new simulator, ns-3, would be a complete rewrite of ns-2 with the portage of some efficient modules. Spotted problems were:

- The lack of scalability mainly due to the use of two different languages and programming paradigms
- The slow learning curve especially for students

- The large architectural differences between the ns-2 network layers and real systems layers
- The accumulation of unmaintained an incompatible modules
- The lack of documentation
- The lack of validation

ns-3. The ns-3 project [12] is aimed at solving the previously mentioned issues. The principal concern of the project is the realism of the simulator. The ns-3 team wants the project to be easy to validate, with code as close as possible to any real network-related code. For this, ns-3 relies on only one language, C++, for the library and the simulation scenarios (although python bindings exist). This helps producing code easier to debug. The various layers are as close as possible to the real ones: real IP addresses are used, sockets resemble real Berkeley Software Distribution (BSD) sockets, and packets are real network bigendian byte arrays. This permits one to easily execute native code and to do emulation.

Other Inactive Projects. As previously mentioned, the beginning of the 21st century saw a lot of network simulation projects. Many of them are not maintained anymore but got much attention.

Among them, GloMoSim [6] was mainly dedicated to the simulation of wireless networks. It was based on the discrete event simulation language Parallel Simulation Environment for Complex Systems (PARSEC) [18]. A commercial version of the project, Qualnet, is distributed by Scalable Network Technologies.

Java in Simulation Time (JiST) [8] and its wireless ad hoc extension Scalable Wireless Ad hoc Network Simulator (SWANS) was a Java-based high-performance and event-based simulation platform. It also relied on the PARSEC language and used it to advertise very fast execution times and low memory footprints.

4.2.2 Analysis

As stated, lots of tools are available to achieve wireless mobile network simulation. The first selection criteria were the accurate modeling of the physical layer, the modular approach, and the mobility models included. Although those criteria are reached by the presented tools, one may additionally want to evaluate the validity of the produced traffic or compare results between those tools. Indeed, validation against real testbeds is important to ensure the realism of produced traffic. The IEEE 802.11 model of the ns-3 simulator was validated in [26] and [57]. Comparably, IEEE 802.11g was validated in OMNeT++ [29]. In [59], a comparison between ns-2, Qualnet, and OPNET against a real data set of wireless communication shows the importance of the OSI physical layer (PHY) modeling. The comparison stresses that the classical two-ray ground plus free-space models commonly used are inappropriate to Wi-Fi indoor and outdoor environments.

Some works also focus on comparing simulators. In [38], the authors compare ns-2 and OPNET in a wireless and mobile setup. They show comparable trends in the results but different absolute values. Garrido et al. [38] also point out difficulties to reproduce identical mobility patterns in the two platforms. In [71], the performances of ns-2, ns-3, OMNeT++, SimPy, and Jist/SWANS are investigated. Results reveal large differences according to both runtime and memory usage. Finally, a comparison between ns-2 and OMNeT++ demonstrates an impossibility to compare results [34]. However, the authors succeeded to wrap a ns-2 module so that it could be used as an OMNeT++ module. That could reproduce almost identically the results from ns-2 with the original module and OMNeT++ with the wrapped module. Those results seem to validate that the core behavior of the two simulators is comparable and that the modules themselves produce the shift in the results, mainly because of the various parameters and default values of considered algorithms.

4.3 MOBILITY SIMULATION

We switch in this section to the simulation of mobility. The main existing mobility models are summarized in Section 4.3.1, while some of the most well-known simulators are pointed out in Section 4.3.2.

4.3.1 Mobility Models

Mobility models aim at reproducing the mobility of real-world entities in simulation. In the present book, those entities may be pedestrians walking in an urban environment and carrying a communicating device, or they may also be vehicles moving on a road network and using on-board devices or any mobile entity equipped with communicating sensors. There are different forms of modeling the mobility: (1) artificial rules, (2) reproducing the exact mobility of real entities using previously captured mobility patterns, and finally (3) a mix of artificial models fed with real input data.

The first category is simplistic and easy to produce and reproduce. Some global characteristics can be carried out from these models. Their drawback is the lack of realism in the generated patterns. The second type of model (exact mobility patterns) attempts to produce an accurate behavior based on real mobility data, but it is limited to the capturing session. They interpolate the data, providing higher resolution between two pieces of real information, but it is not possible to extrapolate the data to go beyond the observations. A typical example is the interpolation of GPS data. The last kind of model is the most interesting and the most difficult to produce. Those models are based on real patterns and various information in order to reproduce and extrapolate the known mobility. The extrapolation is in time (simulation of longer period than the real capture) and in number (more entities than in the capture).

4.3.1.1 Artificial Models. Bai and Helmy [24] proposed four classes of artificial models.

1. *Random models*, mostly inspired by the modeling of physical unpre-dicted models, rely on random and independent variables to produce each entity's mobility. The *random walk* is an adaptation of the classi-cal *Brownian motion* that models the motion of molecules in a gas. The *random waypoint* [30] describes a random process where each mobile picks up a random destination and speed and goes to that point, then another destination is chosen. This became the most popular artificial model in academia, especially for testing routing protocols.

2. *Time resolution dependency* models care about previous mobility vec-tors in order to pick up new ones. These models try to be more realistic than random models, claiming that one's current direction and speed directly influences the new destination. The *Gauss–Markov* model [51] and the *smooth random* model [28] are the most used ones in this category.

3. *Space resolution dependency* models focus on the spacial interaction between mobile devices. They model groups mobility. The *reference point group* model [43] mimics the mobility of a crowd of pedestrians. Sánchez and Manzoni [63] propose a simulation tool that includes three novel mobility models. The *area scanning* mimics pedestrians in a line going in the same direction, just like rescue patrols seeking for sur-vivors after a snow avalanche. In the *pursue-a-target* model, the whole group goes after the same moving target with some randomness in their direction and speed. The *nomadic community* model sketches the behavior of a flock of entities, like birds, moving as a whole in one direction while keeping some distance between them. Another famous flocking model is the *Boids* model by Craig Reynolds [61] with its three rules, that is, separation, alignment, and cohesion.

4. *Geographical dependency* models take into account exterior factors that alter or direct entities mobility. Mainly vehicular mobility depends on the road network topology. Bai et al. [25] propose the *Manhattan model*

with random motion on a lattice constraint area. In [62], real street maps from the TIGER database (U.S Census Bureau) are used to move vehicles with random origins and destinations. Routes are calculated using Dijkstra's algorithm and the speed of the vehicle varies between 5 miles per hour and the speed limit. In the *pathway* mobility model [66], the classical random waypoint model is adapted to fit the geographical constraints of paths or roads. In [45], the *obstacle* mobility model creates possible paths in an area where obstacles alter the mobility. A Voronoï diagram is constructed around the set of obstacles. Finally, the random waypoint is used to determine destinations and the entities move along the edges of the diagram.

4.3.1.2 Real Data Interpolation. This is not a kind of model per se. It is more related to the time and space interpolation and inference of gathered data, whether it is position based (GPS) or connection based (like access point logs). These models depend on the captured data. The Community Resource for Archiving Wireless Data At Dartmouth (CRAWDAD) project [5] aims at centralizing data sets mainly composed of wireless connection logs. The project counts hundreds of published papers using their data sets.

In [40], human mobility is approximated with mobile phones probes. The information about the geolocalization of a cell phone becomes a proxy to the mobility of its owner.

4.3.1.3 Models Based on Real Data. In this type of model, the input data is not simply some sparse GPS trails where it is only necessary to interpolate the missing positions. The data may be of a different nature and thus would require real modeling to end up in mobility traces. As human mobility usually falls into the *real data interpolation* type of model, mostly vehicular mobility, that actually tolerates models constructed from various data sources.

Hertkorn and Wagner [42] rely on an extremely detailed data set to provide an on-demand trip planning model for the city of Cologne, Germany. The data source is composed of three parts:

- The population of the city modeled with agents with an initial location (their home) and sociodemographic characteristics
- The city environment with locations for activities (shops, working places, theaters) described in zones
- An extensive data set of diaries that reports the detailed mobile activity of the inhabitants of the city

This detailed data set is then formatted, sorted, and clustered, to propose an on-demand model that for any agent at any desired time can produce a trip (effective departure time, source, and destination). Paths from source to destination are then computed with Gawron's algorithm [39].

Similarly, Chapter 9 in this book is dedicated to the optimization of a mobility model based on real data from Luxembourg. The model also uses a zoned city environment, but no diary surveys are available. Instead, counting data about road traffic are used.

4.3.1.4 Various Scales of Models. The problem of scales is almost specific to vehicular motion. Indeed, traffic simulation can be considered on different levels, from the macroscopic level, dealing with flows of vehicles on wide areas and wide time windows, to the microscopic level, taking into account speedups and slowdowns of vehicles, lane changes, or traffic lights. The macroscopic level corresponds to the classical notion of mobility model like the ones outlined in this section. The microscopic level is closely related to physical mechanisms around the vehicle and requires specific models plus a lot of computation. The two most popular models are the *intelligent driver model* [67] and the *Krauss model* [49]. They use deterministic dynamical systems that represent the vehicle's position and speed evolution in time. This evolution depends on the actual values of this vehicle's speed and position but also on the behavior of the vehicle in front of that one. Those dynamical systems are numerically solved in simulators with Runge–Kutta methods.

4.3.2   State of the Art of Mobility Simulators

This section focuses on vehicular mobility simulators because only this kind of mobility requires intensive computation and models. Human mobility models are usually simple or artificial and are thus directly implemented into wireless network simulators.

A few human mobility projects can, however, be cited like ParkSim [70], a human mobility simulator for theme parks based on empirical GPS data, or MobiREAL [52], a model-based human mobility simulator coupled with a home-made network simulator.

Vehicular motion simulation is a more complicated task with various levels of complexity. Phenomena like traffic congestion are nontrivial and require specific models.

In the MObility model generator for VEhicular networks (MOVE) project [47], random paths are chosen for vehicles on real maps. The STRAW (street random waypoint) project [33] again uses real maps, and vehicles are given random origins and destinations. The mobility is, however, more realistic with an intersection management. It should, however, not be compared with real microsimulation.

Tools like STRAW and MOVE rely on the US TIGER database to produce realistic maps. Their mobility module is not really accurate since no micro-simulation is implemented. The implemented models are comparable to the ones described earlier in the geographical dependency models section, with an extra nonuniform distribution of vehicle speed.

In [53], GrooveSim is presented as an integrated simulation platform, performing both network and mobility simulation.

CANU mobility simulation environment (CanuMobiSim) is a flexible framework for human mobility modeling [1]. Its extension to vehicular mobility, VanetMobiSim [21], uses both macroscopic and microscopic models to simulate realistic traffic. On the macroscopic level, it can handle TIGER maps or generate artificial ones from Voronoï diagrams. On the microscopic side, it implements the classical Intelligent Driver Model (IDM) dynamical system. The quite high resolution of the produced data is a good input for realistic wireless simulators.

MATSim [9] is an active project for the large-scale agent-based simulation of road traffic.

A number of commercial tools advertise realistic traffic simulation, usually coupled with nice visualization tools. Paramics [17] includes pedestrian microsimulation to the vehicular network for having more realistic urban network simulations. SimTraffic [19] is another commercial microsimulation traffic tool with realistic 3-D viewer. VISSIM [22] is a programming language and execution environment specialized in the simulation of physical nonlinear dynamic systems. It is used in various fields on engineering. It can model road traffic, pedestrians, but also signal propagation. CORridor SIMulation (CORSIM) [3] is a microscopic traffic simulator dedicated to multilane freeways and traffic signal optimization.

SUMO [20, 27] is a space-continuous road traffic simulator. SUMO stands for Simulation of Urban MObility. It is an open-source project (GPL license), mainly developed by the Institute of Transportation Systems at the German Aerospace Centre (DLR) that handles the micromobility level including road interactions such as car-following models, traffic light logic, or overtaking models. Among its various features one can cite:

- The ability to import realistic maps in various popular formats
- A traffic demand approach for the specification of individual vehicle journeys
- A state of the art and efficient microscopic simulation engine for car-following models, lane change, and intersection management

- A variety of global and local (vehicle-based or edge-based) simulation outputs that allow fine-grained statistics
- A standardized Application Programming Interface (API) through a network interface that permits to *drive* the tool from another program with a wide range of details

This last feature is very important as it allows bidirectional interaction with a network simulator.

4.4 CONCLUSION

The aim of this chapter was to provide the reader with basic yet sufficient knowledge about the issues related to mobile network simulation. First, we presented the waves propagation physical phenomena and the main existing techniques to model them, as well as some of the most well-known network simulators. Then, we focused on mobility simulation, describing the most well-known mobility models in the literature and giving an overview of the main existing mobility simulators.

As shown, physical constraints of radio wave propagation are the biggest issue when wishing to achieve realistic simulation. This field has, however, received wide attention for many years. Mostly dedicated to long-distance transmission, the obtained results in terms of modeling apply more or less successfully to medium- and short-range communication technologies like Wi-Fi.

Realistic microsimulation of vehicle mobility was also shown as a challenging field of research where many problems remain unresolved.

When considering network and mobility simulators, only little attention could be given to commercial solutions since documentation is hardly publicly available. Thus a broader focus was put on free and open-source (mainly academic) solutions.

The ns-3 network simulator as well as the SUMO traffic simulator have been identified as favorable tool sets in order to achieve realistic mobile network simulation, based on open-source solutions.

REFERENCES

1. CANU mobility simulation environment (canumobisim). Available at `http://canu.informatik.uni-stuttgart.de/mobisim`. Accessed July 2013.
2. The CNET network simulator. Available at `http://www.csse.uwa.edu.au/cnet`. Accessed July 2013.

3. CORSIM. Available at `http://mctrans.ce.ufl.edu/featured/tsis/Version5/corsim.htm`. Accessed July 2013.

4. COST 231. Available at `http://www.lx.it.pt/cost231/final_report.htm`. Accessed July 2013.

5. CRAWDAD a community resource for archiving wireless data at Dartmouth. Available at `http://crawdad.cs.dartmouth.edu`. Accessed July 2013.

6. Global mobile information systems simulation library (GloMoSim). Available at `http://pcl.cs.ucla.edu/projects/glomosim`. Accessed July 2013.

7. GNS3 graphical network simulator. Available at `http://www.gns3.net`. Accessed July 2013.

8. JiST java in simulation time. Available at `http://jist.ece.cornell.edu`. Accessed July 2013.

9. Multi-Agent Transport Simulation Toolkit (MATSim). Available at `http://www.matsim.org`. Accessed July 2013.

10. NetSim the Cisco network simulator. Available at `http://www.boson.com/netsim-cisco-network-simulator`. Accessed July 2013.

11. The network simulator ns-2. Available at `http://www.isi.edu/nsnam/ns/`. Accessed July 2013.

12. The network simulator ns-3. Available at `http://www.nsnam.org`. Accessed July 2013.

13. OMNEST high performance simulation for all kinds of networks. Available at `http://www.omnest.com`. Accessed July 2013.

14. OMNeT++ Community. Available at `http://www.omnetpp.org`. Accessed July 2013.

15. OPNET. Available at `http://www.opnet.com`. Accessed July 2013.

16. Packet Tracer. Available at `http://www.packettracernetwork.com`. Accessed July 2013.

17. PARAMICS MICROSIMULATION. Available at `http://www.paramics.com`. Accessed July 2013.

18. PARSEC parallel simulation environment for complex systems. Available at `http://pcl.cs.ucla.edu/projects/parsec`. Accessed July 2013.

19. SimTraffic. Available at `http://www.trafficware.com`. Accessed July 2013.

20. Simulation of Urban MObility (SUMO). Available at `http://sumo.sourceforge.net`. Accessed July 2013.

21. VANETMobiSim extension to CanuMobiSim. Available at `http://vanet.eurecom.fr`. Accessed July 2013.

22. VISSIM. Available at `http://www.vissim.com`. Accessed July 2013.

23. A. Abdi, C. Tepedelenlioglu, M. Kaveh, and G. Giannakis. On the estimation of the K parameter for the rice fading distribution. *IEEE Communications Letters*, 5(3):92–94, 2001.

24. F. Bai and A. Helmy. A survey of mobility modeling and analysis in wireless adhoc networks. In *Wireless Ad Hoc and Sensor Networks*, pp. 483–502. Kluwer Academic.

25. F. Bai, N. Sadagopan, and A. Helmy. IMPORTANT: A framework to systematically analyze the impact of mobility on performance of routing protocols for adhoc networks. In *Proceedings of the 22nd Annual Joint Conference of the IEEE Computer and Communications Societies* (IEEE Cat. No.03CH37428). IEEE INFOCOM 2003, Vol. 2, 2003.

26. N. Baldo, M. Requena-Esteso, J. Núñez Martínez, M. Portolès-Comeras, J. Nin-Guerrero, P. Dini, and J. Mangues-Bafalluy. Validation of the IEEE 802.11 MAC model in the ns3 simulator using the EXTREME testbed. In *Proceedings of the 3rd International ICST Conference on Simulation Tools and Techniques (SIMUTools)*, pp. 64:1–64:9, 2010.

27. M. Behrisch, L. Bieker, J. Erdmann, and D. Krajzewicz. SUMO—Simulation of urban mobility: An overview. In *The Third International Conference on Advances in System Simulation (SIMUL)*. IARIA, pp. 55–60. Barcelona, Spain, 2011.

28. C. Bettstetter. Smooth is better than sharp: A random mobility model for simulation of wireless networks. In M. Meo, T. A. Dahlberg, and L. Donatiello, Eds., *Proceedings of the 4th ACM International Workshop on Modeling, Analysis and Simulation of Wireless and Mobile Systems*, pp. 19–27. ACM, New York, 2001.

29. M. Bredel and M. Bergner. On the accuracy of IEEE 802.11g wireless LAN simulations using OMNeT++. In *Proceedings of the 2nd International Conference on Simulation Tools and Techniques (Simutools)*. ICST, pp. 81:1–81:5. Rome, 2009.

30. J. Broch, D. A. Maltz, D. B. Johnson, Y. C. Hu, and J. Jetcheva. A performance comparison of multi-hop wireless ad hoc network routing protocols. In W. P. Osborne and D. Moghe, Eds., *Proceedings of the 4th Annual ACM/IEEE International Conference on Mobile Computing and Networking*, pp. 85–97. ACM, New York, 1998.

31. M. Cesana, L. Fratta, M. Gerla, E. Giordano, and G. Pau. C-VeT the UCLA campus vehicular testbed: Integration of VANET and mesh networks. In *Proceedings of the European Wireless Conference (EW)*, pp. 689–695. IEEE, Lucca, Italy, 2010.

32. J. Chan and E. T. T. Wong. Empirical modelling of received signal strength in indoor localization. In *Proceedings of the International Conference on Automatic Control and Artificial Intelligence (ACAI 2012)*, pp. 978–981. IEEE, Xiamen, 2012.

33. D. R. Choffnes and F. E. Bustamante. An integrated mobility and traffic model for vehicular wireless networks. In *Proceedings of the 2nd ACM International Workshop on Vehicular Ad Hoc Networks (VANET)*, pp. 69–78. New York, ACM, 2005.

34. P. Di, Y. Houri, K. Kutzner, and T. Fuhrmann. Towards comparable network simulations. Interner Bericht 2008-9. Dept. of Computer Science, Universität Karlsruhe (TH), 2008.

35. D. Eckhoff and C. Sommer. A multi-channel IEEE 1609.4 and 802.11p EDCA model for the Veins framework. In *Proceedings of the 5th ACM/ICST International Conference on Simulation Tools and Techniques for Communications, Networks and Systems (SIMUTools): 5th ACM/ICST International Workshop on OMNeT++*. ACM, New York, 2012.

36. D. Eckhoff, C. Sommer, and F. Dressler. On the necessity of accurate IEEE 802.11p models for IVC protocol simulation. In *Proceedings of the 75th IEEE Vehicular Technology Conference (VTC)*, Yokohama, Japan, 2012.

37. G Gaertner, E. ONuallain, and A. Butterly. 802.11 link quality and its prediction—An experimental study. *Personal Wireless*, 3260:147–163, 2004.

38. P. P. Garrido, M. P. Malumbres, and C. T. Calafate. ns-2 vs. OPNET: A comparative study of the IEEE 802.11e technology on MANET environments. In S. Molnár, J. R. Heath, O. Dalle, G. A. Wainer, Eds., *Proceedings of the 1st International Conference on Simulation Tools and Techniques for Communications, Networks and Systems & Workshops (Simutools)*, pp. 37:1–37:10. ICST, Marseille, 2008.

39. C. Gawron. An iterative algorithm to determine the dynamic user equilibrium in a traffic simulation model. *International Journal of Modern Physics C*, 9: 393–408, 1998.

40. M. C. González, C. A. Hidalgo, and A. Barabási. Understanding individual human mobility patterns. *Nature*, 453(7196):779–782, 2008.

41. M. Hata and T. Nagatsu. Mobile location using signal strength measurements in a cellular system. *IEEE Transactions on Vehicular Technology*, 29(2): 245–252, 1980.

42. G. Hertkorn and P. Wagner. The application of microscopic activity based travel demand modelling in large scale simulations. In *Proceedings of the World Conference on Transport Research (WCTR)*, pp. 1–10. Istanbul, 2004.

43. X. Hong, M. Gerla, G. Pei, and C. C. Chiang. A group mobility model for ad hoc wireless networks. In *Proceedings of the 2nd ACM International Workshop on Modeling, Analysis and Simulation of Wireless and Mobile Systems*, pp. 53–60, 1999.

44. International Telecommunication Union (ITU). Propagation data and prediction methods for the planning of indoor radiocommunication systems and radio local area networks in the frequency range 900 MHz to 100 GHz, 2012. P.1238-7. Available at `http://www.itu.int/rec/R-REC-P.1238/`.

45. A. P. Jardosh, E. M. Belding-Royer, K. C. Almeroth, and S. Suri. Real-world environment models for mobile network evaluation. *IEEE Journal on Selected Areas in Communications*, 23(3):622–632, 2005.

46. F. Kaisser, C. Gransart, and M. Berbineau. Simulations of VANET scenarios with OPNET and SUMO. In *Communication Technologies for Vehicles*,

Vol. 7266 of *Lecture Notes in Computer Science*, pp. 103–112. Springer, Berlin and Heidelberg, 2012.

47. F. K. Karnadi, Z. H. Mo, and K. Lan. Rapid generation of realistic mobility models for VANET. In *Proceedings of the IEEE Wireless Communications and Networking Conference (WCNC)*, pp. 2506–2511. IEEE, Hong Kong, 2007.

48. Y.-B. Ko and N. Vaidya. Location aided routing (LAR) in mobile ad hoc networks. *Wireless Networks*, 6:307–321, 2000.

49. S. Krauss, P. Wagner, and C. Gawron. Metastable states in a microscopic model of traffic flow. *Physical Review E*, 55:5597–5602, 1997.

50. S. Kun, W. Ping, and L. Yingze. Path loss models for suburban scenario at 2.3GHz, 2.6GHz and 3.5GHz. In *Proceedings of the 8th International Symposium on Antennas, Propagation and EM Theory (ISAPE)*, pp. 438–441. IEEE, Kunming, 2008.

51. B. Liang and Z. J. Haas. Predictive distance-based mobility management for PCS networks. In *Proceedings of the Eighteenth Annual Joint Conference of the IEEE Computer and Communications Societies (INFOCOM)*, 3:1377–1384, 1999.

52. K. Maeda, A. Uchiyama, T. Umedu, H. Yamaguchi, K. Yasumoto, and T. Higashino. Urban pedestrian mobility for mobile wireless network simulation. *Ad Hoc Networks*, 7(1):153–170, 2009.

53. R. Mangharam, D. S. Weller, D. D. Stancil, R. Rajkumar, and J. S. Parikh. GrooveSim: A topography-accurate simulator for geographic routing in vehicular networks. In *Proceedings of the 2nd ACM International Workshop on Vehicular Ad Hoc Networks (VANET)*, pp. 59–68, 2005.

54. R. Nagel and S. Eichler. Efficient and realistic mobility and channel modeling for VANET scenarios using OMNeT++ and INET-framework. In *Proceedings of the 1st International Conference on Simulation Tools and Techniques for Communications, Networks and Systems & Workshops (Simutools)*, pp. 89: 1–89:8, 2008.

55. N. Nakagami. The *m*-distribution, a general formula for intensity distribution of rapid fading. In W. G. Hoffman, Ed. *Statistical Methods in Radio Wave Propagation*. Pergamon, Oxford, 1960.

56. Y. Okumura, E. Ohmori, T. Kawano, and K. Fukuda. Review of the electrical communication laboratories. *Review of the Electrical Communication Laboratory*, 16:825–873, 1968.

57. G. Pei and T. Henderson. Validation of ns-3 802.11b PHY model. Technical Report. Boeing Research and Technology, 2009.

58. C. E. Perkins and E. M. Royer. Ad-hoc on-demand distance vector routing. In *Proceedings of the 2nd Mobile Computing Systems and Applications (WMCSA)*, pp. 90–100. IEEE, New Orleans, 1999.

59. A. Rachedi, S. Lohier, S. Cherrier, and I. Salhi. Wireless network simulators relevance compared to a real testbed in outdoor and indoor environments. In *Proceedings of the 6th International Wireless Communications and Mobile Computing Conference (IWCMC)*, pp. 346–350. ACM, New York, 2010.

60. T. Rappaport. *Wireless Communications: Principles and Practice*, 2nd ed. Prentice Hall, Upper Saddle River, 2001.

61. C. W. Reynolds. Flocks, herds, and schools: A distributed behavioral model. *Computer Graphics*, 21(4):25–34, 1987.

62. A. K. Saha and D. B. Johnson. Modeling mobility for vehicular ad-hoc networks. In *Proceedings of the 1st ACM International Workshop on Vehicular Ad Hoc Networks (VANET)*, pp. 91–92. ACM, New York, 2004.

63. M. Sánchez and P. Manzoni. ANEJOS: A java based simulator for ad hoc networks. *Future Generation Computer Systems*, 17(5):573–583, 2001.

64. B. Sklar. Rayleigh fading channels in mobile digital communication systems. I. Characterization. *IEEE Communications Magazine*, 35(7):90–100, 1997.

65. C. Sommer, R. German, and F. Dressler. Bidirectionally coupled network and road traffic simulation for improved IVC analysis. *IEEE Transactions on Mobile Computing*, 10(1):3–15, 2011.

66. J. Tian, J. Haehner, C. Becker, I. Stepanov, and K. Rothermel. Graph-based mobility model for mobile ad hoc network simulation. In *Proceedings of the 35th Annual Simulation Symposium (SS)*, pp. 337–344. IEEE Computer Society, New York, 2002.

67. M. Treiber, A. Hennecke, and D. Helbing. Congested traffic states in empirical observations and microscopic simulations. *Physical Review E*, 62:1805–1824, 2000.

68. D. Tse and P. Viswanath. *Fundamentals of Wireless Communication*. Cambridge University Press, Cambridge, 2005.

69. A. Varga. Using the OMNeT++ discrete event simulation system in education. *IEEE Transactions on Education*, 42(4):11, 1999.

70. V. Vukadinovic, F. Dreier, and S. Mangold. A simple framework to simulate the mobility and activity of theme park visitors. In S. Jain, R. R. Creasey Jr., J. Himmelspach, K. P. White, M. C. Fu, Eds., *Proceedings of the 2011 Winter Simulation Conference (WSC)*, pp. 3248–3260. IEEE, Phoenix, 2011.

71. E. Weingärtner, H. vom Lehn, and K. Wehrle. A performance comparison of recent network simulators. In *Proceedings of the IEEE International Conference on Communications (ICC)*, pp. 1–5, 2009.

72. K. Wessel, M. Swigulski, A. Köpke, and D. Willkomm. MiXiM: The physical layer an architecture overview. In *Proceedings of the 2nd International Conference on Simulation Tools and Techniques (Simutools)*, pp. 78:1–78:8, 2009.

PART II

PROBLEMS OPTIMIZATION

5

PROPOSED OPTIMIZATION FRAMEWORK

As introduced in Chapter 4, the development of real MANETs is nowadays still an open issue. Thus, simulators are the most commonly used technique to emulate the behavior of the MANET for evaluating, validating, and optimizing algorithms. It is possible to either use an existing general-purpose simulator (e.g., ns-3) or use or conceive a custom simulator tailored to specific purposes.

Emulating the real behavior of a mobile ad hoc network is a complex task, not only are accurate network simulators required but also realistic mobility generators. Solving optimization problems using realistic simulations for MANETs can be computationally very expensive. However, there might be some problems where such degree of realism in simulations is not needed, for example, the network model is not needed. Thus, depending on the needs of the problem tackled, we differentiate between high accuracy and computationally demanding simulations or low accuracy but fast simulation.

Evolutionary Algorithms for Mobile Ad Hoc Networks, First Edition. Bernabé Dorronsoro, Patricia Ruiz, Grégoire Danoy, Yoann Pigné, and Pascal Bouvry.
© 2014 John Wiley & Sons, Inc. Published 2014 by John Wiley & Sons, Inc.

We introduce in this chapter the optimization framework that we used for all the experiments presented in this book. It presents a simple modular architecture that integrates all the required components to solve an optimization problem related to mobile ad hoc networks. This framework can also be used to ease the early stages of the design and development of an algorithm in mobile ad hoc networks because the optimization module is just a component that might be unplugged if not needed.

We present in Section 5.1 the architecture of the proposed optimization framework. Section 5.2 contains descriptions of all the optimization algorithms used in the book, while the simulators we adopted are highlighted in Section 5.3. We summarize in Section 5.4 the experimental setup that we followed in all chapters. Finally, Section 5.5 concludes the chapter.

5.1 ARCHITECTURE

This section describes the framework we propose for the optimization of problems related to mobile ad hoc networks. Its design is outlined in Fig. 5.1. As can be seen, it is composed of different modules that can be easily plugged in or unplugged, according to the user's needs. To work with such a framework, we first need to select the modules that are required for our experimentation and then define the contents of each one.

First, we need to define the *optimization problem* we want to solve, which must be modeled by a function. This function (usually called the *fitness* function) quantifies the quality of any potential solution, and it is used to guide the search during the optimization process. Additionally, it should ideally reflect to what extent one solution is better than another. Therefore, it must

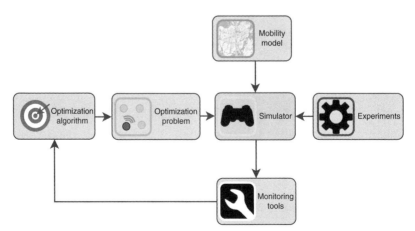

Figure 5.1. Design of the proposed framework.

be carefully defined in order to get good results. As we mentioned before, we rely on simulators to evaluate the quality of potential solutions.

In order to evaluate a solution, the optimization problem relies on simulators. Either network or mobility simulators, or both, might be required by the optimization problem in the *simulator* module. In the latter case, they must be able to interact. The network simulator may need an accurate mobility model to perform realistic simulations. Additionally, in some cases it is required that the network simulator be able to influence the mobility of devices. For instance, imagine the case of a VANET in which vehicles dynamically change their routes according to some messages they receive from the network.

The *mobility model* module contains information about the different mobility patterns that nodes must follow. This depends on the type of network (sensor, vehicular, etc.) and the environment that need to be studied. The mobility model must be very accurate in order to perform realistic simulations.

In the *experiments* module the use we want to study is specified. Usually, the configuration parameters influence the behavior of the algorithm to be optimized, for example, the number of nodes composing the network or the size of the simulation area.

Once the problem to optimize is defined, we need to set the *optimization algorithm* to tackle it. The choice of the optimization algorithm will highly depend on the problem to solve. If it is an NP-hard problem (i.e., no algorithm exists that can solve it in polynomial time), then we must rely on greedy algorithms, heuristics, or better, metaheuristics. In other cases, exact approaches are the most appropriate ones. Then, the algorithm to use will depend on the nature of the problem: if it is combinatorial or continuous, single- or multi-objective, epistatic, multimodal, and so forth. The literature must be consulted in order to choose an appropriate optimization algorithm for the problem at hand. Through out this book, we give some hints to help in this choice.

Finally, we require some *monitoring tools* that take the output of the simulation and process it for the optimization algorithm. For instance, in the case of using stochastic simulators, we can not rely on the results of a single simulation run. We, therefore, need to perform a number of independent simulations for a given solution and compute from all the results one single fitness value that will be used by the optimization algorithm to guide the search. In this case, the monitoring tool will be in charge of performing the independent simulations, process the obtained results, and report the fitness value to the optimization algorithm.

Next, we will describe the optimization algorithms used in this book (Section 5.2), as well as the network and mobility simulators (Section 5.3), and their experimental configurations (Section 5.4). The optimization problem description, as well as the monitoring tools used to feed the optimization algorithm from the simulations results, are specific to the handled problem, and they will be described in every chapter.

5.2 OPTIMIZATION ALGORITHMS

We present in this section the algorithms used during the experiments performed in the following chapters. In every chapter, panmictic, cellular, and cooperative coevolutionary evolutionary algorithms are used. They represent three different kinds of algorithms, and studying all of them will allow us to extract some guidelines about the suitable algorithm to use for the studied problem classes. That discussion is provided in Chapter 10.

5.2.1 Single-Objective Algorithms

We introduce in this section the four optimization algorithms we used for the single-objective problems studied. They are two GAs with panmictic population, namely, the steady-state GA (ssGA) and the generational GA (genGA), and two others with structured populations: the cellular GA (cGA) and the cooperative coevolutionary GA (CCGA).

5.2.1.1 Steady-State Genetic Algorithm. The steady-state GA uses a centralized, also called panmictic, population. In panmictic algorithms, any individual in the population can interact with any other one during the breeding loop. The pseudocode of this algorithm is shown in Pseudocode 5.1. It iterates a process (lines 4–10) in which two parents are selected from the whole population with a given selection criterion (line 5), they are then recombined (line 6), the obtained offsprings are mutated (line 7), and finally they are evaluated (line 8), and one of them is inserted into the population following a given criterion (line 9).

Pseudocode 5.1 Steady-State GA

```
 1: //Algorithm parameters in 'ssga'
 2: InitializePopulation(ssga.pop)
 3: Evaluation(ssga.pop)
 4: while ! StopCondition() do
 5:    parents←Selection(ssga.Pop);
 6:    offspring←Recombination(ssga.Pc,parents);
 7:    offspring←Mutation(ssga.Pm,offspring);
 8:    Evaluation(offspring);
 9:    Add(offspring,ssga.Pop);
10: end while
```

As can be seen in the pseudocode of the algorithm, new individuals generated during the evolution are directly inserted into the current population. Therefore, it is a $(\mu+1)$-GA, meaning that the population is asynchronously being updated with the newly generated individuals.

5.2.1.2   *Generational Genetic Algorithm.*   As the ssGA, the generational GA (genGA) works on a panmictic population. The difference between them lies in the way in which the population is updated with the offspring solutions. While for the ssGA new solutions are inserted into the population just after being evaluated, in the case of genGA the whole population is updated at the same time. Therefore, it is a $(\mu+\lambda)$-GA, with $\mu = \lambda$.

The gGA pseudocode is given in Pseudocode 5.2. As can be seen, it is similar to the ssGA, but offspring solutions are inserted into an auxiliary population of the same size as the main one (line 11). Then, after the auxiliary population is filled with offspring individuals, it becomes the main population for the next generation, typically including some elitist solutions from the previous generation (line 13).

Pseudocode 5.2   Generational GA

```
 1: //Algorithm parameters in 'genga'
 2: InitializePopulation(genga.pop)
 3: Evaluation(genga.pop)
 4: while ! StopCondition() do
 5:    // Perform one generation
 6:    for iterator ← 1 to gen.popSize do
 7:       parents←Selection(genga.Pop);
 8:       offspring←Recombination(genga.Pc,parents);
 9:       offspring←Mutation(genga.Pm,offspring);
10:       Evaluation(offspring);
11:       Add(offspring,genga.AuxPop);
12:    end for
13:    genga.Pop←ReplaceWithElitism
          (genga.Pop,genga.AuxPop);
14: end while
```

5.2.1.3   *Cellular Genetic Algorithm.*   Cellular genetic algorithms (cGAs) [5] are a kind of GA with a structured population in which individuals are spread in a (usually) two-dimensional toroidal mesh, and they are only allowed to interact with their neighbors. As an example, we show in Fig. 5.2 the disposition of the individuals in the population of a cGA, the

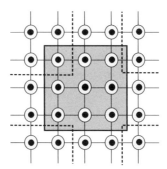

Figure 5.2. cGA with 5 × 5 population and C9 neighborhood.

neighborhood of the center individual (shaded), and of another individual far from the center, in the upper left corner (dashed line).

A canonical cGA follows the pseudocode included in the algorithm shown in Pseudocode 5.3. In this basic cGA, the population is usually structured in a regular grid of d dimensions ($d = 1, 2, 3$), and a neighborhood is defined on it. The algorithm iteratively considers as current each individual in the grid (line 5), and individuals may only interact with individuals belonging to their neighborhood (line 6), so parents are chosen among the neighbors (line 7) with a given criterion. Crossover and mutation operators are applied to the individuals in lines 8 and 9, with probabilities P_c and P_m, respectively. Afterward, the algorithm computes the fitness value of the new offspring individual (or individuals) (line 10) and inserts it (or one of them) instead of the current individual in the population (line 11) following a given replacement policy. This loop is repeated until a termination condition is met (line 4).

Pseudocode 5.3   Canonical cGA

```
 1: //Algorithm parameters in 'cga'
 2: InitializePopulation(cga.pop)
 3: Evaluation(cga.pop)
 4: while ! StopCondition() do
 5:   for individual ← 1 to cga.popSize do
 6:     n_list←Get_Neighborhood
        (cga,position(individual));
 7:     parents←Selection(n_list);
 8:     offspring←Recombination(cga.Pc,parents);
 9:     offspring←Mutation(cga.Pm,offspring);
10:     Evaluation(offspring);
11:     Add(position(individual),offspring,cga);
12:   end for
13: end while
```

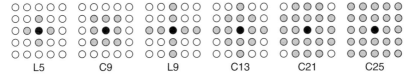

Figure 5.3. Typical neighborhood structures used in cGAs.

Thanks to the limited interactions given by the population topology, some isolation is introduced between distant individuals in the population. The further two individuals are from each other, the longer it would take for them to receive any information from the other. The overlapping neighborhoods allow for a smooth diffusion of information throughout the population. The effect is that cellular GAs perform a slower convergence with respect to ssGA, maintaining a higher diversity of solutions in the population. This will allow cGAs to have a better chance of escaping from local optima in which other algorithms performing faster convergence, as the ssGA, may get trapped.

The main neighborhood structures typically used in cGAs are shown in Figure 5.3 in growing size order, according to the radius metric [7]. The larger the neighborhood radius and the smaller the population radius, the faster the information will be spread throughout the population [6].

5.2.1.4 *Cooperative Coevolutionary Genetic Algorithm.* In
addition to the cellular model, there is another common way for structuring the population of GAs. It consists in splitting the whole population into several subpopulations in which isolated GAs are evolving. These subpopulations exchange some information among them during the run. We study in this book an algorithm following this model, namely CCGA, a cooperative coevolutionary GA.

The main idea behind coevolutionary algorithms is to consider the coevolution of subpopulations of individuals representing specific parts of the global solution, instead of considering a population of similar individuals representing a global solution, like classical genetic algorithms do. The quality of this kind of algorithm has been reported in a large number of studies in the literature. As an example, two different coevolutionary GAs were applied in [32] on a number of well-known test functions, and they were demonstrated to clearly outperform a sequential GA. Similar conclusions were obtained in [10] for the problem of overcoming network partitioning and improving its connectivity in MANETs using bypass links.

Cooperative (also called symbiotic) coevolutionary genetic algorithms (CCGA) involve a number of independently evolving species that together

---

Pseudocode 5.4   Cooperative Coevolutionary GA

```
 1: InitializePopulations(ccga.pop)
 2: for all species_s do
 3:    Evaluation(ccga.pop_s)
 4:    ShareBestLocal(ccga.pop_s)
 5: end for
 6: while !StopCondition() do
 7:    for all species_s do
 8:       parents ← Selection(ccga.pop_s)
 9:       offspring ← Recombination(ccga.pop_s, parents)
10:       offspring ← Mutation(ccga.pop_s, offspring)
11:       Evaluation(ccga.pop_s)
12:       ShareBestLocal(ccga.pop_s)
13:    end for
14: end while
```

---

form complex structures, well-suited to solve a problem (see Pseudocode 5.4). The fitness of an individual depends on its ability to collaborate with individuals from other species. In this way, the evolutionary pressure stemming from the difficulty of the problem favors the development of cooperative strategies and individuals. The CCGA considered here is based on the model proposed by Potter and De Jong [29] in which a number of populations explore different decompositions of the problem, as shown in Fig. 5.4. In this system, each species represents a subcomponent of a potential solution. Complete solutions are obtained by assembling representative members of each of the species (populations). The fitness of each individual depends on the quality of (some of) the complete solutions it participated in, thus measuring how well it cooperates to solve the problem. The evolution of each species is controlled by a separate, independent, evolutionary algorithm. In the initial generation, individuals from a given subpopulation are matched with randomly chosen individuals from all other subpopulations. A fitness for each individual is evaluated (line 3), and the best individual in each subpopulation is found (line 4). The process of *cooperative coevolution* starts from the next generation. For this purpose, in each generation a cycle of operations is repeated in a round-robin fashion (lines 8–12). Only one current subpopulation is active in a cycle, while the other subpopulations are frozen. All individuals from the active subpopulation are matched with the best values of frozen subpopulations. When the evolutionary process is completed, a composition of the best individuals from each subpopulation represents a solution of a problem.

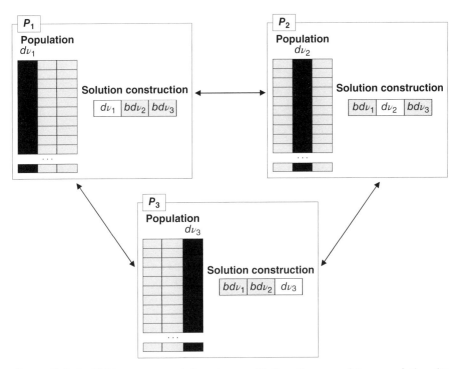

Figure 5.4. In CCGAs, every population shares with the other coevolving populations its best partial solution. The partial solutions are evaluated by building complete solutions with the best partial solutions of the other subpopulations.

5.2.2 Multi-Objective Algorithms

The multi-objective (MO) algorithms used for the experiments in this book are described in Sections 5.2.2.1–5.2.2.3. They are the well-known NSGA-II algorithm, CellDE, a cellular differential evolution algorithm for multi-objective optimization, and CCNSGA-II, a multi-objective cooperative coevolutionary version of NSGA-II.

5.2.2.1 Nondominated Sorting Genetic Algorithm. The

NSGA-II [12] algorithm is, undoubtedly, the reference MO algorithm. Even when nowadays better MO algorithms exist, NSGA-II is still the most referenced one, probably because of its simplicity and good operators and components, adopted by a large number of other MO algorithms.

Pseudocode 5.5 gives the code for NSGA-II. NSGA-II does not implement an external archive of nondominated solutions, but the population itself keeps

---

Pseudocode 5.5   Nondominated Sorting GA-II

```
 1: //Algorithm parameters in 'nsga'
 2: InitializePopulation(nsga.pop);
 3: Evaluation(nsga.pop);
 4: while ! StopCondition() do
 5:   for index ← l to nsga.popSize/2 do
 6:      parents←SelectParents(nsga.pop);
 7:      children←Crossover(nsga.Pc,parents);
 8:      children←Mutate(nsga.Pm,children);
 9:      offspringPop←Add(children);
10:   end for
11:   Evaluation(offspringPop);
12:   union←Merge(nsga.pop, offspringPop);
13:   fronts←SortFronts(union);
14:   (Pop', lastFront)←GetBestCompleteFronts(fronts);
15:   if size(nextPop) < nsga.popsize then
16:     Pop'←BestAccToCrowding(lastFront,
         nsga.popsize-size(Pop'));
17:   end if
18: end while
```

---

the best nondominated solutions found so far. The algorithm starts by generating an initial random population and evaluating it (lines 2 and 3). Then, it enters in the main loop that evolves the population. It starts by generating a second population of the same size as the main one. It is done by selecting two parents (line 6) by binary tournament based on dominance and crowding distance (in the case the two selected solutions are nondominated), applying the recombination operator (typically SBX [12], standing for simulated binary crossover) to generate two new solutions (line 7), which are mutated in line 8 (typically using polynomial mutation [12]) and added to the offspring population (line 9). The number of times this cycle (lines 5–10) is repeated is the population size divided by 2, thus generating the new population with the same size as the main one. This new population is then evaluated (line 11) and merged with the main population (line 12). Now, the algorithm must discard half of the solutions from the merged population to generate the population for the next generation. This is done by selecting the best solutions according to ranking and crowding, in that order. Concretely, ranking consists of ordering solutions according to the dominance level into different fronts (line 13). The first front is composed of the nondominated solutions in the merged population. Then, these solutions in the first front are removed from the merged population, and the nondominated ones of the remaining solutions compose the second front. The algorithm proceeds to iterate like this until all solutions are classified. To build the new population for the next generation, the algorithm adds those solutions in the first front until the population is full or adding a front would exceed the population size (line 14). In the latter case (lines 15–17), the best solutions are selected from the latter front according to crowding distance (i.e., those solutions that are more isolated in the front) to complete the population. The process is repeated until the termination condition is met (lines 4–18).

5.2.2.2 CellDE. CellDE [15] is a multi-objective evolutionary algorithm (MOEA) for three-objective problems. It is a hybrid of MOCell [26], a cellular MO algorithm, and DE [30]. Therefore, it implements a cellular population topology. The pseudocode of CellDE is given in Pseudocode 5.6. As can be seen, it starts by creating and evaluating a random initial solution (lines 2 and 3) and building an initial empty archive of nondominated solutions (line 4). Then, the algorithm iterates to evolve the population until a given termination condition is met (lines 5–13). In every iteration, all individuals are evolved by selecting two different parents (line 8) from the neighborhood of the current individual being evolved and applying a standard differential evolution operator described later (line 9). The resulting offspring individual is then evaluated, and it replaces the current individual in the population if the current one does not dominate it (all individuals are updated at the same time, in a synchronous way). Then, the offspring is inserted into the archive following the strength pareto evolutionary algorithm 2 (SPEA2)

Pseudocode 5.6   CellDE Algorithm

```
 1: //Algorithm parameters in 'cellde'
 2: InitialisePopulation(cellde.pop)
 3: Evaluation(cellde.pop)
 4: CreateFront(cellde.front)
 5: while ! StopCondition() do
 6:   for individual ← 1 to cellde.popSize do
 7:     n_list←Get_Neighborhood(cellde,
        position(individual));
 8:     parents←SelectDifferentParents(n_list);
 9:     offspring←DifferentialEvolution(parents,
        individual);
10:     Evaluation(offspring);
11:     Add(position(individual),offspring,cellde);
12:     AddToArchive(individual);
13:   end for
14:   PopFeedback();
15: end while
```

---

density estimator. Finally, some randomly selected solutions in the archive are moved back at random positions in the population.

The differential evolution operator used in CellDE is defined by Equation (5.1), where u is the offspring, i is the individual index, j is the variable position in the representation, x is the current individual, and p_1 and p_2 are the two parents. Variables F and C_R are two control parameters specific to DE, and they represent the scaling factor for mutation and the control of the recombination operator, respectively.

$$u_{i,j} = \begin{cases} x_{r_0,j} + F(x_{p_1,j} - x_{p_2,j}) & \text{if } \text{rand}(0,1) \le C_R \text{ or } j = j_{\text{rand}} \\ x_{i,j} & \text{otherwise} \end{cases}. \quad (5.1)$$

5.2.2.3 Cooperative Coevolutionary Nondominated Sorting Genetic Algorithm.
We present in this section the design of the CCNSGA-II algorithm. It was presented and validated versus other multi-objective algorithms from the state of the art on continuous functions and on a scheduling problem in [13] and [14], respectively.

As in single-objective CCGAs, every subpopulation is focused on the optimization of a subset of the problem variables, and a multi-objective GA is run in every subpopulation to evolve the population of solutions to the corresponding subproblem. Every subpopulation will locally look for its own approximation to the Pareto front. At the end of the run, the obtained solution sets of every subpopulation are merged into a single one that will be the output of the CCNSGA-II. Therefore, the Pareto approximations in every subpopulation are obtained in a decentralized way.

The merging process of the solution sets, found by all the subpopulations, is achieved by choosing one of them and then adding to it all the solutions from the others. In case the resulting approximation set is full, a policy based on the crowding distance [12] is used to remove the solution that contributes less to promote diversity. This scheme performs well when solving bidimensional problems, as the ones studied in this work.

Besides the archives management in the subpopulations, another difference of the multi-objective design with respect to the single-objective one is the way in which complete solutions are built for evaluation. As previously mentioned, in the case of single-objective optimization, the evaluation of a partial solution in a subpopulation is achieved by composing a complete solution with the best partial solutions from all the other subpopulations. In the case of multi-objective optimization, in most cases there will be more than a single best solution, that is, a set of nondominated ones. One could think on solving the problem by randomly choosing one of the nondominated solutions in every subpopulation, as is done in other previous

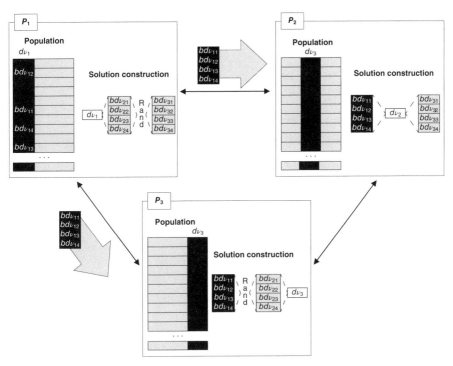

Figure 5.5. In our CCNSGA-II, every population (e.g., P_1) shares with the other coevolving populations (P_2 and P_3) its four best partial solutions (bdv_{11} to bdv_{14}). The partial solutions are evaluated by building complete solutions with random partial solutions of the other two subpopulations (bdv_{2X} and bdv_{3Y}).

works [9, 19, 21, 22, 25, 35]. However, it does not provide the different subpopulations with enough diversity to get accurate Pareto front approximations, as is suggested in [14]. It therefore highly restricts the search performed by the algorithm, resulting in solution sets with poor accuracy and diversity.

In CCNSGA-II, every subpopulation shares a number N_s of solutions randomly chosen from the nondominated ones found so far. An example of how one subpopulation, P_1, shares its best solutions with the others is shown in Fig. 5.5, where $N_s = 4$. If the local Pareto front contains less than N_s nondominated solutions, the set of N_s solutions is completed by other individuals randomly taken from the rest of the population.

Another consequence of sharing multiple partial solutions is the high number of possible combinations available to build complete solutions. Indeed, for a given subpopulation, N_s partial solutions are received from every other subpopulation, therefore, there are $N_s^{N_P-1}$ possible combinations, where N_P is the number of subpopulations. Building and evaluating all the possible solutions would be extremely costly. In CCNSGA-II, a complete solution is

---

Pseudocode 5.7   CCNSGAII Algorithm

```
1: InitialisePopulations(ccnsgaII.pop)
2: for all species_s do
3:   Evaluation(ccnsgaII.pop_s)
4:   Share20BestLocal(ccnsgaII.pop_s)
5: end for
6: while ! StopCondition() do
7:   for all species_s do
8:     NSGAIIGeneration(Pop_s(gen))
9:     Evaluation(ccnsgaII.pop_s)
10:    Share20BestLocal(ccnsgaII.pop_s)
11:  end for
12: end while
13: mergeSubpopulations( ) // Generate the final Pareto
    front approximation
```

---

built for every solution in subpopulation s by using a random partial solution from every other island bdv_{ij} (i is the identifier of the population the solution belongs to, and j is the index of the solution in the shared list with the N_s partial solutions). An example is provided in Fig. 5.5 on how population P_1 builds its complete solutions with bdv_{2X} and bdv_{3Y}, $\forall X, Y \in \{1, 2, 3, 4\}$.

Similar to single-objective CCGAs, the CCNSGA-II is easily parallelizable since it is composed of several subpopulations evolved by independent instances of NSGA-II. In order to improve the computational performance of CCNSGA-II, we designed a parallel implementation for multicore architectures in [14]. One thread is created per subpopulation, and a few synchronization points are kept in order to reproduce exactly the same behavior as the sequential algorithm. Asynchronous communications could also be implemented, as we proposed in [27].

The proposed CCNSGA-II implementation is shown in Pseudocode 5.7. The different subpopulations are initialized in line 1. This initialization process creates new subpopulations of random partial solutions. After that, partial solutions are evaluated using random partial solutions from the other subpopulations (line 3). Then, each subpopulation shares 20 partial solutions, randomly selected from the best local ones (line 4) [14], unlike the single-objective CCEA presented in Section 5.2.1.4 in which each species shares only the local best solution. The algorithm enters now in its main loop (the cooperative loop), from which it will not exit until the termination criterion is met. In every iteration of the loop, the subpopulations perform one generation of NSGA-II in parallel (line 8) and then evaluate their partial solutions using one random partial solution from those shared by the other species (line 9) and publish their best local partial solutions (line 10). At the end, we build a single Pareto front approximation from the solutions in the local Pareto front approximations in every subpopulation (line 13). This final Pareto front approximation will be the output of the algorithm.

5.3 SIMULATORS

We used for the experiments carried out for this book two advanced network and mobility simulators. After surveying the related literature (see Chapter 4), we decided to rely on ns-3 for the simulation of wireless communication networks and SUMO for generating realistic mobility traces in real scenarios. They are described next. Less accurate but faster approaches might also be needed to model both mobility and network communications. Such an approach based on graphs is also presented.

5.3.1 Network Simulator: ns-3

The strong concern for realism present in the ns-3 project design, as described in Chapter 4, guided us on the decision to choose it for some of the developed works in this book.

The architecture of ns-3 is split into independent modules that can be exposed in two parts. The core part that gathers the general behavior allowing the discrete event scheduling, and the simulation part that describes and holds the components of a scenario. We present these two parts and then go through some specific implementations that are interesting for our concerns.

The Core. This central part, independent of any kind of network being simulated, gathers the commonly needed components. The discrete event simulation core handles and schedules the events created by the user in its scenario.

The Object Model. On top of the core discrete event model lies the actual networking one. It is an object-oriented model where components share as few dependencies as possible, in order to maximize interoperability and code reuse. The communication between the various modules is ensured by a callback mechanism. The main entities of this object model are presented next:

- *Node* mimics a communicating device. Other components are plugged to it like network devices, applications, or mobility models.

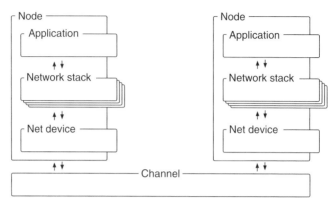

Figure 5.6. Overview of the ns-3 object model.

- *Device* represents a physical networking interface. It mostly models the behavior of the driver of a real network interface.
- *Channel* is the way the physical medium is modeled. This object holds all the nonsoftware part of the network, from electronic transmission in wires to electromagnetic wave propagation in the air. The device model is tightly linked to the channel since network interfaces depend on the type of physical medium used.
- *Socket* is very similar to a real socket. It is the logical medium through which data go from upper layers to lower layers and the other way around.
- *Application* is at the top of the communication stack. Communication starts from applications that initiate networking activity.

Figure 5.6 illustrates the basic communication model between two nodes. Data transmissions start from applications, and they follow the network stack through sockets. When reaching the physical layer, data is handled by the channel object as a physical phenomenon. All the upper layers are part of the nodes.

Some Existing Implementations. The simulator implements a variety of models, protocols, and devices. We will here only provide a brief overview of the models that are useful to the problems tackled in this book.

We first focus on the wireless implementation. It implements the IEEE 802.11 [2] set of standards. These standards span over the two first layers of the OSI model, the PHY and the MAC. According to the ns-3 object model, 802.11 appears both in the *device* model (MAC layer) and the *channel* model (PHY layer).

- The PHY layer models both the physical states of the device (TX, SYNC, CCA_BUSY, and IDLE) and the physical transmission of the signal through the air. In this part, the propagation models are gathered, that is, Friis, two-ray ground, log-distance, Nakagami, Okumura-Hata, ITU indoor/outdoor, and Kun 2.6 GHz. All these models are described in Chapter . Some basic (constant speed and random) propagation delays are also implemented.
- The MAC layer implements the collision avoidance algorithm, as the Distributed Coordination Function (DCF). It handles *infrastructure* and ad hoc modes with beaconing, probing, and association mechanisms.

One may also stress the implementation of acknowledged routing protocols (e.g., Ad hoc On-Demand Distance Vector (AODV), Optimized Link State Routing (OLSR), Destination-Sequenced Distance Vector (DSDV)), as well as an energy consumption framework.

Another important feature is the ability for the simulator to handle mobility of devices. It has an implementation for the common artificial mobility models (constant velocity, constant acceleration, Gauss–Markov, random position, random walk, random waypoint, and steady-state random waypoint). Nodes may also have no specified mobility and can be driven by an external application. The following section is dedicated to the study of the SUMO mobility model, which can be used together with ns-3.

5.3.2 Mobility Simulator: SUMO

The development of the project started in 2001 with a first public release in 2002. Even if main funding and the core team come from the German Aerospace Centre (DLR), a large open-source community also contributed. Mostly universities (Erlangen-Nürnberg, Innsbruck, Berlin, Lübeck, Cologne, Munich, Wroclaw, Bombay, Turin) are participants to the project, which is a good indicator of SUMO's popularity in academia.

As the main design guideline is for the project to be *fast* and *portable*, the code is only composed of standard C++ with no extra platform-specific dependencies. Dealing with the *fast* guideline, SUMO does not rely on any graphical interface. Tools in their basic usage are command-line-based only, and configuriation is done through XML files. Although there exists a fast and useful graphical version of SUMO, it is not necessary.

In order to start using SUMO, at least two sources of information are needed: the definition of a road network and some traffic demand related to this network. Road networks are passed to SUMO through an XML file with a dedicated format. There are two ways to get such a file: by generating it with the *netgen* tool or by converting it from another file format with *netconvert*. The tool can read and translate a number of formats from other simulators (e.g., VISUM, VISSIM, openDRIVE, MATsim) or from database formats (e.g., ArcView's shapefiles, OpenStreatMap's OSM files). When it comes to traffic demand, the format is yet another XML file with a simple specification that can be created by other applications. SUMO provides a number of ways to generate traffic demand depending on the input data source used.

5.3.2.1   The Architecture. There are three main components in the architecture of SUMO: the network, vehicles, and the traffic demand, which defines where and when vehicles move in the network.

Network. A SUMO network contains the geographical information about roads as well as other useful information. From a graph theory point of view, roads are edges and intersections are vertices, but this is not enough to gather all the useful road network information. Some other logic is thus used where roads are still *edges* (one for each direction of the road) and intersections are named *junctions*. Some extra data is used to encode the possibility to go from one edge to another with *connections* that indicate to what other edges one is connected. Edges have attributes that indicate their nature (type of road and type of traffic allowed). They are composed of lanes on which vehicles drive. Each lane can have an attribute that indicates the maximum allowed speed on it. Junctions mainly hold the intersection priority rule attributes. If a junction has to be controlled by a traffic light, it will bear the identifier of that device. Traffic lights can also be defined and identified in the network file with an associated logic.

Vehicles. They have a unique identifier. Each one has a set of attributes (directly specified or specified through a vehicle type). The color, the length, the maximum speed, the acceleration, the deceleration, and a CO_2 profile can be given. Since vehicles move in the network, they also hold microscopic mobility models. In SUMO, vehicles have two models: a car-following model (a variant of the Krauss model [24]) and a lane change model (originally designed by SUMO).

Traffic Demand. One single traffic demand is a set of parameters that gives, for only one vehicle, its *trip* over the network at a given time. A trip is identified by at least:

- A vehicle ID
- Optionally, a vehicle *type*
- An initial position (the ID of an edge on the network)

- A start *date* in simulation time (in seconds)
- A destination node ID

Depending on the use case, a demand may also be identified with a *route*, which is a list of adjacent edges (IDs in the network) starting from the initial position of the vehicle and ending at its destination.

Demand files can be produced by an external application since traffic demand requires external information, like socioeconomic schemes or population densities. SUMO, however, provides a set of tools to deal with common sources of information and finally produces the necessary traffic demand files.

5.3.2.2   *TraCI, the Bidirectional Interaction.*   One of the most useful extra features of the project is probably its ability to interact with other tools. *TraCI* (traffic control interface) allows remote control of a running SUMO simulation. The interface uses a TCP client/server architecture so that any network-capable application can interact with it. There is no constraint in terms of language since the communication is done through the network protocol. Moreover, the other program can run on another machine. The only constraint is that a client has to be implemented in the other program's language [1].

The main use case when considering mobile networks is to couple the traffic simulator with a network simulation. When dealing with intelligent transportation systems (ITS), such coupling becomes an essential need. Indeed, simulating traffic management applications, such as traffic congestion avoidance, requires to modify vehicles mobility at runtime (e.g., changing the predefined route of a vehicle if a congestion appears). On the one hand, the traffic simulator provides the mobility of the vehicles (position, direction, and speed) while the network simulator computes the corresponding wireless network according to the given position and mobility. On the other hand, the network application may decide a change in the route of a vehicle and ask the traffic simulation to modify this vehicle mobility. Figure 5.7 illustrates this bidirectional interaction between mobility simulation and wireless network simulation.

To achieve this integration and allow online simulation, some middleware is needed.

- *TraNS* performed the integration of ns-2 with SUMO. It was probably the first middleware proposed but is not maintained anymore.
- *Veins* [34] performs the integration with OMNeT++. It actually does more than a simple middleware integration since the authors claim to have proposed the first complete implementation on a simulator of the IEEE 802.11p stack.

Figure 5.7. Online simulation with a bidirectional interaction between mobility and wireless network.

- In the *iTETRIS* project [31], an open-source system called *iCS* (iTETRIS control system) was proposed to integrate SUMO with ns-3.
- Another integration tool with ns-3 is the OVNIS framework [28]. It offers the same fundamental functionality as iCS but adds an adaptation of ns-3 channel for the simulation of wide-area environments. This feature reduces the computation complexity in time inherent to the classical channel behavior, where all nodes in the network are considered for each packet, that is, $O(n^2)$.

5.3.3   Graph-Based Simulations

When the accuracy of a realistic simulator is not mandatory, then it is a common usage in the field of mobile networks to rely on the analogy of graphs and dynamic graphs as a way to model both the mobility of stations and the connection network. Nodes of such graphs are stations evolving in a two- or three-dimensional environment, and edges between nodes represent communication links no matter if wired or wireless connections are considered. The graph analogy does not provide the accuracy and realism that dedicated networks and mobility simulators offer, however, graphs are abstractions that provide rapid modeling and typically run faster than realistic simulators.

  In this book, when the constraint of realism gets mitigated by computation time constraints, then the tackled problems are solved using such graph-based simulations. More precisely, we here rely on GraphStream [3, 17], a software library written in Java for the modeling and manipulation of dynamic graphs. The library design is based on the concept of event-driven graph dynamics. It is generic and application independent, thus easily adaptable to any application domain. Moreover, since GraphStream is written in Java the interconnection with the optimization framework (also Java based) is made easily.

GraphStream handles static and most importantly dynamic graphs (i.e., graphs that evolve over time). If nodes are moving stations, and edges are volatile communications, then the resulting graph is highly dynamic with nodes and edges being added, modified, or removed. Information related to nodes and edges (called attributes) are dynamic as well. The fact that a modification appears in the graph is called an event, and thus, a dynamic graph is an ordered list or a stream of such graph events.

There are various ways to consider and manipulate these streams of events. One interesting feature is that such streams may be produced by another tool or simulator. On the contrary, output streams produced by GraphStream may be injected in another tool. The simplest way to enable interconnection between various simulators is an offline link with the help of files.

When an online connection is necessary, it is possible to connect Graph-Stream in real time with another tool so that it can send to it, or receive from it, some graph events. A network protocol, NetStream [4], allows the transport of graph events between tools, which can be written in different languages and not necessarily located on the same machine. Indeed, realistic simulators like SUMO or ns-3 are easily connected to GraphStream by this mean.

5.4 EXPERIMENTAL SETUP

We describe in this section the setup we adopted in all our experiments for this book, unless the opposite is mentioned in the corresponding chapter.

Our framework has been executed on the HPC facilities of the University of Luxembourg `http://hpc.uni.lu/`, specifically, on the 2.26 GHz Intel Xeon L5640 8 core processor nodes, having 24 GB random-access memory (RAM). These nodes run Debian Linux version 6.0.5 (with kernel 2.6.32-5-amd64) and Java version 1.6.0_25.

In Table 5.1, we show the generic parameters used for all the algorithms in our experiments in this book. All of them have a single population of 100 individuals, except for the CCGA and CCNSGA-II algorithms, using subpopulations of 100 individuals for each of the 8 islands used. The termination condition is achieving 10, 000 fitness function evaluations. The recombination and mutation operators will be specified in every chapter since they are dependent on the problem encoding. Recombination is applied with probability $p_c = 1.0$, while the probability for mutation is $p_m = 1/\texttt{chrom\_length}$.

The two parents are selected using a binary tournament, except for the cellular algorithms, for which one of them is considered to be the current individual itself. A specific parameter of this cellular model is the neighborhood. We used C9 (9 closest individuals measured in Manhattan distance; see

TABLE 5.1. Generic Parameters Used for the Studied Algorithms

Population size	100 (ssGA, NSGAII)
	10×10 (cGA, CellDE)
	$100 \times$ number of subpopulations
	(CCGA, CCNSGAII)
Termination Condition	$10,000$ function evaluations
Selection	Binary tournament (BT)
	Current individual + BT for cGA
Neighborhood	C9 for cellular topologies
Crossover probability	$p_c = 1.0$
Mutation probability	$p_m = 1/\texttt{chrom\_length}$

Fig. 5.2). In the case of CellDE, the same C9 neighborhood is used, and two of the three parents are randomly selected from the neighborhood (forced to be different) and the third one is the current individual itself, as suggested in [15]. We adopt the original values proposed by the authors for the rest of the parameters in NSGA-II, CellDE, and CCNSGA-II, with the exceptions of those cases when the values are explicitly mentioned.

Single-objective experiments were conducted using the JCell framework [5], a Java-based evolutionary optimization framework. Originally introduced to work with cGAs, it also includes panmictic models (generational and steady-state GA). The cooperative coevolutionary GA extension of JCell was implemented by the authors. For the multi-objective experiments, another Java-based framework for metaheuristics was used, jMetal [16]. Similarly to JCell, the cooperative coevolutionary variants are not part of the standard distribution and were implemented in jMetal by the authors.

In order to evaluate the quality of the Pareto front approximations provided by the MO algorithms, different metrics are typically used in the literature. None of them is perfect, and it is normal to use several in the comparison of the algorithms in the literature. In this book, we adopt three common metrics from the literature, measuring the accuracy of the Pareto front approximations, their diversity, and both of them at the same time. These quality indicators are the unary additive epsilon ($I_{\varepsilon+}^1$), SPREAD (Δ), and hypervolume (HV):

- *Hypervolume (HV) [37].* Calculates the m-dimensional volume (in the objective space) covered by the solutions in the evaluated Pareto front Q and a dominated reference point W. Mathematically, for each solution $i \in Q$, a hypercube v_i is constructed with the reference point W (e.g., constructed with a vector of worst objective function values) and the solution i as the diagonal corners of the hypercube. Thereafter, a union

of all hypercubes is found and its hypervolume is calculated, as shown
in Equation (5.2). Algorithms with the highest HV value perform best
as this metric takes its maximum value when all the solutions in the
evaluated Pareto front belong to the optimal one.

$$HV = \text{volume} \left(\bigcup_{i=1}^{|Q|} v_i \right). \tag{5.2}$$

- *SPREAD.* This indicator [12] measures the extent of spread by the set of
  computed solutions. It is defined as

$$\Delta = \frac{d_f + d_l + \sum_{i=1}^{N-1} \left| d_i - \bar{d} \right|}{d_f + d_l + (N-1)\bar{d}}, \tag{5.3}$$

where d_i is the Euclidean distance between consecutive solutions, $\bar{d}$ is
the mean of these distances, and d_f and d_l are the Euclidean distances to
the *extreme* solutions of the optimal Pareto front in the objective space.
This indicator takes a zero value for an ideal distribution, pointing out a
perfect spread of the solutions in the Pareto front.

- *Unary Additive Epsilon ($I^1_{\varepsilon+}$) Indicator [23].* Provides a measure of the
  convergence, that is, of the distance to the optimal Pareto front. Given an
  approximation set of a problem, S, the $I^1_{\varepsilon+}$ indicator is a measure of the
  smallest distance needed to translate every point in S so that it dominates the true Pareto front of the problem S^*. More formally, given
  $\mathbf{e}^1 = (e^1_1, \ldots, e^1_m)$ and $\mathbf{e}^2 = (e^2_1, \ldots, e^2_m)$, where m is the number of
  objectives,

$$I^1_{\varepsilon+}(S) = \inf_{\varepsilon \in \mathbb{R}} \{ \forall \mathbf{e}^2 \in S^* \exists \mathbf{e}^1 \in S : \mathbf{e}^1 \prec_\varepsilon \mathbf{e}^2 \} \tag{5.4}$$

where $\mathbf{e}^1 \prec_\varepsilon \mathbf{e}^2$ if and only if $\forall 1 \leq i \leq m : e^1_i < \varepsilon + e^2_i$.

Before applying these metrics, the evaluated Pareto front approximation is
normalized with the maximum and minimum values in the true Pareto front
for every objective. This is done to avoid some bias due to the (possible)
high differences in the order of magnitude of the different objectives. In the
case of the problems considered in this book, the optimal Pareto front is not
known. Therefore, we build a *reference* Pareto front by merging all the Pareto
front approximations found by all the tested algorithms in every independent
run into one single front. The crowding method is used to discard solutions
when the reference Pareto front is full. This method has been reported to be
appropriate for two- and three-objective problems [8, 11], as those considered

TABLE 5.2. Configuration of ns-3 for
the Simulations

Devices/km^2	100–200–300
Speed	[0, 2] m/s
Size of the area	500 m × 500 m
Default transmission power	16.02 dBm
Direction and speed change	every 20 s
Simulation time	40 s

in this book. The reference Pareto front is then used to normalize the Pareto front approximations found by the algorithms.

Regarding the experimental setup used for ns-3, the mobility model used to emulate the movements of the devices is either the *random walk* (also known as *brownian motion mobility model* [20]) for simulation of MANETs, or SUMO for VANETs related problems. In random walk, nodes move with a randomly chosen speed and direction during a fixed amount of time (20 seconds in our case). After that, other random values for the speed and direction are chosen. The simulation environment used is a square area of 500 m side, and the transmission power of devices is set to 16.02 dBm. The speed of the nodes can vary from 0 to 2 m/s (i.e., between 0 and 7.2 km/h).

We consider three different network densities. The first one is a sparse network with 100 devices/km^2, the second one has 200 devices/km^2, and finally the densest one with 300 devices/km^2. All the configuration parameters are summarized in Table 5.2.

Experiments requiring a lower level of accuracy have been conducted with the dynamic graph library GraphStream in an offline fashion. The realistic mobility of the nodes or the simulation environment (e.g., the road network) were provided as inputs for the simulation. The parameter settings are quite different and thus described in the corresponding experimental chapters.

Finally, in order to provide concluding results, we perform the Wilcoxon unpaired signed-ranks test [18, 33, 36] to look for significant differences on the results provided by the algorithms and protocols, compared pairwise. In the case of MO optimization algorithms, the test is applied on the results obtained by the quality indicators. This test is a nonparametric alternative to the student's *t* test. This method is used to check whether two data samplings belong to different populations or not. Therefore, we can use it to compute if there are statistically significant differences between the data reported by two different algorithms after the independent runs. The null hypothesis for this test is that the median difference between pairs of observations in the underlying populations represented by the samples of results provided by the algorithms is zero.

In this book, we use the symbols ▲, ▽, and – to show existing significant differences in the pairwise comparison of the algorithms according to the Wilcoxon test. These symbols will be arranged in tables. Symbol ▲ means that the algorithm in that row is statistically better than the algorithm in the corresponding column with 95% confidence level. On the contrary, ▽ stands for significantly worse results of the algorithm in that row compared to the algorithm in the column. Finally, – indicates that no statistical differences were found between the corresponding algorithms.

5.5 CONCLUSION

This chapter was dedicated to the description of the optimization framework and the experimental setup that was used throughout all the experiments reported in this book. The framework is generic enough to be suitable to the needs of most designers interested on optimizing problems related to mobile ad hoc networks.

All the single- and multi-objective optimization algorithms used have first been presented. Network and mobility simulators have also been described, considering two levels of accuracy: the selected high accuracy but computationally demanding simulation with ns-3 and SUMO, and low accuracy but fast simulation with the GraphStream graph library. The configurations adopted for all of them is given, as well as the method followed to statistically compare the performance of algorithms and protocols.

REFERENCES

1. traci4j. Available at http://sourceforge.net/projects/traci4j. Accessed July 2012.

2. IEEE standard for information technology — Telecommunications and information exchange between systems — Local and metropolitan area networks — Specific requirements — Part 11: Wireless LAN medium access control (MAC) and physical layer (PHY) specifications. IEEE Std 802.11-2007 (Revision of IEEE Std 802.11-1999), pp. 1–1076, 12 2007.

3. GraphStream a dynamic graph library. Available at http://github.com/graphstream/gs-netstream. Accessed July 2013.

4. The NetStream protocol. Available at http://graphstream-project.org. Accessed July 2013.

5. E. Alba and B. Dorronsoro. *Cellular Genetic Algorithms*. Operations Research/Compuer Science Interfaces. Springer-Verlag, Heidelberg, 2008.

6. E. Alba, B. Dorronsoro, M. Giacobini, and M. Tomassini. Decentralized cellular evolutionary algorithms. In S. Olariu and A. Zomaya, Eds., *Handbook of Bioinspired Algorithms and Applications*, Chapter 7, pp. 103–120. CRC Press, Boca Raton, FL, 2006.

7. E. Alba and J. M. Troya. Cellular evolutionary algorithms: Evaluating the influence of ratio. In M. Schoenauer, Ed., *Proceedings of the Parallel Problem Solving from Nature (PPSN-VI)*, Vol. 1917 of *Lecture Notes in Computer Science*, pp. 29–38. Springer, Heidelberg, 2000.

8. C. A. Coello Coello, G. B. Lamont, and D. A. Veldhuizen. *Evolutionary Algorithms for Solving Multi-Objective Problems*, 2nd edition. Springer, New York, 2007.

9. C. A. Coello Coello and M. Reyes Sierra. A coevolutionary multi-objective evolutionary algorithm. In *Proceedings of the IEEE Congress on Evolutionary Computation (CEC)*, Vol. 1, pp. 482–489. IEEE, Piscataway, 2003.

10. G. Danoy, B. Dorronsoro, and P. Bouvry. Overcoming partitioning in large ad hoc networks using genetic algorithms. In *Proceedings of the Genetic and Evolutionary Computation Conference (GECCO)*, pp. 1347–1354. ACM, New York, 2009.

11. K. Deb. *Multi-Objective Optimization Using Evolutionary Algorithms*. Wiley, Hoboken, 2001.

12. K. Deb, A. Pratap, S. Agarwal, and T. Meyarivan. A fast and elitist multiobjective genetic algorithm: NSGA-II. *IEEE Transactions on Evolutionary Computation*, 6(2):182–197, 2002.

13. B. Dorronsoro, G. Danoy, P. Bouvry, and A. J. Nebro. Multi-objective cooperative coevolutionary evolutionary algorithms for continuous and combinatorial optimization. In P. Bouvry, H. González-velez, and J. Kolodziej, Eds., *Intelligent Decision Systems in Large-Scale Distributed Environments*, Vol. 362 of *Studies in Computational Intelligence*, Chapter 3, pp. 49–74. Springer, Berlin and Heidelberg, 2011.

14. B. Dorronsoro, G. Danoy, A. J. Nebro, and P. Bouvry. Achieving super-linear performance in parallel multi-objective evolutionary algorithms by means of cooperative coevolution. *Computers & Operations Research*, 40(6):1552–1563, 2013.

15. J. J. Durillo, A. J. Nebro, F. Luna, and E. Alba. Solving three-objective optimization problems using a new hybrid cellular genetic algorithm. In G. Rudolph, T. Jensen, S. Lucas, C. Poloni, and N. Beume, Eds., *Proceedings of the Parallel Problem Solving from Nature—PPSN X*, Vol. 5199 of *Lecture Notes in Computer Science*, pp. 661–670. Springer, Heidelberg, 2008.

16. J. J. Durillo and A. J. Nebro. jmetal, a java framework for multiobjective optimization. *Advances in Engineering Software*, 42:760–771, 2011.

17. A. Dutot, F. Guinand, D. Olivier, and Y. Pigné. Graphstream: A tool for bridging the gap between complex systems and dynamic graphs. In *Proceedings of Emergent Properties in Natural and Artificial Complex Systems. Satellite Conference within the 4th European Conference on Complex Systems (ECCS'2007)*, 2007.

18. S. García, D. Molina, M. Lozano, and F. Herrera. A study on the use of non-parametric tests for analyzing the evolutionary algorithms' behaviour: A case study on the CEC'05 special session on real parameter optimization. *Journal of Heuristics*, 15:617–644, 2009.

19. C.-K. Goh and K. C. Tan. A coevolutionary paradigm for dynamic multiobjective optimization. In *Evolutionary Multi-Objective Optimization in Uncertain Environments*, Vol. 186 of *Studies in Computational Intelligence (SCI)*, pp. 153–185, 2009.

20. R. B. Groenevelt, E. Altman, and P. Nain. Relaying in mobile ad hoc networks: The brownian motion mobility model. *Journal of Wireless Networks*, 12(5):561–571, 2006.

21. A. W. Iorio and X. Li. A cooperative coevolutionary multiobjective algorithm using non-dominated sorting. In *Proceedings of the Genetic and Evolutionary Computation Conference (GECCO)*, pp. 537–548, 2004.

22. N. Keerativuttitumrong, N. Chaiyaratana, and V. Varavithya. Multi-objective co-operative co-evolutionary genetic algorithm. In *International Conference on Parallel Problem Solving from Nature (PPSN)*, Vol. 2439 of *Lecture Notes in Computer Science (LNCS)*, pp. 288–297. Springer-Verlag, Heidelberg, 2002.

23. J. Knowles, L. Thiele, and E. Zitzler. A tutorial on the performance assessment of stochastic multiobjective optimizers. TIK Report 214. Computer Engineering and Networks Laboratory (TIK), Zurich, February 2006.

24. S. Krauss, P. Wagner, and C. Gawron. Metastable states in a microscopic model of traffic flow. *Physical Review E*, 55:5597–5602, 1997.

25. K. Maneeratana, K. Boonlong, and N. Chaiyaratana. Multi-objective optimisation by co-operative co-evolution. In *Proceedings of the International Conference on Parallel Problem Solving from Nature (PPSN)*, pp. 772–781, 2004.

26. A. J. Nebro, J. J. Durillo, F. Luna, B. Dorronsoro, and E. Alba. Mocell: A cellular genetic algorithm for multiobjective optimization. *International Journal of Intelligent Systems*, 24(7):726–746, 2009.

27. S. S. Nielsen, B. Dorronsoro, G. Danoy, and P. Bouvry. Novel efficient asynchronous cooperative co-evolutionary multi-objective algorithms. In *Proceedings of the IEEE Congress on Evolutionary Computation (CEC), part of World Conference in Computational Intelligence (WCCI)*, pp. 2784–2790, 2012.

28. Y. Pigné, G. Danoy, and P. Bouvry. A platform for realistic online vehicular network management. In *Proceedings of the IEEE International Workshop on Management of Emerging Networks and Services*, pp. 615–619. IEEE Computer Society, New York, 2010.

29. M. A. Potter and K. De Jong. A cooperative coevolutionary approach to function optimization. In *International Conference on Parallel Problem Solving from Nature (PPSN)*, Vol. 866 of *Lecture Notes in Computer Science (LNCS)*, pp. 249–257. Springer, Berlin and Heidelberg, 1994.

30. K. V. Price, R. M. Storn, and J. A. Lampinen. *Differential Evolution—A Practical Approach to Global Optimization. Natural Computing Series.* Springer, Berlin and Heidelberg, 2005.

31. M. Rondinone, J. Maneros, D. Krajzewicz, R. Bauza, P. Cataldi, F. Hrizi, J. Gozalvez, V. Kumar, M. Röckl, O. Lin, L.and Lazaro, J. Leguay, J. Haerri, S. Vaz, Y. Lopez, M. Sepulcre, M. Wetterwald, R. Blokpoel, and F. Cartolano. iTETRIS: A modular simulation platform for the large scale evaluation of cooperative ITS applications. In *Simulation Modelling Practice and Theory.* Vol. 34 pp. 99–125, Elsevier, May 2013.

32. F. Seredynski, A. Y. Zomaya, and P. Bouvry. Function optimization with coevolutionary algorithms. In *Proceedings of the International Intelligent Information Processing and Web Mining Conference, Advances in Soft Computing series,* Vol. 22, pp. 13–22. Springer, Berlin and Heidelberg, 2003.

33. D. J. Sheshin. *Handbook of Parametric and Nonparametric Statistical Procedures.* CRC Press, Boca Raton, FL, 2003.

34. C. Sommer, R. German, and F. Dressler. Bidirectionally coupled network and road traffic simulation for improved IVC analysis. *IEEE Transactions on Mobile Computing,* 10(1):3–15, 2011.

35. K. C. Tan, Y. J. Yang, and C. K. Goh. A distributed cooperative coevolutionary algorithm for multiobjective optimization. *IEEE Transactions on Evolutionary Computation,* 10(5):527–549, 2006.

36. J. H. Zar. *Biostatistical Analysis.* Prentice Hall, Upper Saddle River, 1999.

37. E. Zitzler and L. Thiele. Multiobjective evolutionary algorithms: A comparative case study and the strength pareto approach. *IEEE Transactions on Evolutionary Computation,* 3(4):257–271, 1999.

6

BROADCASTING PROTOCOL

One of the most important low-level operations in networking is broadcasting, especially when dealing with unstructured MANETs. The reason is that, due to the limited communication range of devices, together with their mobility, the topology of such networks may change quickly and in unpredictable ways. This dynamical behavior constitutes one of the main obstacles for performing efficient communications. Therefore, in this chapter we address the optimization of the delayed flooding with cumulative neighbors (or DFCN for short) broadcasting protocol [6]. DFCN is a smart broadcasting protocol that reduces the number of forwarded messages with very low penalization on the final coverage. This is achieved by dropping the message when a high percentage of the device's neighbors has already received it. Additionally, once the forwarding decision is taken, the device waits for an arbitrary amount of time before performing the action, which is canceled in case another neighbor forwards the message during this time.

Evolutionary Algorithms for Mobile Ad Hoc Networks, First Edition. Bernabé Dorronsoro,
Patricia Ruiz, Grégoire Danoy, Yoann Pigné, and Pascal Bouvry.
© 2014 John Wiley & Sons, Inc. Published 2014 by John Wiley & Sons, Inc.

The DFCN protocol was already optimized in a previous work [1] with a simple multi-objective cellular GA, and using the custom Madhoc simulator [5] for fitness evaluations. However, in this chapter we optimize it with different types of more advanced highly efficient optimization techniques, such as NSGA-II, CellDE, and CCNSGA-II (refer to Chapter 5 for details). Additionally, the protocol has been implemented in the ns-3 simulator in order to perform much more realistic simulations. Three different network densities have been considered in this work.

Optimizing a broadcasting strategy implies multiple conflicting goals to be satisfied at the same time, such as maximizing the number of devices reached (coverage), minimizing the network use (bandwidth), minimizing the duration of the process, and the like. In this work, we tackle these three objectives, thus, we are facing a multi-objective optimization problem.

This chapter is structured as follows. Section 6.1 gives a description of DFCN and defines the optimization problem we will tackle to enhance the behavior of the protocol. Section 6.2 summarizes the comparison of the performance of the considered evolutionary algorithms on this problem. Results are later analyzed and discussed in Section 6.3. Finally, our main conclusions are pointed out in Section 6.4.

6.1 THE PROBLEM

The problem we study in this chapter is to, given an input MANET, determine the most adequate parameters for the DFCN broadcasting strategy. In Section 6.1.1 we first present DFCN [6]. Then, in Section 6.1.2 we define the optimization problem we tackle to find good configurations of the protocol.

6.1.1 DFCN Protocol

Williams and Camp [14], as well as Stojmenovic and Wu [13], proposed two of the most frequently referenced analysis of broadcasting protocols. Williams and Camp [14] categorized the protocols into four families: simple flooding, probability-based methods, area-based methods, and neighbor knowledge methods. In their proposal, Stojmenovic and Wu [13] state that protocols can be classified according to their algorithmic nature — determinism (no use of randomness), reliability (guarantee of full coverage) — or the information required by their execution (network information, "hello" messages content, broadcast messages content). Similarly, Wu and Lou [15] categorized protocols as *centralized* [9] and *localized* ones. On the one hand, centralized protocols require a global or quasi-global knowledge of the network. They are hence not scalable. On the other hand, localized protocols are those that require some knowledge of the network at only 1 or 2 hops.

Using the classifications presented here, DFCN [6] is a deterministic algorithm, fully localized, which defines heuristics based on 1-hop information (neighbor knowledge). This permits DFCN to achieve great scalability. "Hello" messages interchanged by the nodes do not carry any additional information. Only broadcast messages must embed the list of the node's neighbors.

In order to be able to run the DFCN protocol, the following assumptions must be met.

- Like many other neighbor-knowledge-based broadcasting protocols (Flooding With Self-Pruning (FWSP) Scalable Broadcast Algorithm (SBA), etc.) [8, 10], DFCN requires the knowledge of a 1-hop neighborhood. This is obtained by the use of "hello" packets at a lower network layer. The set of neighbors of the device s is named $N(s)$.
- Each message m carries — embedded in its header — the set of IDs of the 1-hop neighbors of its most recent sender.
- Each device maintains local information about all messages received. Each instance of this local information consists of the following items:
  ◦ The ID of the message received
  ◦ The set of IDs of the devices that are known to have received the message
  ◦ The decision of whether the message was forwarded or not
- DFCN requires the use of a random delay before possibly reemitting a broadcast message m. This delay, called random assessment delay (RAD), is intended to prevent collisions. More precisely, when a device s emits a message m, all the devices in $N(s)$ receive it at approximately the same time. It is then likely that all of them forward m simultaneously, and this simultaneity entails network collisions. The RAD aims at randomly delaying the retransmission of m. As every device in $N(s)$ waits for the expiration of a different RAD before forwarding m, the risk of collisions is hugely reduced.

DFCN is an event-driven algorithm that can be divided into three main parts: the first two deal with the handling of outcoming events, which are (1) new message reception and (2) detection of a new neighbor. The third part (3) consists of the decision making for emission as a followup of one of the two previous events. The behavior resulting from message reception is referred to as *reactive* behavior; when a new neighbor is discovered, the behavior is referred to as *proactive* behavior.

Let s_1 and s_2 be two devices in the neighborhood of one another. When s_1 sends a packet to s_2, it attaches to the packet the set $N(s_1)$. At reception, s_2 hence knows that each device in $N(s_1)$ has likely received the packet. The set of known devices that has *potentially* not yet received the packet is then $N(s_2) - N(s_1)$. If s_2 reemits the packet, the *effective* number of devices newly reached is maximized by the heuristic function: $h(s_2, s_1) = |N(s_2) - N(s_1)|$.

In order to minimize the network use caused by a possible packet re-emission, a message is forwarded only if the number of potentially reached devices $h(s_2, s_1)$ is greater than a given threshold. This threshold is a function of the number of devices in the neighborhood (the local network density) of the recipient device s_2. It is written "threshold(n)." The decision made by s_2 to reemit the packet received from s_1 is defined by the Boolean function:

$$B(s_2, s_1) = \begin{cases} \text{true} & h(s_2, s_1) \geq \text{threshold}(n) \\ \text{false} & \text{otherwise.} \end{cases}$$

If the threshold is exceeded, the recipient device s_2 becomes an emitter in turn. The message is effectively sent when the random delay (defined by the RAD) expires. The threshold function, which allows DFCN to facilitate the message rebroadcasting when the connectivity is low, depends on the size of the neighborhood n, as given by

$$\text{Threshold}(n) = \begin{cases} 1 & n \leq \text{safeDensity} \\ \text{minGain} * n & \text{otherwise,} \end{cases}$$

where safeDensity is the maximum number of neighbors for which the network is considered to be sparse, thus, DFCN always rebroadcasts. minGain is a parameter of DFCN used for computing the minimum threshold for forwarding a message, that is, the ratio between the number of neighbors that have not received the message and the total number of neighbors.

Each time a device s discovers a new neighbor, the RAD for all messages is set to zero and, therefore, the messages are immediately candidates for emission. If $N(s)$ is greater than a given threshold, which we have called *proD*, this behavior is disabled, so no action is undertaken on new neighbor discovery.

6.1.2 Optimization Problem Definition

From the description of DFCN in the previous section, we identify the following parameters to be tuned.

minGain is the minimum gain for rebroadcasting. This is the most important parameter for tuning DFCN since minimizing the bandwidth should be highly dependent on the network density. It ranges from 0.0 to 1.0.

lowerBoundRAD,upperBoundRAD define the RAD value (random delay for rebroadcasting). The two parameters take values in the interval [0.0, 10.0] seconds, and lowerBoundRAD ≤ upperBoundRAD.

proD is the maximum number of neighbors (proD ∈ [0, 100]) for which it is still needed to use proactive behavior (i.e., reacting on new neighbors) for promoting the dissemination in sparse networks.

safeDensity defines the maximum value of the local network density for rebroadcasting all messages. It ranges from 0 to 100 devices.

These five parameters compose the five decision variables that correspond to a DFCN configuration, and, therefore, they characterize the search space. We have set wide enough intervals for the values of these parameters in order to include all the reasonable possibilities we can find in a real scenario. The objectives to optimize are: minimizing the duration of the broadcasting process, maximizing the network coverage, and minimizing the number of transmissions. Thus, we have defined a triple objective MOP, which is formally defined as:

$$
\begin{aligned}
&s : \text{ instance of the ns-3 simulator} \\
&\text{minG} = g \in \mathbb{R} | g \in \text{minGain} \\
&\text{lowRAD} = \texttt{l\_RAD} \in \mathbb{R} | \texttt{l\_RAD} \in \text{lowerBoundRAD} \\
&\text{uppRAD} = \texttt{u\_RAD} \in \mathbb{R} | \texttt{u\_RAD} \in \text{upperBoundRAD} \\
&\text{proact} = d \in \mathbb{I} | d \in \text{proD} \\
&\text{safeDens} = s_d \in \mathbb{I} | s_d \in \text{safeDensity} \\
&z = (c, b, t) = s(\text{minG,lowRAD,uppRAD,proact,safeDens})
\end{aligned}
$$

$$
f(\text{minG,lowRAD,uppRAD,proact,safeDens}) = \begin{cases} \max\{c\} \\ \min\{b\} \\ \min\{t\} \end{cases}, \qquad (6.1)
$$

where z is the set of objectives, c stands for coverage, b for number of broadcastings, and t is the broadcasting time. The domains of the variables minGain, lowerBoundRAD, upperBoundRAD, proD, and safeDensity are presented in detail in Table 6.1.

TABLE 6.1. Domain of the Variables
to Optimize

minGain	[0.0, 1.0]
lowerBoundRAD	[0.0, 10.0] seconds
upperBoundRAD	[0.0, 10.0] seconds
proD	[0, 100] devices
safeDensity	[0, 100] devices

6.2   EXPERIMENTS

We present in this section the results obtained during our experimentation process. Section 6.2.1 presents the configuration used for our algorithms, which are later compared in Section 6.2.2.

6.2.1   Algorithm Configurations

Because we are dealing with a multi-objective problem, in this chapter we use CellDE, NSGA-II, and CCNSGA-II algorithms to look for the optimal configuration of the DFCN parameters (defined in Section 6.1.2) in order to get the best possible performance of the considered broadcasting protocol. The configuration of the different algorithms is the one suggested by their authors, and it can be found in Chapter 5. The evaluation function of this problem is expensive (it takes around 10 s), therefore the algorithms stop after performing 10,000 evaluations.

Solutions are represented as an array of five real variables, corresponding to the minimum gain, the RAD interval (minimum and maximum values in the range), proD, and the safe density (the details for these variables can be found in Section 6.1.2). The last two variables are integer values in DFCN, and therefore we take the integer part of the real value proposed by the algorithm before evaluating the solution. This is done for simplicity since it allows us to avoid the use of heterogeneous chromosomes that would require specific operators.

In the case of CCNSGA-II, the values of these variables have been discretized because we need a number of variables to be optimized by every island [11]. Consequently, real-coded variables are discretized into 16-bit strings (minGain, lowerBoundRAD, upperBoundRAD), while integer ones are coded with 8 bits (proD, safeDensity). Two classical recombination and mutation operators for binary representations were implemented, namely two-point crossover and bit-flip mutation. Both of them were introduced in Chapter 2. Eight islands are used to decompose the problem, and therefore every island is focused on the optimization of 8 bits of the chromosome of individuals.

To evaluate the quality of solutions found, the protocol is run with every solution in ns-3 in 10 different networks (the same 10 networks are used for all tentative solutions), and the average value of the 10 runs obtained for coverage, time, and number of forwardings is considered as the fitness value of that solution.

We use the ns-3 configuration provided in Chapter 5 for the simulation of the broadcasting algorithm, using the *random-walk* mobility model. In the simulations, the network evolves for 30 s in order to have the nodes uniformly distributed in the area. Then, after these 30 s, a node starts the broadcasting process. The simulation stops after 40 s.

6.2.2 Comparison of the Performance of the Algorithms

In Tables 6.2–6.4 we present the results we obtained (as mean and standard deviation) with CellDE, NSGA-II, and CCNSGA-II for the three considered problem densities according to the HV, SPREAD, and $I_{\varepsilon+}^1$ quality metrics (already presented in Chapter 5). Those values shadowed in dark gray color

TABLE 6.2. Comparison of Algorithms according to HV

	CellDE	NSGA-II	CCNSGA-II
100 Dev.	$6.46e - 01_{3.7e-03}$	$6.32e - 01_{9.3e-03}$	$5.50e - 01_{8.5e-03}$
200 Dev.	$7.66e - 01_{4.0e-03}$	$7.42e - 01_{8.3e-03}$	$3.98e - 01_{1.5e-02}$
300 Dev.	$8.21e - 01_{2.9e-03}$	$8.09e - 01_{5.2e-03}$	$3.31e - 01_{1.4e-02}$

TABLE 6.3. Comparison of Algorithms according to SPREAD

	CellDE	NSGA-II	CCNSGA-II
100 Dev.	$5.30e - 01_{2.8e-02}$	$7.43e - 01_{4.5e-02}$	$6.73e - 01_{4.7e-02}$
200 Dev.	$5.65e - 01_{3.3e-02}$	$7.39e - 01_{4.6e-02}$	$6.52e - 01_{4.6e-02}$
300 Dev.	$6.32e - 01_{3.9e-02}$	$7.96e - 01_{5.6e-02}$	$6.59e - 01_{3.1e-02}$

TABLE 6.4. Comparison of Algorithms according to $I_{\varepsilon+}^1$

	CellDE	NSGA-II	CCNSGA-II
100 Dev.	$1.04e + 00_{1.3e-01}$	$1.25e + 00_{2.3e-01}$	$4.22e + 00_{4.7e-01}$
200 Dev.	$1.84e + 00_{2.5e-01}$	$2.40e + 00_{5.1e-01}$	$6.82e + 00_{3.4e-01}$
300 Dev.	$3.14e + 00_{3.8e-01}$	$3.72e + 00_{5.2e-01}$	$1.09e + 01_{5.5e-01}$

TABLE 6.5. Comparison of Algorithms according to Wilcoxon Unpaired Signed-Ranks Test for HV, SPREAD, and $I^1_{\varepsilon+}$ on Three Network Densities

		NSGA-II	CCNSGA-II
HV	CellDE	▲ ▲ ▲	▲ ▲ ▲
	NSGAII		▲ ▲ ▲
SPREAD	CellDE	▲ ▲ ▲	▲ ▲ ▲
	NSGAII		▽ ▽ ▽
$I^1_{\varepsilon+}$	CellDE	▲ ▲ ▲	▲ ▲ ▲
	NSGAII		▲ ▲ ▲

represent the best obtained results, while the second best ones are over light gray background. As can be seen, CellDE is the best algorithm for all densities on the three quality indicators used. CCNSGA-II is the second best one according to SPREAD, and NSGA-II is the second most accurate one.

Table 6.5 presents the results obtained by the Wilcoxon test on the comparison of the algorithms for the three considered network densities. In every cell, the three symbols refer to the 100, 200, and 300 devices/km^2 densities, in that order. The Wilcoxon test found statistically significant differences in all cases. CellDE outperforms the other algorithms according to the three studied metrics for all the problem densities. In the comparison between NSGA-II and CCNSGA-II, the coevolutionary algorithm is better in terms of SPREAD and worse for HV and $I^1_{\varepsilon+}$, for the three densities.

6.3   ANALYSIS OF RESULTS

After performing all our experiments, we get 90 Pareto front approximations (3 algorithms, and 30 independent runs for each) for every considered network density, containing approximately 100 accurate DFCN configurations each. Analyzing all 9000 solutions for every density is a tedious task for the decision maker to get the best one for his/her needs. Therefore, it is necessary to choose among all solutions a subset of representative ones to be analyzed. For that, we will build an aggregated Pareto front of 100 solutions from all the solutions reported by the algorithms. This step is not only required in the case of the study we make in this book, when several algorithms are used and a final Pareto front approximation is built from all the results obtained, but also when one single MO algorithm is used to solve the problem. The reason is that MOEAs are stochastic processes, and, therefore, we must run them several times in order to avoid possible low-quality results obtained from one single unsuccessful run.

We present in Section 6.3.1 a discussion on some appropriate techniques to gather a representative set of solutions from all the obtained ones in the experimentation process. Then, we analyze the set of selected representative solutions built in Section 6.3.2, and we propose in Section 6.3.3 some of them as new improved configurations for DFCN, analyzing and comparing them versus the original one.

6.3.1 Building a Representative Subset of Best Solutions

In order to extract a set of representative solutions among all those found during experimentation, a final Pareto front approximation can be built from all the solutions reported by the algorithms in every independent run. This can be done by simply generating an empty front of limited size (i.e., 100 solutions) and start adding all the obtained solutions in it. Building such Pareto front approximation from all the solutions found in the different runs will provide a better front than just choosing the best one reported by the algorithm according to some quality metric.

There are several density estimators in the literature to discard solutions from the densest areas in case a new solution is inserted in an already full front [2, 3]. However, it is worth mentioning that this density estimation method used to discard nondominated solutions might influence the results.

To illustrate this, in Fig. 6.1 we show the Pareto front approximations obtained when using three well-known density estimators in the multi-objective optimization literature, namely *strength raw fitness* [16], *adaptive grid* [7], and *crowding* [4]. The plots correspond to the densest studied networks, as a representative case, and the default configuration of DFCN is represented as a black square. The three fronts provide similar quality results, none of them contain solutions that are dominated by any other solution from the other fronts, and this conclusion is also extensible to the other two densities. However, they provide different numbers of solutions dominating DFCN: 5, 7, and 9 for strength raw fitness, for the three studied densities (from sparser to denser), 1, 6, and 5 for crowding, and 10, 0, and 6 in the case of adaptive grid. Additionally, not all of them provide a high diversity of solutions in the covered area, and some of them even dismiss solutions at the borders of this area, shrinking it. This is important because the decision maker may think that no solutions exist in these uncovered areas, when in fact they were found during the experimentations.

As can be seen, the front built with strength raw fitness is the one that provides a higher diversity of solutions. The adaptive grid technique provides

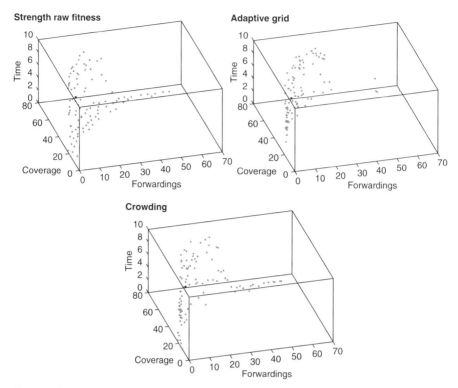

Figure 6.1. Pareto front approximations obtained after combining all the reported results in every run by the three EAs with three different density estimators for the 300 devices/km^2 networks. The performance of the default DFCN configuration is shown as a black square.

poor diversity for high forwarding and coverage values, with a large empty area. Additionally, there is also an important gap in the lowest part of the front, corresponding to solutions with short broadcasting times. Regarding the front generated with crowding, we can observe some denser regions than in the front generated by strength raw fitness, and therefore there are some gaps that are not covered, especially the area corresponding to short times, as in the previous case. These observations are supported by the SPREAD metric in the 300 devices/km^2 network, which gives values 0.2781, 0.4766, and 0.4933 for the fronts generated by strength raw fitness, crowding, and adaptive grid techniques, respectively. For the other densities, we obtained similar results, with strength raw fitness providing the best diversity front, followed by, crowding, and adaptive grid, in that order. The values obtained are 0.1687, 0.3611, and 0.5012 for the three techniques on the 100 devices/km^2 density and 0.3055, 0.4141, and 0.5201 for the 200 devices/km^2 networks.

Even when many solutions are dismissed in the process, it is still recommended to build one single Pareto front approximation from all the results obtained in the experimentation. The reason is that it can give an overview of a representative set of solutions available that can be analyzed by the decision maker. Dealing with all the nondominated solutions without any preselection is hard to handle, especially when a large number of runs of the MOEA(s) is performed, as is recommended. Once a certain region of appropriate solutions is identified, then it is possible to find all the dismissed solutions in this area to perform a deeper study.

6.3.2 Interpretation of the Results

In order to visually show the different solutions found by the EAs with respect to the original DFCN configuration, in Fig. 6.2 we plot the best solutions found in our experiments, obtained by merging all the Pareto front approximations found by the three EAs in all the independent runs. The number of solutions was limited to 100, so nondominated solutions in the densest regions were discarded according to the strength raw fitness method [16], with the aim of offering a wide set of diverse solutions. In the plots, we differentiate the solutions provided by the different algorithms, therefore, those solutions found by NSGA-II are represented as black points, while gray ones are solutions from CellDE and the + symbol represents the solutions provided by CCNSGA-II.

The default configuration of DFCN is [6]: minGain = 0.4, RAD $\in$ [0.0, 7.0], proD = 4, and safeDensity = 12 [12]. DFCN was dominated by 5, 7, and 3 solutions out of the 100 reported by EAs for the 100, 200, and 300 devices/km^2 densities, respectively. Notice that these solutions outperform the original DFCN configuration in all objectives, so they provide higher coverage with lower number of forwardings in less time. In addition, 11, 11, and 7 solutions are better if we put time aside, and 40, 30, and 26 are better in terms of coverage, for the three densities.

However, we found that the number of solutions dominating DFCN reported by the three algorithms in the 30 independent runs is considerably higher than that. In this sense, CellDE, NSGA-II, and CCNSGA-II found 123, 127, and 12 different solutions dominating DFCN, respectively, for the 100 devices/km^2 density, 134, 95, and 4 for 200 devices/km^2, and 84, 101, and 0 for 300 devices/km^2. The total number of different solutions dominating DFCN found in our experiments increases to 262, 233, and 185 for the 100, 200, and 300 devices/km^2. All of them are plotted as black points in Fig. 6.3. Consequently, a high number of solutions dominating DFCN

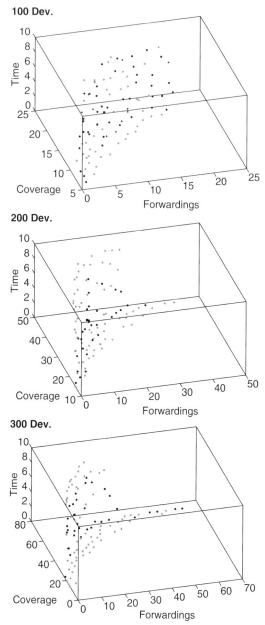

Figure 6.2. Best nondominated solutions found and the performance of the default DFCN configuration (represented as black square). Solutions provided by NSGA-II, CellDE, and CCNSGA-II are represented with symbols and black points, gray points, and +, respectively.

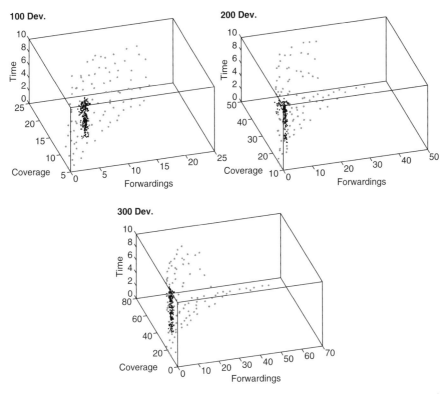

Figure 6.3. Best nondominated solutions found (gray points) and the performance of the default DFCN configuration (black square), together with all the solutions dominating DFCN that were found in our experiments (black points).

is lost when building the final Pareto front approximation. The reasons are that (i) a number of these solutions are dominated by the ones chosen for the final set of solutions, (ii) its size is limited to 100, so nondominated solutions in the most crowded regions are discarded, and (iii) representative solutions from the whole Pareto front area must be selected, as was discussed in Section 6.3.1, including those extreme solutions with highly accurate values for one of the objectives, but that are low compared to the others. These solutions are nondominated ones, so they are still interesting from the multi-objective optimization point of view, although they are worse than DFCN in some of the objectives. It is then the choice of the decision maker to implement some solution that does not dominate DFCN but is nondominated with it. As an example, a solution with higher coverage than DFCN and less network use, at the cost of longer broadcasting time, could be acceptable in our case.

6.3.3   Selected Improved DFCN Configurations

In Table 6.6 we compile all the solutions from the Pareto front that were
found to dominate the original DFCN configuration. Their corresponding fitness values are listed in Table 6.7 (where forwardings and coverage values are
expressed as the percentage of devices in the network). From Table 6.6, one
of the most outstanding issues we can see is the high values the EAs assigned
to the proD parameter, ranging from 11 to 88, while the original configuration of DFCN suggests using a value of 4. This means that the algorithms
found that the proactive behavior of the protocol, consisting on resetting the
RAD delay to rebroadcast the messages when a new device arrives in the
neighborhood, is always advisable even in dense areas. Indeed, we tested
the same solutions with a very high value for this parameter — we used
proD = 100 — and the results obtained where exactly the same ones in all
cases, with the exceptions of solutions Sol9 and Sol10, both of them for the
200 devices/km^2 networks. Therefore, we can conclude that the EAs find that
this proactive behavior is generally advisable for DFCN, and they are simply
choosing high enough values for proD in order to always enable this feature
of the protocol.

Indeed, enabling always the proactive behavior of the protocol makes the
broadcasting process faster since the RAD does not expire but is stopped
when a new neighbor is found. That is the reason why even when the value
of the RAD in Sol11 is higher than in Sol12 because of the values of the
lowerBoundRAD and upperBoundRAD, the difference in the broadcast time
is not so important. In Sol11, the RAD is fixed to 10 s while it is less than
2.8308 s in Sol12 (more than three times lower), but the broadcast process is
finally only 0.212 s slower for Sol11.

With regard to the other protocol variables optimized, we can see that the
value suggested by the EAs for minGain is in all cases close to the one set by
the protocol designer. We do not find a pattern in the values assigned by the
EAs to the safeDensity parameter. However, we observe that very low values
are assigned for some solutions (i.e., Sol2), indicating that in some cases
it might be a good idea to disable flooding capability of the protocol. For
instance, Sol2 is suggesting to disable the flooding mode but at the same time
promoting the dissemination by canceling the RAD when a new neighbor is
met (as we mentioned before, all the solutions gave the same results with
proD equal to 100 except Sol9 and Sol10).

We observe that small intervals are assigned to RAD, in general. The
extreme is Sol6, which removes this feature from the protocol. Configurations with low RAD interval provide fast solutions, while those with the
highest intervals are the slowest ones. In this sense, there are four solutions

TABLE 6.6. Solutions Found That Outperform DFCN Original Configuration for Three Objectives

dev./km²	Solution	minGain	RAD	proD	safeDensity	Algorithm
	DFCN	0.4	[0.0, 7.0]	4	12	—
100	Sol1	0.2559279959314381	[0.37838939855767806, 9.1205896205331833]	84	3	NSGA-II
	Sol2	0.3106136104098672	[0.0, 3.77622653439971]	11	0	CellDE
	Sol3	0.3137985713985266	[0.0, 1.8166803587138693]	88	7	CellDE
	Sol4	0.2956905050280863	[0.28417307413411563, 1.87903803838884]	62	5	NSGA-II
	Sol5	0.30190793008451416	[0.002167250712626841, 0.17757117483530718]	82	9	NSGA-II
200	Sol6	0.5244789246681958	[0.0, 0.0]	68	12	CellDE
	Sol7	0.23262266938338613	[10.0, 10.0]	67	12	CellDE
	Sol8	0.45138885098745435	[0.005853573465718576, 1.4167981490052637]	73	5	NSGA-II
	Sol9	0.35188367053794545	[10.0, 10.0]	18	24	CellDE
	Sol10	0.2935923314536946	[10.0, 10.0]	23	10	CellDE
	Sol11	0.2874099031627282	[10.0, 10.0]	43	3	CellDE
	Sol12	0.48537600157429095	[0.4216484850009434, 2.8308110208460655]	37	11	NSGA-II
300	Sol13	0.46147023817982497	[0.010781467931704425, 4.261884410159036]	74	2	NSGA-II
	Sol14	0.41084724320088	[2.5014487499316895, 4.601211573914485]	38	13	CellDE
	Sol15	0.4977711892032174	[0.06103145898364451, 0.5542608402159395]	79	10	NSGA-II

TABLE 6.7. Solutions Found that Outperform DFCN
Original Configuration for Three Objectives[a]

dev./km^2	Solution	Forwardings (%)	Coverage (%)	Time
100	DFCN	25.60	54.80	5.1212
	Sol1	22.80	58.40	4.8054
	Sol2	22.80	58.00	3.2082
	Sol3	20.40	57.20	1.7476
	Sol4	24.40	63.20	2.3648
	Sol5	25.60	57.60	0.2682
200	DFCN	13.80	49.40	6.0320
	Sol6	12.40	52.00	0.0042
	Sol7	12.60	69.00	6.0276
	Sol8	13.60	55.60	1.3358
	Sol9	11.20	58.20	5.1376
	Sol10	9.00	55.00	5.2180
	Sol11	8.00	52.00	4.1517
	Sol12	12.60	53.40	3.9389
300	DFCN	10.27	50.27	6.2294
	Sol13	7.20	52.53	4.0212
	Sol14	10.27	58.93	5.0449
	Sol15	8.40	51.73	0.6933

[a]Forwardings and coverage are shown as the percentage of devices in the network.

(Sol7, Sol9, Sol10, and Sol11), all of them for the 200 devices/km^2 networks, forcing this RAD time to be 10 s (i.e., the interval is set to [10.0, 10.0]). These solutions provide, in general, high coverage with a low number of reemissions, but at the cost of longer times, although, as previously mentioned, the difference in time is not that high.

6.4 CONCLUSION

In this chapter we show how evolutionary algorithms can be applied to fine-tune broadcasting protocols in order to maximize the achieved coverage in the broadcasting process, while minimizing the network use and the time required. We focus here on the DFCN protocol as an example, explain it, and identify the parameters that have a major influence on its performance.

The cellular algorithm, CellDE, clearly outperformed the panmictic (NSGA-II) and cooperative coevolutionary (CCNSGA-II) algorithms for the three network densities considered and the three quality indicators used. The bad performance of the CCNSGA-II algorithm, only better than NSGA-II for SPREAD and the worst algorithm for the other metrics is probably due to the high epistasis introduced in the discretization of the variables. This was necessary due to the small number of variables identified in the problem.

As a result, a number of solutions were found that outperform the original configuration of DFCN for all objectives. Among them, we select and analyze a representative subset with different characteristics.

The algorithms suggest that the proactive behavior included in DFCN for promoting the dissemination of the message in sparse areas is, indeed, suitable for any kind of network. The performance of the protocol was measured in terms of coverage, number of forwardings, and broadcasting time. Therefore, the algorithms provide a new simpler version of the protocol that outperforms the original one.

REFERENCES

1. E. Alba, B. Dorronsoro, F. Luna, A. J. Nebro, P. Bouvry, and L. Hogie. A cellular multi-objective genetic algorithm for optimal broadcasting strategy in metropolitan MANETs. *Computer Communications*, 30(4):685–697, 2007.

2. C. A. Coello Coello, G. B. Lamont, and D. A. Veldhuizen. *Evolutionary Algorithms for Solving Multi-Objective Problems*. 2nd ed. Springer, New York, 2007.

3. K. Deb. *Multi-Objective Optimization Using Evolutionary Algorithms*. Wiley, Hoboken, 2001.

4. K. Deb, A. Pratap, S. Agarwal, and T. Meyarivan. A fast and elitist multi-objective genetic algorithm: NSGA-II. *IEEE Transactions on Evolutionary Computation*, 6(2):182–197, 2002.

5. L. Hogie. The madhoc simulator. Technical Report. Le Havre University, 2005.

6. L. Hogie, F. Guinand, and P. Bouvry. A heuristic for efficient broadcasting in the metropolitan ad hoc network. In M. Gh. Negoita, R.J. Howlett, and L.C. Jain, Eds., *8th International Conference on Knowledge-Based Intelligent Information and Engineering Systems*, Vol. 3215 of *Lecture Notes In Artificial Intelligence (LNAI)*, pp. 727–733. Springer-Verlag, Berlin and Heidelberg, 2004.

7. J. Knowles and D. Corne. Approximating the nondominated front using the Pareto archived evolution strategy. *Evolutionary Computation*, 8(2):149–172, 2001.

8. H. Lim and C. Kim. Multicast tree construction and flooding in wireless ad hoc networks. In A. Boukerche, M. Meo, and C.Tropper, Eds., *Proceedings of the ACM International Workshop on Modelling, Analysis and Simulation of Wireless and Mobile Systems (MSWIM)*, pp. 61–68, ACM, New York, 2000.

9. A. Pelc. Broadcasting in wireless networks. In I. Stojmenovic, Ed., *Handbook of Wireless Networks and Mobile Computing*, pp. 509–528. Wiley, Hoboken, 2002.

10. W. Peng and X.-C. Lu. On the reduction of broadcast redundancy in mobile ad hoc networks. In R. L. Pickholtz, S. K. Das, R. Cáceres, and J. J. Garcia-Luna-Aceves, Eds., *MobiHoc '00: Proceedings of the 1st ACM International Symposium on Mobile Ad Hoc Networking & Computing*, pp. 129–130. ACM, New York, 2000.

11. M. Potter. The design and analysis of a computational model of cooperative coEvolution. PhD thesis. George Mason University, Fairfax, VA, 1997.

12. P. Ruiz, B. Dorronsoro, P. Bouvry, and L. Tardón. Information dissemination in VANETs based upon a tree topology. *Ad Hoc Networks*, 10:111–127, 2012.

13. I. Stojmenovic and J. Wu. Broadcasting and activity scheduling in ad hoc networks. In S. Basagni, M. Conti, S. Giordano, and I. Stojmenovic, Eds., *Mobile Ad Hoc Networking*, pp. 205–229. John Wiley & Sons, Inc., Hoboken, 2004.

14. B. Williams and T. Camp. Comparison of broadcasting techniques for mobile ad hoc networks. In J.-P. Hubaux, J. J. Garcia-Luna-Aceves, and D. B. Johnson, Eds., *Proceedings of the ACM International Symposium on Mobile Ad Hoc Networking and Computing (MOBIHOC)*, pp. 194–205. ACM, New York, 2002.

15. J. Wu and W. Lou. Forward-node-set-based broadcast in clustered mobile ad hoc networks. *Wireless Communications and Mobile Computing*, 3(2):155–173, 2003. Special issue on algorithmic, geometric, graph, combinatorial, and vector.

16. E. Zitzler, M. Laumanns, and L. Thiele. SPEA2: Improving the strength Pareto evolutionary algorithm. Technical Report 103. Computer Engineering and Networks Laboratory (TIK), Zurich, 2001.

7

ENERGY MANAGEMENT

As mentioned in Chapter 6, broadcasting is considered one of the most important low-level operations in networking, as many applications and even other protocols rely on its service. In the case of wireless networks, these dissemination algorithms are generally associated with the broadcast storm problem [2]. However, when designing broadcast protocols for mobile ad hoc networks apart from the broadcast storm problem, we should also take into account the intrinsic limitations of ad hoc networks.

In Chapter 1, the main characteristics of MANETs were presented. As stated there, one of the main drawbacks is the dependence on the battery life of the devices, because this energy limitation highly influences the network behavior: When devices run out of battery power the network capabilities decrease and might lead to the disappearance of the network. Therefore, many researchers focus on reducing the energy consumption of devices conforming the MANET [1, 4].

Evolutionary Algorithms for Mobile Ad Hoc Networks, First Edition. Bernabé Dorronsoro, Patricia Ruiz, Grégoire Danoy, Yoann Pigné, and Pascal Bouvry.
© 2014 John Wiley & Sons, Inc. Published 2014 by John Wiley & Sons, Inc.

In this chapter, we are tackling the optimization of an energy-efficient broadcasting algorithm. We are considering the enhanced distance-based broadcasting algorithm (AEDB hereinafter), an energy-aware and distance based broadcasting algorithm that uses a cross-layer design to reduce energy consumption [3]. In previous work, some metaheuristics were used in order to find out the optimal configuration of its parameters [5, 6]. In this chapter, three different evolutionary algorithms are used for the optimization of AEDB, giving a comparison between performance of each algorithm and a deep analysis on the behavior of the solutions found.

The chapter is organized as follows: Section 7.1 describes the energy-aware protocol, AEDB, and the optimization problem we are tackling to find its optimal configuration. Section 7.2 summarizes the comparison of the performance of the considered evolutionary algorithms on this problem. Results are later analyzed and discussed in Section 7.3. Different solutions from the Pareto front are selected and analyzed in Section 7.4. Finally, our main conclusions are pointed out in Section 7.5.

7.1 THE PROBLEM

The core of AEDB relies on decisions such as whether to forward the message or not and what transmission power to use for each retransmission. The algorithm's performance is highly influenced by the value of those thresholds, which originally were experimentally chosen. In this work, we optimize the values of these thresholds using some multi-objective techniques, and some of the proposed solutions are analyzed. In this section, we first introduce the protocol and then the optimization problem is presented.

7.1.1 AEDB Protocol

In the minimum energy broadcasting problem, every node is able to adjust its transmission range in order to reduce the power consumption of the dissemination process while still guaranteeing full coverage in the network. In a real scenario with obstacles, moving devices, signal fading, path loss, packet loss, and the like, ensuring full coverage might be very ambitious, impossible (due to network partitioning), and in some cases even unnecessary. For disseminating safety, control, or important messages, it might be worth the overhead needed for delivering the message to all nodes in the network. But for all the other messages (information, advertisment, etc.), it would rather be more efficient to consider the possibility of relaxing the full coverage constraint and, thus, saving all the overhead derived from acknowledgments, retransmissions, and so forth. In this work, we consider this second family of protocols, where full coverage is not required.

The adaptive enhanced distance-based broadcasting algorithm (AEDB) considered in this work aims at saving energy in both sparse and dense networks. AEDB [3] is an extension of enhanced distance broadcasting(EDB) [4, 7], a broadcasting algorithm that reduces the transmission power for disseminating a message. As any distance-based broadcasting algorithm, nodes are candidates to forward the message if the distance to the source node is higher than a predefined threshold. Thus, there exists a forwarding area, and only nodes located in it are potential forwarders. In this case, we are using a cross-layer technique that informs the upper layers about the signal strength of messages received. Therefore, the decision is not taken in terms of distance (m) but power (dBm). This predefined value for the energy is called the `borders_Threshold`.

The EDB protocol tries to save energy by reducing the transmission power when forwarding the broadcasting message. The new transmission power is the one that reaches the furthest neighbor. The energy needed is estimated according to the reception energy detected in the beacons exchanged (every 1 s). In order to be aware of the nodes mobility, an extra fixed amount of energy is added to the one estimated. This is called the `margin_Threshold`.

In denser networks, the probability of having a node close to the limit transmission range is high, therefore, the probability for EDB to reduce the transmission power is low. Indeed, when the network is very dense the connectivity is usually very high. Thus, reducing the transmission power allowing the loss of some one-hop neighbors will save energy without any detriment in the performance of the broadcasting process. On the contrary, when the network is sparse, the node must maintain the network connectivity, as not doing so would make it more difficult to spread a message through the whole network.

The AEDB protocol considers the possibility of discarding some neighbors from the one-hop neighborhood in dense networks. In fact, the algorithm is able to adapt its behavior to the network density. Potential forwarders set a random delay before resending. If, during this time, many nodes located in the forwarding area are detected (called `neighbors_Threshold`), the transmission range is reduced and some one-hop neighbors are discarded. The new furthest neighbor is the node located in the forwarding area that is the closest one to the source node. A more detailed explanation can be found in [3], and Pseudocode 7.1 gives the AEDB code.

Pseudocode 7.1   AEDB Algorithm

Data: *m*: the incoming broadcast message.

Data: *r*: the node receiving *m*.

Data: *s*: the node that sent *m*.

Data: *p*: the received signal strength of m sent by *s*.

Data: *pmin*: the minimum signal strength received from any *s*.

Data: *potentialForwarders*: # neighbors in the forwarding area.

```
 1: if m is received for the first time then
 2:    calculate p
 3:    update pmin
 4:    if  pmin > borders_Threshold then
 5:      r → drop message m
 6:    else
 7:      waiting ← true
 8:      wait time rand ∈ [delay interval]
 9:    end if
10: else if  waiting then
11:    calculate p
12:    if  p > pmin then
13:      update pmin
14:    end if
15: end if
16: if  pmin > borders_Threshold then
17:    r → drop message m
18: else
19:    if potentialForwarders > neighbors_Threshold then
20:      estimate p to reach closest neighbor to
          borders_Threshold
21:    else
22:      discard s from the one-hop neighbors list
23:      estimate p to reach furthest neighbor
24:    end if
25:    transmit m
26: end if
27: waiting ← false
```

7.1.2   Optimization Problem Definition

As mentioned in Section 7.1.1, AEDB has a set of fixed parameters whose values determine the behavior of the protocol. Those thresholds are explained after and listed here: borders_Threshold, margin_Forwarding, the delay interval, and neighbors_Threshold.

- The value of the `borders_Threshold` sets the size of the forwarding area. The higher the threshold, the higher the number of potential forwarders, the coverage, the network resources used, and the number of collisions.
- The `margin_Forwarding` is related to both the energy saved and the coverage achieved. It is the extra amount of energy added to the estimated transmission power. The higher the margin value, the higher the coverage reached as well as the energy used.
- The value of the `delay` interval sets the waiting time and also affects the behavior of the protocol. We split this threshold into two different variables: `minimum delay` and `maximum delay` referring to the lower and upper value of the interval, respectively. If the delay is very high, the time used to spread the message will be high, but if it is very small, the number of collisions will probably increase.
- Finally, the `neighbors_Threshold` fixes the minimum number of neighbors in the forwarding area needed to consider the network is dense enough to discard some nodes. It affects the use of the network and the energy used. The lower the value, the lower the energy used and the higher the number of forwardings.

We choose an interval for each parameter in order to find reasonable solutions and limit the search space. These values are shown in Table 7.1, and they are large enough to cover the most suitable solutions. The algorithm originally creates a set of random feasible solutions (values chosen from the intervals shown in Table 7.1), and automatically evolves them to better solutions.

The quality of the performance of a broadcasting algorithm in ad hoc networks is usually related to some standard measurements. The aspects we are considering and that are the most common ones in this kind of protocols are:

1. The **coverage** obtained, that is, the number of devices that, after the dissemination process, receive the broadcast message
2. The **energy used** by the broadcast process, measured as the sum of the energy every device consumes to forward the message

TABLE 7.1. Domain of Variables to Optimize

minimum delay	[0, 1] s
maximum delay	[0, 5] s
border_Threshold	[−95, −70] dBm
margin_Threshold	[0, 3] dBm
neighbors_Threshold	[0, 50]

3. The number of **forwardings**, considered as the amount of nodes that after receiving the broadcasting message decide to resend it

4. And the **broadcast time**, considered as the time needed to spread a message in the network, since the source node sends the message until the last node receives it

From the point of view of the designer of the broadcasting algorithm, the higher the number of objectives the more complex the decision making and the optimization process. Thus, in this work instead of optimizing the protocol in terms of the previously mentioned four different objectives, we consider three objectives and a constraint. Previous work observed that the best solutions found on the same scenarios do not take longer than 2 s for disseminating the broadcasting message [5]. Therefore, in the evaluation process of the optimization, we consider a solution is no longer valid if the broadcasting time is higher than 2 s, and analyze the following three objectives: (1) energy used, (2) coverage achieved, and (3) number of forwardings used.

Unlike in Chapter 5.5, in this work we are showing how to find the most suitable values of the parameters subject to a specific restriction. In our case, we only consider the broadcasting time constraint, but more constraints could be easily added to the optimization algorithms.

The purpose of this work is, therefore, to tune all these parameters using multi-objective techniques (based on Pareto dominance) in order to obtain the best possible behavior of the protocol, considering the three objectives and the constraint explained above. Below, we include a formal definition of the problem.

$$s : \text{ instance of the ns3 simulator}$$

$$dmin = d_1 \in \mathbb{R} | d_1 \in \text{minimum delay}$$

$$dmax = d_2 \in \mathbb{R} | d_2 \in \text{maximum delay}$$

$$b = b_1 \in \mathbb{R} | b_1 \in \text{border\_Threshold}$$

$$m = m_1 \in \mathbb{R} | m_1 \in \text{margin\_Threshold}$$

$$n = n_1 \in \mathbb{R} | n_1 \in \text{neighbor\_Threshold}$$

$$z = (e, c, nb, t) = s(d\min, d\max, d, m, n)$$

$$f(d\min, d\max, b, m, n) = \begin{cases} \min\{e\} \\ \max\{c\} \\ \min\{nb\} \end{cases} ; \ \text{s. t. } t < 2 \qquad (7.1)$$

where z is the set of objectives, e stands for energy saved, c for coverage, nb for number of broadcastings, and t is the broadcasting time.

The domains of the variables `minimum delay`, `maximum delay`, `border_Threshold`, `margin_Threshold`, and `neighbor_Threshold` are presented in detail in Table 7.1.

7.2 EXPERIMENTS

As mentioned before, optimizing four objectives makes both the optimization process and the analysis of the results more complex. Thus, we use broadcasting time as a constraint and consider that any solution that takes more than 2 s is no longer valid. As in the case of Chapter 6, we deal here with a three-dimensional problem, composed of a number of real-coded and integer variables. Hence, we tackle the problem with the same algorithms: NSGA-II, CellDE, and CCNSGA-II.

7.2.1 Algorithm Configurations

Measuring the quality of a given parameter configuration (i.e., a tentative solution to the problem) is a complex task that must evaluate the solution in terms of the coverage, the energy used, the number of forwarded messages, and the broadcasting time obtained by the optimized protocol in any network configuration.

We adopt the same experimental setup and algorithm configurations as in Chapter 6. Therefore, we rely on the ns-3 simulator to evaluate every solution. As an attempt to obtain concluding results in the evaluation of solutions, we simulate every protocol configuration (i.e., every solution) on 10 different networks. The fitness value for every objective is defined as the average of the values obtained for the 10 networks in every objective. We always used the same 10 different seeds in our ns-3 simulations to evaluate the solutions, thus, we analyze the behavior of AEDB over the same 10 different networks.

We use the original configurations proposed by the authors for the three optimization algorithms, previously detailed in Chapter 5. The termination condition of the algorithms was set to 10,000 evaluations performed. Individuals are encoded as an array of 5 real values, and the value used for evaluation for the integer variable (`neighbor_Threshold`) is the integer part of the real value. Therefore, the real-coded variables are `minimum delay`, `maximum delay`, `border_Threshold`, and `margin_Threshold`. In the case of CCNSGA-II, variables were discretized into 16 and 8 bits (for real and integer variables, respectively), as was the case in Chapter 6. The population is decomposed into 8 islands, each of them being in charge of the optimization of 32 bits of the chromosome of each individual.

Regarding the configuration of ns-3 for the simulation of the broadcasting algorithm, we use the same as in Chapter 6. They are described in Section 6.2.1.

7.2.2 Comparison of the Performance of the Algorithms

The performance of the three algorithms is compared in Tables 7.2–7.4, in terms of the mean and standard deviation for the three quality metrics we consider in this book: HV, SPREAD, and $I_{\varepsilon+}^1$ (please refer to Chapter 5). Those values shaded in dark gray color represent the best obtained results, while the second best ones are shaded in a light gray background. The results of the Wilcoxon test are shown in Table 7.5.

As can be seen, the most accurate algorithm is NSGA-II, significantly outperforming CCNSGA-II and CellDE for HV and $I_{\varepsilon+}^1$ on the three densities. The only exception is CellDE in the densest network for $I_{\varepsilon+}^1$. In that case, we did not find significant differences in the performance of the two algorithms.

In terms of the diversity of solutions in the Pareto front approximation, NSGA-II is clearly the worst performing one, with significant differences with the other two algorithms in all cases. In the comparison between CellDE

TABLE 7.2. Comparison of the Algorithms according to HV

	CellDE	NSGA-II	CCNSGA-II
100 Dev.	$5.52e-01_{2.0e-03}$	$5.59e-01_{2.9e-03}$	$5.31e-01_{5.1e-03}$
200 Dev.	$5.50e-01_{3.8e-03}$	$5.66e-01_{2.3e-03}$	$5.23e-01_{1.2e-02}$
300 Dev.	$6.33e-01_{3.8e-03}$	$6.46e-01_{4.1e-03}$	$6.06e-01_{6.6e-03}$

TABLE 7.3. Comparison of Algorithms according to SPREAD

	CellDE	NSGA-II	CCNSGA-II
100 Dev.	$7.35e-01_{3.6e-02}$	$8.71e-01_{6.2e-02}$	$7.94e-01_{6.6e-02}$
200 Dev.	$7.98e-01_{4.7e-02}$	$9.76e-01_{5.6e-02}$	$7.88e-01_{5.7e-02}$
300 Dev.	$7.68e-01_{4.4e-02}$	$1.02e+00_{4.5e-02}$	$7.79e-01_{8.6e-02}$

TABLE 7.4. Comparison of Algorithms according to $I_{\varepsilon+}^1$

	CellDE	NSGA-II	CCNSGA-II
100 Dev.	$1.48e+00_{2.0e-01}$	$3.64e+00_{6.2e+00}$	$5.22e+00_{4.4e+00}$
200 Dev.	$3.17e+00_{3.4e-01}$	$3.27e+00_{4.3e+00}$	$6.23e+00_{2.6e+00}$
300 Dev.	$7.78e+00_{5.2e+00}$	$7.31e+00_{2.0e+00}$	$1.45e+01_{7.3e+00}$

TABLE 7.5. Comparison of Algorithms according to Wilcoxon Unpaired Signed-Ranks Test for HV, SPREAD, and $I_{\varepsilon+}^1$ on Three Network Densities

		NSGA-II	CCNSGA-II
HV	CellDE	▽ ▽ ▽	▲ ▲ ▲
	NSGA-II		▲ ▲ ▲
SPREAD	CellDE	▲ ▲ ▲	▲ – –
	NSGA-II		▽ ▽ ▽
$I_{\varepsilon+}^1$	CellDE	▽ ▽ –	▲ ▲ ▲
	NSGA-II		▲ ▲ ▲

and CCNSGA-II, the former was found to be statistically better only for the sparsest density, and no significant differences were found for the other densities.

7.3 ANALYSIS OF RESULTS

We analyze in this section the quality of the obtained results and validate them with the performance of the original AEDB configurations. The values assigned to this original configuration are: $[0.0, 1.0]$ seconds for the delay interval, -90 dBm for border_Threshold, 0.5 dBm for margin_ Threshold, and 8, 10, and 12 devices for neighbor_Threshold for the 100, 200, and 300 devices/km^2 densities, respectively.

As in Chapter 6, all the different solutions obtained for each optimization algorithm were considered to build one single Pareto front approximation with the best nondominated solutions found for every network density. They are displayed in Fig. 7.1. The maximum size for these fronts was set to 100 solutions, so when more than 100 nondominated solutions are available, the best 100 ones, according to the strength raw fitness method, are selected. In the different plots, the black square is the result obtained by the default configuration of AEDB [3, 6].

In the Pareto front approximations shown in Fig. 7.1, it stands out that the fronts have two clear sets of solutions in the three scenarios. For the lowest energy values in the approximated range $[-20, 20]$ dBm, solutions provide very low coverage and a high number of forwardings, following a linear relationship between these two objectives in which the coverage value is similar to the number of forwardings. These are typically solutions in which devices are only broadcasting the message to their closest one, and therefore the number of forwardings is very close to the number of devices

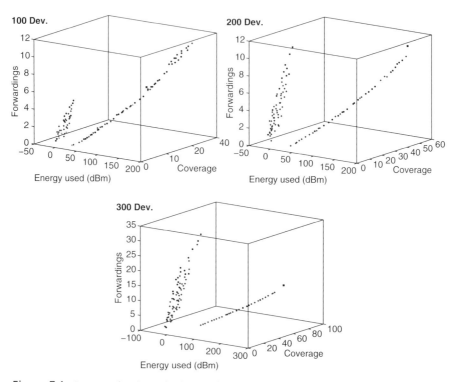

Figure 7.1. Best nondominated solutions found and the performance of the default AEDB configuration (represented as black square). Solutions provided by NSGA-II, CellDE, and CCNSGA-II are represented with symbols and black points, gray points, and +, respectively.

receiving the message (i.e., the coverage). However, for higher energy values over 20 dBm, the shape of the Pareto front changes, and we can see a clearly defined front of solutions in which coverage values are growing much faster than the number of forwardings. This region of the front is the one in which we are more interested, since it is providing high coverage at a reasonable number of forwardings and energy requirements.

We compared these Pareto front approximations to the solution obtained with the original configurations of AEDB for the three network densities. Looking for fair comparisons, AEDB with the initial settings was executed on 10 different networks using the same seeds as in the optimization algorithms. The average values for each of the objectives is compared to the solutions of the Pareto front. In case at least one objective of the solution is better than AEDB and better or equal for the rest of the objectives, the solution is said to be dominant. We found 8, 11, and 1 solutions dominating the original config- uration of AEDB (i.e., providing better results for the three objectives) for the three different configurations: 100, 200, and 300 devices/km^2, respectively.

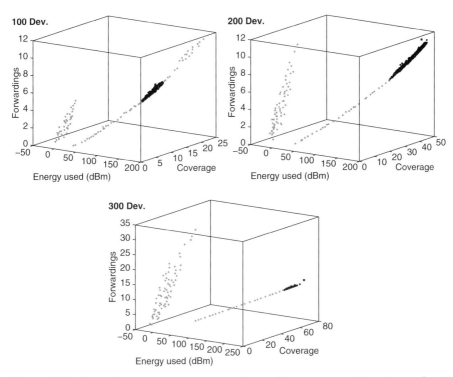

Figure 7.2. The reference Pareto fronts obtained after merging all the Pareto front approximations obtained with all dominating solutions. Black filled circles are the solutions that dominate the original AEDB configuration.

As in Chapter 6, we proceed now to study all the solutions outperforming the original configuration of AEDB. We considered all the solutions found by each algorithm in the 30 executions and we found out that CellDE outperforms AEDB in 201 solutions, NSGA-II in 349, and CCNSGA-II in 116 for the 100 devices configuration. From these 666 solutions, 17 were nondominated with the solutions in the Pareto front. For the 200 devices configuration, CellDE outperforms AEDB in 349 solutions, NSGA-II in 539, and CCNSGA-II in 280. From this set of 1168 solutions, 33 were nondominated. In case of the 300 devices network, CellDE dominates AEDB in 29 solutions, NSGA-II found 53 better solutions, and CCNSGA-II 30. From those 112 solutions, 2 were nondominated solutions with those in the Pareto front. In Fig. 7.2, the solutions found that dominate AEDB are plotted as black dots.

From Fig. 7.2, we can see that in both the Pareto front of 100 and 300 devices networks, the dominating solutions that were added are localized in a small area. However, in the 200 devices case we can see that the solutions are more spread along the Pareto front. The reason is that the original configuration of AEDB is not as fine tuned as in the case of the other network densities.

7.4   SELECTING SOLUTIONS FROM THE PARETO FRONT

The main goal of the multi-objective optimization process we follow is to have a complete view of the protocol behavior in terms of different objectives. So that depending on the situation or the specific needs, the designer can tune the protocol for promoting one objective or another. Additionally, this process allows him/her to fine-tune the protocol for different scenarios or even to make it adaptive to the circumstances (changing from a very crowded place to a more empty one).

All the solutions in the Pareto front approximations are nondominated, that is, none is better than another. However, from the point of view of the protocol designer, a decision must be taken to choose the most appropriate one according to the expected performance.

We can apply restrictions to the Pareto front solutions in order to focus on one part of the front, that is, targeting a minimum coverage or network usage. It is also possible to apply these restrictions during the optimization process such that all the solutions found by the optimization algorithm fit in this part of the front (as we did with the broadcast time). However, including the restriction during the optimization will prevent the designer from a complete view of the protocol behavior mentioned before. That is the case here with the broadcast time, that is, we do not know the performance of the protocol for solutions taking longer than 2 s.

In this work, we want to have a comprehensive idea of the protocol for all the different objectives (that is why no more constraints were added) and then focus on one small area to better understand the behavior of the protocol. For that, we selected some solutions from the Pareto front and applied some restriction considering we are using a broadcasting algorithm in an ad hoc network. Therefore, we assess that the coverage must be at least 80% of the total number of devices, and the number of forwardings should be less than 30%. From the remaining solutions fulfilling those constraints, we compute the energy saved per forwarding (in milliwatts), and consider the 10 best ones. The solutions obtained and the values for their parameters are shown in Table 7.6. Additionally, the quality of the solutions appears in the last 3 columns. The first one, represents the percentage of the energy saved per forwarding. The second, the percentage of the coverage reached, and the last one, the percentage of nodes that forwarded the message. Solutions in **bold** dominate the original configuration of AEDB.

	Parameters					Objectives		
	minD	maxD	bordersT	marginT	neighborsT	%Es	%C	%F
AEDB	0.0	1.0	−90.0	0.5	8	58.6	75.2	24.8
100dSol1	0.1796	0.6389	−90.9565	0.4686	24.4182	11.0	85.2	24.0
100dSol2	0.0928	0.8193	−90.5793	0.3923	24.6660	40.8	90.0	28.4
100dSol3	0.2882	0.8802	−90.5645	1.2530	28.5137	17.5	89.2	27.2
100dSol4	0.3799	0.6743	−90.6264	0.1654	25.4845	27.6	84.4	23.2
100dSol5	0.1307	0.7251	−91.4043	0.5598	16.0962	22.6	84.0	22.8
100dSol6	0.2703	0.4440	−90.9450	0.1701	44.4758	25.5	88.8	27.2
100dSol7	0.3579	0.6742	−90.5978	0.1355	34.3880	29.4	88.4	26.8
100dSol8	0.3684	0.6310	−90.6968	0.0775	22.1308	36.1	87.2	26.0
100dSol9	0.1698	0.6378	−90.9297	0.2342	26.4092	33.8	86.4	25.6
AEDB	0.0	1.0	−90.0	0.5	8	33.1	92.4	22.8
200dSol1	0.2679	0.5308	−93.5228	0.2751	32.7293	31.9	92.8	12.6
200dSol2	0.4894	0.5929	−91.9719	0.9398	10.6796	23.7	100.0	18.6
200dSol3	0.0133	0.5883	−92.2266	0.2404	12.0021	29.1	99.6	18.4
200dSol4	0.3107	0.7424	−93.6534	0.2234	29.1790	37.6	88.0	10.4
200dSol5	0.2328	0.5508	−93.0524	0.3565	19.5563	23.6	98.6	10.8
200dSol6	0.2426	0.5618	−93.3382	0.2899	44.1326	26.6	96.2	14.8
200dSol7	0.2568	0.5394	−93.7108	0.1750	31.8875	30.2	88.8	10.8
200dSol8	0.0000	0.6734	−92.9580	0.8386	40.3794	31.7	95.8	14.2
200dSol9	0.0928	0.4158	−92.9908	0.1787	45.6975	34.9	95.6	14.2
200dSol10	0.2368	0.3712	−93.6204	0.0962	10.9326	23.8	89.4	11.2
AEDB	0.0	1.0	−90.0	0.5	12	20.6	100	18.66
300dSol1	0.3304	0.9755	−93.8238	1.0391	15.5752	31.2	93.1	8.3
300dSol2	0.0043	0.6865	−92.5747	2.4238	12.1417	18.2	99.9	12.5
300dSol3	0.0844	0.3344	−92.0849	0.0176	28.0880	25.9	100.0	13.7
300dSol4	0.1242	0.6474	−94.0484	0.6994	10.2404	38.1	86.5	6.8
300dSol5	$2.81E-4$	0.7205	−93.9438	0.9199	5.5229	31.2	88.5	7.1
300dSol6	0.2361	0.7497	−93.7313	1.1220	15.3702	17.1	93.6	8.8
300dSol7	0.4102	0.5029	−94.0152	0.6055	1.9229	25.1	82.1	6.1
300dSol8	0.2188	0.3125	−93.0334	1.8721	10.9504	15.2	97.9	10.1
300dSol9	0.0212	0.9739	−93.0191	1.7999	13.2432	25.6	99.5	10.9
300dSol10	0.1300	0.9242	−92.7375	2.1095	5.1715	17.2	99.7	11.3

The energy saved per forwarding is calculated as

$$EgSaved = DefTx \ (mW) - EgPerForwarding(mW);$$

$$EgPerForwarding = \frac{EgUsed}{\#forwardings + 1}. \qquad (7.2)$$

That is, the difference between the energy used in case all the nodes sending the message are using the default transmission power `DefTx`, and the actual energy used by the protocol (in milliwatts) `EgUsed`, divided by the number of forwardings.

Analyzing the values of the solutions obtained we can extract several conclusions:

- As the network density grows, the value of the `borders_Threshold` decreases. This behavior was expected as for dense networks, the dissemination of the message is easier, and a lower percentage of nodes is required to resend the message. Thus, the smaller the area of forwarding, the lower the number of potential forwarders.

- The value of the `neighbors_Threshold` is very high for the two sparsest densities (100 and 200 devices/km^2). In fact, this high value is disabling the mechanism for excluding neighbors from the one-hop neighborhood. Only in the densest network, there are four solutions where this adaptive behavior is allowed. They are 300dSol5, 300dSol7, 300dSol8, and 300dSol10.

- The solutions obtaining the highest value of coverage are not necessarily the ones consuming the most (i.e., the percentage of energy saved for 300dSol3 is higher than in the case of 300dSol8) but are the ones with higher number of forwardings.

- The configurations with high values of forwardings are not always saving less energy (i.e., 100dSol2 has the highest value of forwardings as well as the highest value for the energy saved per forwarding). We must clarify that this is happening because we are showing the energy saved per forwarding. Even when the energy used is high, if the number of forwardings is also high, it could mean that many nodes forward with low transmission power, therefore, obtaining a high value of the energy saved per forwarding.

Additionally, we would like to emphasize that in the table we are including the percentage of energy saved per forwarding. Therefore, high-energy saving will appear in solutions where the total energy used is not necessarily low, but the number of forwardings is high. Additionally, solutions that tend to use high transmission power but a low number of forwarding will present low energy savings. That is the reason why 100devSol1 (in **bold**) dominates AEDB, but the values presented for the energy savings is lower (58.8% and 11% for AEDB and 100devSol1, respectively).

From the values obtained, we can conclude that, finding an optimal configuration of the parameters is a complex task. Even after analyzing the obtained values, we can conclude that there is no general rule we can apply for obtaining one specific behavior. Therefore, we confirm that multi-objective optimization is needed for optimally configuring the parameters of any protocol.

7.4.1 Performance of the Selected Solutions

The values of the solutions shown in Table 7.6 were obtained after optimizing the dissemination algorithm in 10 different networks. The optimization algorithm looks for a combination of parameters that gives the best possible performance of the protocol on those networks. Therefore, very sensitive solutions are obtained. Small changes in the value of the parameters highly influence the behavior of the algorithm.

We select now some solutions from this small area of the Pareto front we are studying in depth and test them in 100 different networks in order to evaluate the robustness of the solutions. For the selection process, at least one of the solutions that dominate the AEDB original configuration was chosen, as well as the solution with the highest value for the coverage and forwarding (it is always the case). Analyzing the behavior of solutions that obtained a high value of coverage using a low number of forwardings is also desired (a very sensitive solution).

The average broadcast time for 100 executions of all the above solutions is lower than 2 s. In Table 7.7, the quality of some selected solutions is presented. We can see the values obtained for the different objectives for the optimized 10 networks and also when the solutions are evaluated in 100 different networks. A drop in the quality of solutions is expected as the parameters were optimized for those 10 networks.

Solutions with high coverage but a low value of number of forwardings are very sensitive as they were really fine tuned for those 10 networks. Therefore, their coverage values for 100 networks decrease. This is the case for 100dSol5, 200dSol5, and 300dSol8.

The biggest changes are noticed in the 100 devices configuration as it is the network where the dissemination process is harder. Therefore, good configurations require exhaustive fine tuning, and small changes highly influence the behavior of the protocol.

TABLE 7.7. Quality of Selected Solutions in 100
Networks

	10 runs			100 runs		
	%Es	%C	%F	%Es	%C	%F
AEDB	58.6	75.2	24.8	38.4	81.1	29.0
100dSol2	40.8	90.0	28.4	29.3	79.0	26.8
100dSol4	27.6	84.4	23.2	32.1	80.2	26.4
100dSol5	22.6	84.0	22.8	27.2	75.8	22.7
AEDB	33.1	92.4	22.8	32.9	93.0	15.4
200dSol2	23.7	100.0	18.6	30.6	89.4	16.2
200dSol3	29.1	99.6	18.4	28.1	93.5	16.6
200dSol5	23.6	98.6	10.8	19.1	79.0	11.4
AEDB	20.6	100.0	18.7	26.7	98.1	18.3
300dSol3	25.9	100.0	13.7	27.0	98.8	13.6
300dSol4	38.1	86.5	6.8	38.0	72.4	5.6
300dSol8	15.2	97.9	10.1	9.4	91.9	10.4

In order to provide statistical confidence to our results, we employ the
Wilcoxon matched-pairs signed-rank test. This method is used to check
whether two data samplings belong to different populations or not. Therefore, it can be used to compute if there are statistically significant differences
between the data reported by two different protocol configurations on the 100
studied networks. The null hypothesis for this test is that the median difference between pairs of observations in the underlying populations represented
by samples of results provided by the protocol is zero. In Table 7.8 the comparison between the original configuration and the three selected solutions
of each density is shown. Each solution is compared to AEDB in terms of
the three different objectives. The symbol ▲ means that there is a statistical difference and the solution found by the EAs is better. On the contrary,
▽ represents statistical differences but the original configuration of AEDB
performs better. Finally, the em dash (—) stands for no differences found.

The original configuration of AEDB was experimentally chosen. Therefore, different configurations were manually tested and the best one was
selected. From Table 7.8, we can see that this initial setting highly promotes
the number of devices reached. Indeed, none of the solutions found by the
evolutionary algorithms perform better than AEDB in terms of the coverage
achieved (from the three selected ones) in any density on the 100 networks.
Other solutions from the Pareto front should be chosen in case achieving high
coverage is the main priority for the protocol, over the energy and the number of forwardings. On the contrary, 8 out of 9 solutions behave better than

TABLE 7.8. Comparison between the AEDB Original Configurations and Selected Solutions in 100 Different Networks in Terms of Three Objectives

	EnergyUsed	Coverage	Forwardings
100dSol2	–	–	–
100dSol4	▲	–	▲
100dSol5	▲	▽	▲
200dSol2	▲	▽	▲
200dSol3	▲	–	▲
200dSol5	▲	▽	▲
300dSol3	▲	–	▲
300dSol4	▲	▽	▲
300dSol8	▲	▽	▲

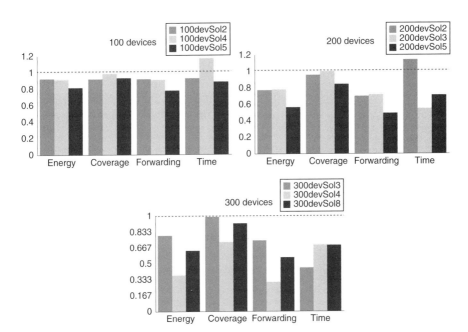

Figure 7.3. Relative value of the different solutions with respect to the original AEDB setting.

AEDB with statistical significance in terms of the other 2 objectives (energy and number of forwardings).

For a better understanding of the behavior of the different solutions, Fig. 7.3 we shows the relative values to the original configuration of AEDB for all the selected solutions. We plot the relative performance for the three optimized objectives as well as for the broadcast time. We should remark that all the solutions presented have an average value of the broadcasting time lower than 2 s. A dashed line marks the behavior of AEDB using the original settings. On the one hand, in case of maximization (coverage) values above the dashed line means an improvement. On the other hand, minimizing (energy used, number of forwarding, and broadcast time) values below the dashed line represent a better performance than the original configuration of AEDB.

As we mentioned before, we can see that, on average, none of the solutions outperform AEDB with the original settings in terms of the coverage achieved. Some solutions are very close to the dashed line, but none is over it. Oppositely, all the solutions outperform it for the two other optimized objectives (energy used and number of forwarding). Regarding the broadcast time, a couple of solutions take longer to disseminate the message, but we should remark that the broadcast time was a constraint not an objective in the optimization process.

7.5 CONCLUSION

In this chapter, an adaptive energy-efficient and distance-based broadcasting algorithm was optimized in terms of three different objectives: (1) the energy used for the dissemination process, (2) the coverage achieved by the message, and (3) the number of forwardings used to get the mentioned coverage. An upper bound for the broadcast time was set (i.e., 2 s). Therefore, we have included a constraint in our optimization process. The set of parameters proposed by the optimization algorithm is only a feasible solution if the broadcasting time is lower than 2 s. Otherwise, the solution is discarded.

We used three different optimization algorithms, namely, NSGA-II, CellDE, and CCNSGA-II, and compared them in terms of three different metrics: (1) Hypervolume, (2) SPREAD, and (3) unary additive epsilon indicator.

Considering the point of view of the protocol designer, we selected and analyzed a small subset of solutions from a specific area of the Pareto front. Bearing in mind that the protocol is a dissemination algorithm, we analyzed solutions with a coverage value higher than 80% of the total number of devices. We also restricted the solutions to have less than 30% number of forwarding. Finally, from all the remaining solutions we calculated the energy saved per forwarding and selected the 10 best solutions. We could see that there is no general rule we can apply for obtaining one specific behavior, thus, the optimization process was needed.

Additionally, some selected solutions were executed in 100 different networks to check their robustness. As expected, we noticed that the deterioration of solutions depends on the density of the network, as well as on how sensitive the solutions are. Nevertheless, they are still very competitive and outperform the original configuration of AEDB.

REFERENCES

1. X. Li, T. D. Nguyen, and R. P. Martin. Using adaptive range control to optimize 1-hop broadcast coverage in dense wireless networks. In I. Akyildiz, D. Estrin, D. Culler, and M. Srivastava, Eds., *Proceedings of the 1st international conference on Embedded networked sensor systems (SenSys)*, pp. 314–315. ACM, New York, 2003.
2. S.-Y. Ni, Y.-C. Tseng, Y.-S. Chen, and J.-P. Sheu. The broadcast storm problem in a mobile ad hoc network. In H. Kodesh, V. Bahl, T. Imielinski, and M. Steenstrup, Eds., *Proceedings of the 5th Annual ACM/IEEE International Conference on Mobile Computing and Networking*, pp. 151–162. ACM, New York, 1999.
3. P. Ruiz and P. Bouvry. Distributed energy self-adaptation in ad hoc networks. In H. Wang, J.Thompson, and M. Singhal, Eds., *proceedings of IEEE International workshop on Management of Emerging Networks and Services (MENS), in conjunction with IEEE Globecom*, pp. 539–543. IEEE Computer Society, New York, 2010.
4. P. Ruiz and P. Bouvry. Enhanced distance based broadcasting protocol with reduced energy consumption. In W. W. Smari, Ed., *Proceedings of the Workshop on Optimization Issues in Energy Efficient Distributed Systems (OPTIM), part of the 2010 International Conference on High Performance Computing and Simulation (HPCS)*, pp. 249–258. IEEE Computer Society, New York, 2010.
5. P. Ruiz, B. Dorronsoro, and P. Bouvry. Optimization and performance analysis of the AEDB broadcasting algorithm. In H. Wang, Ed., *Proceedings of the International Workshop on Wireless Mesh and Ad Hoc Networks, in conjunction with International Conference on Computer Communication Networks (ICCCN)*, pp. 1–6. IEEE Computer Society, New York, 2011.
6. P. Ruiz, B. Dorronsoro, and P. Bouvry. Finding scalable configurations for AEDB broadcasting protocol using multi-objective evolutionary algorithms. *Cluster Computing*, 16(3):527–544, 2013.
7. P. Ruiz, B. Dorronsoro, G. Valentini, F. Pinel, and P. Bouvry. Optimisation of the enhanced distance based broadcasting protocol for MANETs. *Journal of Supercomputing. Special Issue on Green Networks*, 62(3):1213–1240, 2012.

8

NETWORK TOPOLOGY

The limited radio range of MANETs nodes as well as their mobility cause a highly fluctuating topology that can induce severe degradation of the quality of service or even lead to network partitioning, that is, no path is available between some pairs of nodes.

In order to leverage such issues, many authors proposed to study or create small-world properties in wireless networks as they are assumed to improve some quality of service metrics, for example, end-to-end throughput [7] or robustness to failure [3].

The main problem is, however, to find a practical way to establish any communication link in an ad hoc network, which is characterized by bounded transmission ranges. TO this end, we introduce the notion of injection points, which are nodes equipped with an additional communication interface. All the injection points are assumed to be fully connected, that is, any injection point can directly communicate with another one. This new paradigm based on an overlay graph approach is proposed to cope with Watts original

Evolutionary Algorithms for Mobile Ad Hoc Networks, First Edition. Bernabé Dorronsoro, Patricia Ruiz, Grégoire Danoy, Yoann Pigné, and Pascal Bouvry.

rewiring process [9]. It extends some of our previous work [4–6] with a more realistic injection point model.

In this chapter, we focus on the VANET class, where vehicles can either communicate with each other, in a peer-to-peer fashion, or with roadside units that allow access to back-end systems. The scenario used here is the vehicular traffic in the center of the city of Luxembourg. This scenario is motivated by the existence of Wi-Fi access points spread all over the city center [1]. Thus, this preexisting infrastructure allows to actually implement the notion of injection point. In addition, the realistic network topologies studied in this chapter were obtained using the VehILux mobility model for Luxembourg, whose parameter optimization is presented in Chapter 9.

The tackled problem consists in finding the best set of *injection points* to create a fully connected overlay network that unpartitions a VANET and maximizes the resulting network small-world properties. This leads to the optimization of three different objectives:

1. The maximization of the clustering coefficient (CC) so that it approaches the CC of a corresponding regular graph
2. The minimization of the difference between the average path length (APL) of the generated graph and the APL of a corresponding random graph
3. The minimization of the number of injection points in order to limit communication overheads

In this chapter, we consider the usage of a scalar approach in which this multi-objective problem is transformed into a singleobjective one. More precisely, we use an aggregation approach through the linear combination of the three objectives.

The problem is optimized in a centralized way, assuming that global knowledge of the network is known. The suitability of this approach for the real world might be debatable. It would require efficient mechanisms to communicate the network status to the server, as well as a fast optimization algorithm to dynamically make decisions on the vehicles to use as injection points. However, this allows one to better understand the problem and find state-of-the-art and highly accurate solutions. These solutions are then used to assess the performance of four online heuristics (i.e., to be implemented in the devices), one centralized and three decentralized, proposed to solve the problem in a computationally efficient way.

The remainder of this chapter is organized as follows. Section 8.1 describes the problem at hand, and the heuristics used for solving it are explained in Section 8.2. The experimental setup is presented in Section 8.3, and the results obtained are later analyzed in Section 8.4. Finally, Section 8.5 concludes the chapter.

8.1 THE PROBLEM

The problem studied in this chapter is to, provided a snapshot of a VANET, determine the best set of vehicles to join the overlay in order to unpartition the corresponding network graph and maximize its small-world properties. Section 8.1.1 first provides details on the injection network problem definition and used metrics. Then Section 8.1.2 defines the tackled optimization problem.

8.1.1 Injection Networks

The injection networks problem considers hybrid VANETs where each vehicle can potentially have both vehicle-to-vehicle and vehicle-to-infrastructure (e.g., using Wi-Fi hotspots) communications. Nodes elected as injection points (i.e., nodes connected to the infrastructure) form a fully connected overlay network that aims at increasing the connectivity and robustness of the VANET. Injection points, respectively, permit one to efficiently disseminate information from distant and potentially disconnected nodes and prevent costly bandwidth overuse with redundant information. An example network is presented in Fig. 8.1. However, the number of chosen injection points must be minimized since these induce additional communication costs.

In addition, we consider that the small-world properties of the network should be maximized. Small-world networks [9] are a class of graphs that combines the advantages of both regular and random networks with, respectively, a high clustering coefficient (CC) and a low average path length (APL). The APL is defined as the average of the shortest path length between any two nodes in a graph $G = (V, E)$, that is,

$$\text{APL} = \frac{1}{n(n-1)} \sum_{i,j} d(v_i, v_j)$$

with $d(v_i, v_j)$ the shortest distance between nodes $v_i, v_j \in V$. It thus indicates the degree of separation between the nodes in the graph. The local CC of node v with k_v neighbors is

$$\text{CC}_v = \frac{|E(\Gamma_v)|}{k_v(k_v - 1)}$$

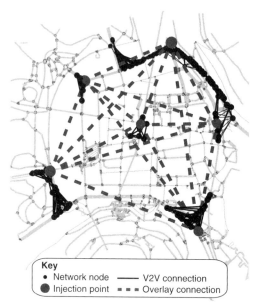

Key
- Network node ——— V2V connection
- Injection point ▪ ▪ ▪ Overlay connection

Figure 8.1. Network with 248 nodes including 6 injection points composing the overlay network.

where $|E(\Gamma_v)|$ is the number of links in the relational neighborhood of v and $k_v(k_v - 1)$ is the number of possible links in the relational neighborhood of v. The global clustering coefficient is the average of all local CC in the network, denoted as

$$CC = \frac{1}{n}\sum_v CC_v.$$

The CC measures the extent to which strongly interconnected groups of nodes exist in the network, that is, groups with many edges connecting nodes belonging to the group, but very few edges leading out of the group.

We here consider Watts original definition of the small-world phenomenon in networks with $APL \approx APL_{random}$ and $CC \gg CC_{random}$, where APL_{random} and CC_{random} are, respectively, the APL and CC of random graphs with similar number of nodes and average node degree k.

8.1.2 Optimization Problem Definition

The proposed optimization problem can be formalized as follows. The solution to this problem is a binary vector sol of size n (number of nodes in the network), sol[1..n] where sol[i] = 1 if node v_i is an injection point, and sol[i] = 0 if v_i is not an injection point. The decision space is thus of size 2^n.

In this work, we consider two single-objective definitions of the problem, F_1 and F_2. F_1 only considers the optimization of the network small-world properties, CC and APL, regardless of the number of injection points to use. Optimizing F_1 will permit to have an empirical bound on the small-world values reachable in the network. F_2 considers the minimization of the number of injection points in addition to the maximization of the small-world properties. The solution maximizing F_2 will then be a compromise between these three objectives.

In case the obtained network is unpartitioned, the aggregative objective function F_1 is defined as

$$F_1 = \left(0.5 + \frac{cc_{diff}}{2}\right) + \left[1 - \left(0.5 + \frac{apl_{diff}}{2 \times d}\right)\right], \tag{8.1}$$

where d is the diameter of the obtained graph G, that is, the longest shortest path between any two nodes; cc_{diff} is the absolute difference between the CC of the resulting network and the CC of the equivalent random graph: $cc_{diff} = |cc - cc_{random}|$. Similarly, apl_{diff} is the absolute difference between the APL of the resulting network and the APL of the equivalent random graph: $apl_{diff} = |apl - apl_{random}|$. For each overlay network instance evaluated in this work, the apl_{random} and cc_{random} is obtained by averaging the APL and CC of 30 corresponding random graphs using Watts random rewiring procedure [9] with probability $p = 1$. Each random graph is created based on the number of devices and average network degree.

No priority is given to one objective over the other. The weights are thus defined in order to normalize the two different objectives to be maximized in the [0,1] interval.

The second function F_2 is defined as

$$F_2 = F_1 + \left(1 - \frac{inj}{n}\right), \tag{8.2}$$

where inj is the number of chosen injection points and n is the total number of nodes in the graph.

Finally, in case the graph is still partitioned, the solution is considered invalid and is thus penalized as the opposite of the number of remaining partitions P:

$$F_1 = -P; \quad F_2 = -P. \tag{8.3}$$

In order to optimize this single-objective problem, we rely on the following four evolutionary algorithms, generational GA, steady-state GA, cellular GA, and cooperative coevolutionary GA described in detail in Chapter 5. The results with these metaheuristics are then used to assess the performance of five heuristics, two centralized and three decentralized, proposed to compute solutions in a computationally efficient way. These heuristics are presented in the next section.

8.2 HEURISTICS

In this section we describe the five different heuristics we propose to quickly solve the injection networks problem. The three presented in Section 8.2.2 are decentralized and require local knowledge; therefore, they can be actually implemented to solve the problem in a real system.

8.2.1 Centralized

We first propose two basic centralized heuristics designed to minimize the number of injection points in the solution. Since the overlay network induced by the injection points is a clique, the smallest valid solution set consists in selecting one injection point in each connected component, that is, unpartitioned graph.

8.2.1.1 *Random Injection Point per Connected Component.*
This heuristic, referred as RandPerComp, selects a random node in each connected component without any consideration for small-world properties (i.e., the average clustering coefficient or the average path length). This heuristic is centralized since it necessitates a global knowledge of the network. Choosing a set of random points permits one to obtain a lower bound for minimum size solutions, that is, solutions with the minimum number of injection points. Indeed, any other minimum-size centralized solution that does not perform better than the random one can directly be considered as useless.

8.2.1.2 *Connected Component Centers.* This second centralized
heuristic, referred as CenterComp, also aims at selecting the smallest set of injection points. The main difference with RandPerComp resides in the fact that we select the center of each connected component in order to optimize the average path length to some extent. The center of a connected component is the node $u \in V$ characterized by the smallest aggregated graph distance,

composed of all graph distances between u and all the other nodes of the same connected component. This can be formalized as follows:

$$\text{center} = \arg \min_{u \in V} \sum_{v \in V \setminus \{u\}} d_G(u, v).$$

8.2.2 Distributed

In this chapter, we propose and evaluate the performance of solutions that can be practically implemented in real VANETs, that is, distributed and localized approaches.

This means that in a realistic situation, no global knowledge can be assumed and each vehicle must rely on local information, that is, information from its neighbors, to decide whether or not it should be an injection point. Indeed in a real VANET context, the access to neighbor information is limited in distance for scalability reasons, since collecting further information would require intensive bandwidth usage to the expense of the application communications. This available information is generally quantified in number of hops, that is, how far in graph distance. As an example, 1-hop information refers to information received from the direct neighbors, while 2-hop information additionally contains data from the neighbors of the neighbors. The first proposed heuristic to solve the injection networks problem is one 1-hop and the other two are 2-hop. These are detailed later.

8.2.2.1 Highest Degree. This very simple heuristic evaluates in its direct (i.e., 1-hop) neighborhood whether its related vehicle has the highest degree, thus number of neighbors. The vehicle becomes an injection point if this evaluation is positive. In the eventuality of ties, the vehicle with the highest unique identifier (ID) is selected. The underlying idea of this heuristic is that having an injection point with a high number of neighbors will help reduce the APL of the local graph, which may also positively affect the APL of the whole graph.

8.2.2.2 Highest Clustering Coefficient. This second heuristic is based on a similar idea, but instead of selecting vehicles based on their number of neighbors, it relies on the highest clustering coefficient. In case of a tie, the highest unique identifier is selected. The underlying idea is that if we select the highest local clustering coefficient (CC), the overall CC can only increase as the overlay network is fully connected.

8.2.2.3   KHOPCA.   The last heuristic is based on KHOPCA, a dynamic multihop clustering algorithm for mobile wireless networks proposed by Brust et al. [2]. KHOPCA creates trees of a maximum depth k, meaning that the maximum graph distance between the root and its farthest leaf is k. This algorithm is based on the repetition of very simple rules in a distributed and localized fashion. The proposed adaptation consists in considering that each root should be selected as an injection point.

8.3   EXPERIMENTS

We describe in this section the methodology we followed for our experiments. Solutions are represented as a binary string, every bit representing one vehicle. Those genes set to 1 mean that the corresponding vehicles act as injection points, while a 0 value indicates the contrary.

8.3.1   Algorithm Configurations

In terms of network, we have used realistic VANETs instances in the center of Luxembourg, simulated using the VehILux mobility model [8]. VehILux accurately reproduces the vehicular mobility in Luxembourg by exploiting both realistic road network topology (OpenStreetMaps) and real traffic counting data from the Luxembourg Ministry of Transport. The six studied networks represent snapshots of a simulated area of 0.6 km^2, three snapshots are taken between 6:00 a.m. and 6:15 a.m., and the three others between 7:00 a.m. and 7:15 a.m. These six network instances are named using their corresponding timestamp, starting from 21900 to 26099. In the case of Luxembourg, this time range is characterized by monotonously increasing number of vehicles due to very dense commuting activity. The properties of the instances are shown in Table 8.1.

8.3.2   Comparison of the Performance of the Algorithms

The algorithms' averaged best solutions over the 30 runs are presented in Tables 8.2 and 8.3 for the six problem instances, when optimizing F_1 and F_2, respectively. Values shaded in dark gray represent the best obtained results, while the second best ones are shaded in light gray. The results of the corresponding Wilcoxon test are shown in Table 8.4.

Considering F_1, it can be first noticed that the CCGA is performing worse than the other three GAs with statistical confidence for the small- and

TABLE 8.1. Network Instances

| | Surface | 0.6 km^2 | |
	Coverage Radius	100 m	
6 a.m.	Network number	21900	22200	22500
	Number of nodes	40	62	60
	Partitions	10	8	6
	Solution space	1^{12}	4.61^{18}	1.15^{18}
7 a.m.	Network number	25500	25800	26099
	Number of nodes	223	248	301
	Partitions	10	6	7
	Solution space	1.34^{67}	4.52^{74}	4.07^{90}

TABLE 8.2. Comparison of the Average Best per Algorithm Using F_1

Instance	genGA	ssGA	cGA	CCGA
21900	$1.3007_{\pm 7.6e-3}$	$1.2983_{\pm 3.9e-3}$	$1.3033_{\pm 6.8e-3}$	$1.2783_{\pm 3.5e-2}$
22200	$1.3568_{\pm 1.4e-2}$	$1.3590_{\pm 1.2e-2}$	$1.3633_{\pm 5.9e-4}$	$1.3389_{\pm 1.4e-2}$
22500	$1.3312_{\pm 4.9e-4}$	$1.3272_{\pm 6.7e-3}$	$1.3307_{\pm 3.3e-3}$	$1.3215_{\pm 1.6e-2}$
25500	$1.2969_{\pm 7.9e-3}$	$1.2972_{\pm 2.4e-3}$	$1.2761_{\pm 7.0e-2}$	$1.2285_{\pm 2.3e-1}$
25800	$1.3088_{\pm 1.3e-2}$	$1.3005_{\pm 6.3e-3}$	$1.3038_{\pm 1.6e-3}$	$1.3037_{\pm 1.0e-2}$
26900	$1.3199_{\pm 2.2e-3}$	$1.3157_{\pm 6.9e-3}$	$1.3094_{\pm 3.7e-3}$	$1.4814_{\pm 7.8e-3}$

TABLE 8.3. Comparison of the Average Best per Algorithm Using F_2

Instance	genGA	ssGA	cGA	CCGA
21900	$2.0329_{\pm 8.9e-16}$	$2.0329_{\pm 8.9e-16}$	$2.0329_{\pm 8.9e-16}$	$2.0225_{\pm 3.9e-2}$
22200	$2.1738_{\pm 1.1e-2}$	$2.1738_{\pm 1.1e-2}$	$2.1748_{\pm 7.7e-4}$	$2.1578_{\pm 5.5e-2}$
22500	$2.1579_{\pm 1.8e-4}$	$2.1574_{\pm 3.5e-4}$	$2.1578_{\pm 2.2e-4}$	$2.1539_{\pm 3.6e-3}$
25500	$2.1845_{\pm 7.6e-2}$	$2.0585_{\pm 1.9e-1}$	$2.1993_{\pm 2.7e-4}$	$2.1222_{\pm 1.6e-1}$
25800	$2.2205_{\pm 1.2e-3}$	$2.2198_{\pm 1.4e-3}$	$2.2207_{\pm 1.1e-3}$	$2.2181_{\pm 2.2e-3}$
26900	$1.7200_{\pm 1.6e-1}$	$1.7893_{\pm 1.9e-1}$	$2.2269_{\pm 1.0e-3}$	$2.0070_{\pm 2.1e-1}$

TABLE 8.4. Comparison of Algorithms according to Wilcoxon Unpaired Signed-Ranks Test for F_1 and F_2 on the Six Network Instances

		ssGA	cGA	CCGA
F_1	genGA	$- - - - \blacktriangle -$	$\triangledown \triangledown - \blacktriangle \blacktriangle \blacktriangle$	$\blacktriangle \blacktriangle \blacktriangle \blacktriangle \blacktriangle \triangledown$
	ssGA		$\triangledown \triangledown - \blacktriangle - \blacktriangle$	$\blacktriangle \blacktriangle \blacktriangle \blacktriangle \triangledown \triangledown$
	cGA			$\blacktriangle \blacktriangle \blacktriangle \blacktriangle \blacktriangle \triangledown$
F_2	genGA	$- - \blacktriangle \blacktriangle \blacktriangle \triangledown$	$- \triangledown - \triangledown - \triangledown$	$\blacktriangle \blacktriangle \blacktriangle \blacktriangle \blacktriangle \triangledown$
	ssGA		$- \triangledown \triangledown \triangledown \triangledown \triangledown$	$\blacktriangle \blacktriangle \blacktriangle - \blacktriangle \triangledown$
	cGA			$\blacktriangle \blacktriangle \blacktriangle \blacktriangle \blacktriangle \blacktriangle$

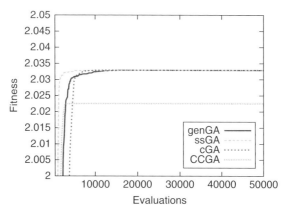

Figure 8.2. Convergence plots of F_2 on the 21900 instance.

medium-size problem instances, that is, from 21900 to 25500. When increasing the problem size, CCGA improves its quality, first outperforming the ssGA in 25800 and then outperforming all on the most complex instance (26099). The cGA is significantly the best on the first two instances, whereas it is outperformed by the two panmictic GAs on the 22500 instance and by the genGA on the 25800.

When optimizing F_2, the CCGA behavior is similar, as it is significantly outperformed by all algorithms for all instances except for the largest one where it is in second place, after the cGA. No difference has been found between the three other algorithms on the first instance. They indeed all found the same average with the same standard deviation. The cGA significantly performs better than all the algorithms on half of the instances (22200, 25500, and 26099) and than the ssGA on the remaining two instances.

Figures 8.2 and 8.3 present the convergence of the four algorithms when optimizing F_2 on the smallest and largest instances, respectively. These two plots are chosen since they are representative of the behavior of the algorithms on the other instances and other fitness function F_1. It clearly appears that on the small problem the CCGA has one of the fastest convergence but is the first to get trapped in some local optima. The three other algorithms all converge to the same average value, the cGA being the fastest to reach it, after 10800 evaluations as opposed to 16100 for genGA and 17200 for ssGA. When tackling the largest instance, the two EAs with structured population, that is, cGA and CCGA clearly outperform the other two EAs.

Finally, Table 8.5 presents the overall best result obtained per algorithm and problem instance among the 30 independent runs. It appears that for the three small-problem instances all algorithms found the same best or second best solution, indicating that the problem is easier to solve. The performance is less homogeneous for the larger instances. The genGA finds the

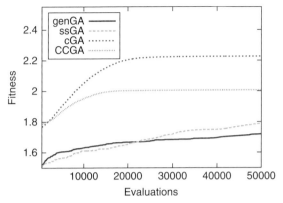

Figure 8.3. Convergence plots of F_2 on the 26099 instance.

TABLE 8.5. Comparison of Overall Best per Algorithm

Instance	F_1				F_2			
	genGA	ssGA	cGA	CCGA	genGA	ssGA	cGA	CCGA
21900	1.3174	1.3174	1.3174	1.3238	2.0329	2.0329	2.0329	2.0329
22200	1.3635	1.3635	1.3635	1.3635	2.1751	2.1751	2.1751	2.1736
22500	1.3316	1.3316	1.3316	1.3789	2.1579	2.1579	2.1579	2.1572
25500	1.3015	1.3013	1.2879	1.2976	2.1995	2.1993	2.1995	2.1990
25800	1.3121	1.3109	1.3069	1.3108	2.2219	2.2217	2.2219	2.2215
26900	1.3228	1.3234	1.3143	1.4892	2.1984	2.1989	2.2286	2.2265

best solution for the next two instances, while CCGA and cGA do for the 26099 with F_1 and F_2, respectively, which also indicates that the EAs with structured population performed better on the most complex instances.

8.4 ANALYSIS OF RESULTS

After conducting all the experiments, we first propose in Section 8.4.1 to analyze the values of the underlying objectives in F_1 and F_2 from the best solution found for each problem instance. Then in Section 8.4.2 the results obtained by the proposed heuristics are compared to these empirical bounds obtained with the EAs.

8.4.1 Analysis of the Objective Values

In this section we are interested in analyzing the objective values of the best solutions obtained during the optimization process. As previously defined,

TABLE 8.6. Objective Values Analysis for F_1

Instance	Fitness	APL	APL_{rand}	CC	CC_{rand}	Inj. Pts
21900	1.3174	3.1026	2.8833	0.8874	0.2159	14
22200	1.3635	2.4918	2.7179	0.9574	0.3056	32
22500	1.3789	2.4915	2.8418	0.8810	0.2108	20
25500	1.3015	2.4910	2.7266	0.8580	0.3334	114
25800	1.3121	2.4656	2.7355	0.8697	0.3244	133
26099	1.4892	2.4933	2.7521	0.8671	0.3078	153

TABLE 8.7. Objective Values Analysis for F_2

Instance	Fitness	APL	APL_{rand}	CC	CC_{rand}	Inj. Pts
21900	2.0329	3.3590	3.0853	0.7680	0.1631	10
22200	2.1751	3.8361	3.1063	0.8351	0.1356	8
22500	2.1579	4.2203	3.0894	0.7713	0.1424	6
25500	2.1995	3.6396	2.8828	0.7752	0.1755	13
25800	2.2219	3.7044	2.8842	0.7739	0.1744	8
26099	2.2286	4.2200	2.9248	0.7615	0.1365	9

the fitness functions F_1 and F_2 are weighted sums of, respectively, two and three objectives: small-world metrics with clustering coefficient and average path length and the number of injection points. We thus propose to analyze the values of these objectives in the best solution obtained per instance, as presented in Tables 8.6 and 8.7 for F_1 and F_2, respectively.

Since F_1 only considers small-world (SW) properties, the APL and CC values are to be considered as empirical bounds. We can observe that the required number of injection points to reach the best SW values is very high, that is, close to half of the nodes, ranging from 14 out of 40 nodes for the instance 21900 to 153 out of 301 nodes for 26099. Except for the first instance, the APL values are quite low and similar, with an average of 2.589 and a standard deviation of $2.5e^{-1}$. Indeed, the APL is also lower than the average APL of equivalent random graphs (APL_{rand}), which means that the defined weighted fitness function focuses on the minimization of this objective. The CC values obtained are very high, with an average of 0.8868, which correspond to the desired SW values since we aim at $CC \gg CC_{random}$.

As expected, when including minimization of the number of injection points in the fitness function, that is, F_2, the SW values change drastically. The average APL is now 3.829, meaning an increase of 47.8% with a highest difference of 69.3% in instance 22500. It is also significantly higher than the APL_{rand}, with an average increase of 27.8% and a worst-case difference of 44.2% in the 26099 instance. The CC difference is also noticeable, with an average of 0.7808, which means a decrease of 11.9% but remains much higher than the CC_{random}. However, the number of required injection points has also been drastically reduced, even to the minimum possible. Indeed it is equal to the number of connected components in the network for the three small instances, and it only requires 13, 8, and 9 injection points for, respectively, 10, 6, and 7 connected components, for the large instances.

8.4.2 Comparison with Heuristics

This section first presents the results obtained with the five heuristics on the same six VANET snapshots and then compares them to the empirical bounds obtained with the EAs. Since the RandPerComp and the KHOPCA heuristics include some randomness, they are averaged over 30 different runs. The other three heuristics are only run once since they are deterministic. Finally, KHOPCA is used with a depth of $k = 2$.

8.4.2.1 Heuristics Performance. Tables 8.8 and 8.9 present the average results of the heuristics on the 6-h instances and 7-h instances, respectively. In terms of fitness, not surprisingly, the two centralized heuristics perform better than the decentralized ones for F_2. This is thanks to their global knowledge of the network that permits to have the minimum number of injection points, that is, as many as the number of connected components in the network. On the contrary, this low number of injection points limits the

TABLE 8.8. Average Heuristics Results on the 6-h Instances

	RndPerComp	CenterComp	HigherCC	HigherDeg	KHOPCA
CC	0.7863	0.7882	0.7799	0.7832	0.7976
APL	4.1875	3.7732	3.2904	3.5145	3.4001
Inj.	8.0000	8.0000	17.0000	10.6667	12.200
F_1	1.2588	1.2724	1.2397	1.2627	1.2497
F_2	2.0992	2.1127	1.9157	2.0567	2.0145

TABLE 8.9. Average Heuristics Results on the 7-h Instances

	RndPerComp	CenterComp	HigherCC	HigherDeg	KHOPCA
CC	0.7672	0.7675	0.7622	0.7641	0.7622
APL	5.2339	5.1365	3.6343	3.7402	3.5093
Inj.	7.6667	7.6667	17.0000	14.0000	14.8000
F_1	1.2276	1.2296	1.2282	1.2408	1.2363
F_2	2.1968	2.1988	2.1605	2.1859	2.1779

quality of the SW values and thus has the opposite effect on F_1, for which the decentralized heuristics perform better on average.

KHOPCA, whose main target is to maximize the CC, obtains the best CC average on the small density networks, but with a higher number of injection points. For the larger networks that represent some traffic jam condition, the CC values obtained are all very similar, probably because selecting nodes in a very dense network does not impact much the average CC. Despite their low number of injection points, the centralized heuristics obtain good CC values, which could be explained by the fact that adding more injection points might not necessarily increase the average CC.

The APL results show that the HigherCC and KHOPCA are the best for this objective, most likely because they have the highest number of injection points. On the other hand, the two centralized heuristics perform the worst because of their low number of injection points. The worst one is the Rand-PerComp, which shows that randomly choosing the injection points makes it highly improbable to obtain good results for the APL.

When considering the number of injection points, the HigherCC shows its limits as it has the highest value in all cases. Obviously, the two centralized approaches have the same values since they are equal to the number of connected components. These provide some lower bound and permit to show the good quality of HigherDeg and KHOPCA. This ranking is the same for both the 6-h and 7-h instances.

8.4.2.2 Heuristics Compared to EAs.

We now compare the performance of the heuristics to the empirical bounds found by the EAs on the two most different instances, that is, 21900 and the 26099.

Tables 8.10 and 8.11 present the three objective values (CC, APL, and injection points) and the corresponding fitness values F_1 and F_2 of the five heuristics on the two problem instances. The last two columns provide the best solution found by the EAs for each fitness function.

When comparing the fitness values, it first appears that the heuristics can have excellent performance on the small instances. Indeed, the CenterComp that best performs on 21900 is only 3% worse than the EA on F_1 and

TABLE 8.10. Comparison of Heuristics and EAs on the 21900 Instance

	RndPerComp	CenterComp	HigherCC	HigherDeg	KHOPCA	Best F_1	Best F_2
CC	0.7711	0.7723	0.8162	0.7632	0.7783	0.8874	0.7680
APL	3.7444	3.3590	2.9743	3.3589	3.1983	3.1026	3.3590
Inj	10.0000	10.0000	16.0000	11.0000	12.2667	14.0000	10.0000
F_1	1.2622	1.2818	1.2474	1.2396	1.2424	1.3174	
F_2	2.0120	2.0318	1.8474	1.9646	1.9357		2.0329

TABLE 8.11. Comparison of Heuristics and EAs on the 26099 Instance

	RndPerComp	CenterComp	HigherCC	HigherDeg	KHOPCA	Best F_1	Best F_2
CC	0.7615	0.7619	0.7532	0.7577	0.7551	0.8671	0.7615
APL	6.2215	6.0900	3.9267	4.0667	3.6129	2.4933	4.2200
Inj.	7.0000	7.0000	16.0000	15.0000	15.7333	153.0000	9.0000
F_1	1.2214	1.2248	1.2082	1.2290	1.2404	1.4892	
F_2	2.1981	2.2015	2.1550	2.1792	2.1882		2.2286

0.0015% worse on F_2. But considering decentralized heuristics, the accuracy decreases with HigherCC being 5.5% worse on F_1 and HigherDeg 3.4% worse on F_2. Also the more complex the problem, the more difference between the heuristics and the EAs. For the 26099 instance, KHOPCA, which performs best on F_1, is 17% worse and RndPerComp, which performs best on F_2, is 1.4% worse.

When comparing to the optimal small-world properties, that is, the results obtained with F_1, the HigherCC is the closest on the 21900 instance, but it requires two additional injection points to reach a smaller APL but also CC. As can be seen on the 26099 instance, the small-world quality degrades with the size of the instances but is justified by the fact that half of the nodes must be injection points to reach this optimum, which is not applicable in a real setting.

Finally, the comparison with the best found compromise solutions on the three objectives, that is, with F_2, demonstrates that simple decentralized solutions like HigherDeg on 21900 can reach very similar values. Indeed the difference in CC is only 0.6%, close to 0 on the APL and just requiring one additional injection point. When tackling the larger instance, the best decentralized heuristic is KHOPCA, whose SW values are also close to the ones found by the best EA, with a CC only 1% worse and an APL 15% better. However, these come at the expense of a drastic increase in number of injection points, as they require 15 injection points compared to the 9 of the EA, thus 67% more.

8.5   CONCLUSION

This third experimental chapter has proposed to apply evolutionary algorithms on a topology control problem in VANETs. The objective is to select so-called injection points that provide connectivity to road-side units and create a fully connected overlay network of back-end systems, to unpartition the network, and optimize its small-world properties.

We have proposed a single-objective formulation for this new problem as a weighted sum of the three objectives, and we used two different scenarios representing realistic vehicular networks in the center of Luxembourg. The six problem instances were first tackled using four EAs to provide some empirical bounds on the SW values and number of injection points.

The performance of the algorithms was compared in terms of the quality and convergence speed of solutions and concluded that the genGA and ssGA perform well on all instances but the largest one, where both structured population algorithms, that is, cGA and CCGA perform the best.

Using such algorithms with a global knowledge of the network is not applicable in a real situation since it would imply the usage of central servers to optimize this hard problem in real time and require large communication overhead. However, the obtained results can be used to assess quality on the results of other more suitable algorithms to solve the problem.

Five heuristics were proposed and compared to the solutions provided by the evolutionary algorithms. Three heuristics are fully decentralized, meaning that these could be implemented in real systems. Experiments demonstrated that heuristics are able to obtain highly accurate results with CC and APL values close to the optimal ones but at the expense of a higher number of injection points.

REFERENCES

1. The HotCity network. Available at `http://www.hotcity.lu`. Accessed July 2013.
2. M. R. Brust, H. Frey, and S. Rothkugel. Dynamic multi-hop clustering for mobile hybrid wireless networks. In *Proceedings of the International Conference on Ubiquitous Information Management and Communication (ICUIMC)*, pp. 130–135. ACM, New York, 2008.
3. M. R. Brust, D. Turgut, C. H. C. Riberio, and M. Kaiser. Is the clustering coefficient a measure for fault tolerance in wireless sensor networks? In *Proceedings of the IEEE International Conference on Communications—Ad-Hoc and Sensor Networking Symposium (ICC)*, pp. 183–187, 2012.
4. G. Danoy, E. Alba, and P. Bouvry. Optimal interconnection of ad hoc injection networks. *Journal of Interconnection Networks (JOIN)*, 9(3):277–297, 2008.
5. G. Danoy, E. Alba, P. Bouvry, and M. R. Brust. Optimal design of ad hoc injection networks by using genetic algorithms. In H. Lipson, Ed., *Conference on Genetic and Evolutionary Computation (GECCO)*, pp. 2256–2256. ACM, New York, 2007.
6. G. Danoy, P. Bouvry, and L. Hogie. Coevolutionary genetic algorithms for ad hoc injection networks design optimization. In D. Srinivasan and L. Wang, Eds.,

Proceedings of the IEEE Congress on Evolutionary Computation (CEC), pp. 4273–4280, 2007.

7. S. Filiposka, D. Trajanov, and A. Grnarov. Analysis of small world phenomena and group mobility in ad hoc networks. In T. Sobh, K. Elleithy, A. Mahmood, and M. Karim, Eds., *Innovative Algorithms and Techniques in Automation, Industrial Electronics and Telecommunications*, pp. 425–430. Springer, Dordrecht, 2007.

8. Y. Pigné, G. Danoy, and P. Bouvry. A vehicular mobility model based on real traffic counting data. In T. Strang; A. Festag, A. Vinel, R. Mehmood, C. Rico Garcia, and M. Röckl, Eds., *Proceedings of the 3rd International Conference on Communication Technologies for Vehicles (Nets4Cars/Nets4Trains)*, Vol. 6596, pp. 131–142. Springer, Berlin and Heidelberg, 2011.

9. D. J. Watts and S. H. Strogatz. Collective dynamics of small-world networks. *Nature*, 393(6684):440–442, 1998.

9

REALISTIC VEHICULAR MOBILITY

Vehicular ad hoc networking opens new services perspectives, including safety, infotainment, and real-time traffic information. The emergence of such networks has raised new research challenges that differ from regular ad hoc networks. These are motivated by the high speed of the vehicles, which creates complex mobility and network connectivity patterns.

In order to provide efficient and reliable services, dedicated solutions like new communication standards and information dissemination algorithms are required. As discussed in Chapter 4, their evaluation can either be achieved through experimental testbeds or simulations. Testbeds permit one to obtain measures in real-world conditions but are limited in scale due to reproducibility and economic and technological constraints. Simulations are, therefore, preferred but require realistic network and mobility models. This chapter focuses on the latter.

The importance of having accurate mobility models in VANET simulation is well acknowledged, and many vehicular mobility models have thus been

Evolutionary Algorithms for Mobile Ad Hoc Networks, First Edition. Bernabé Dorronsoro, Patricia Ruiz, Grégoire Danoy, Yoann Pigné, and Pascal Bouvry.
© 2014 John Wiley & Sons, Inc. Published 2014 by John Wiley & Sons, Inc.

proposed in the literature. Initially limited to simple artificial models such as the Manhattan model [3], traces can now be generated on real road topologies by microscopic mobility simulators. The reader may refer to Chapter 4 for a detailed survey of mobility models and mobility simulators.

As mentioned in [7], the current challenge in mobility modeling is the generation of large-scale traces, such as a citywide area. Two such models have recently been proposed in the literature, one for the city of Cologne (see Chapter 4) and the other for the city of Luxembourg [4, 5], referred to as VehILux in the remainder of this chapter.

VehILux relies on two real-world sources of information: detailed geographic maps and traffic volume counts. A set of probabilistic geographic attraction points is used to select the destination of each vehicle. These values depend on the considered scenario specified by the geographic area and the traffic volume counts.

In this chapter, we thus propose to optimize these probabilities using our optimization framework and demonstrate how it is possible to improve the accuracy of the model.

The remainder of this chapter is organized as follows. Section 9.1 provides a detailed description of the VehILux mobility model and of the corresponding optimization problem. Then, Section 9.2 presents the experimental design, the configuration of the single-objective optimization algorithms, and a comparison of the algorithm's performance. A detailed analysis is then provided in Section 9.3. Finally, conclusions and future works are given in Section 9.4.

9.1 THE PROBLEM

This section first provides a detailed description of the VehILux mobility model and is followed by the definition of the corresponding optimization problem.

9.1.1 Vehicular Mobility Model

VehILux is a realistic vehicular macromobility model that permits one to generate city or regionwide traffic flows based on real geographic and traffic volume count data. Since traffic counts only provide local information, VehILux includes a probability-based destination model exploiting geographic information. A general overview of the VehILux architecture is shown in Fig. 9.1 and a detailed description of its components is then provided.

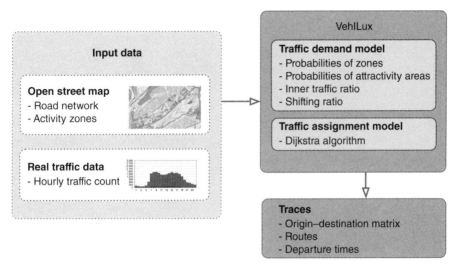

Figure 9.1. VehILux mobility model overview.

9.1.1.1 Input Data. VehIlux relies on two sources of real-world information. The first one is hourly traffic volume counts made available by the Luxembourg Ministry of Transport. These are gathered by count-ing devices (a.k.a., counting loops) spread around Luxembourg. Each traffic count provides quantitative information (i.e., the number of vehicles that passed through the count) and qualitative information (i.e., differentiation between cars and trucks/buses).

The second source of information is detailed geographic maps from Open-StreetMap (OSM) [1]. VehILux exploits OSM accurate information on the road network, speed limits, and traffic lights. It additionally benefits from OSM land-use information through a classification of geographic zones by type: (1) commercial, (2) industrial, and (3) residential. Figure 9.2 presents a map of Luxembourg with the corresponding counting loops and different zones. These two sources of input data are used by VehILux traffic demand and assignment models described hereafter.

9.1.1.2 Traffic Demand and Traffic Assignment Models. A traf-fic demand model must provide information on the vehicles start time and the origin and destination of each vehicle trip. However, as previously men-tioned, traffic volume counts do not provide such geographic information. The VehILux model thus uses two types of origins of traffic, that is, count-ing loops located at the edges of the map (see Fig. 9.2), referred to as *outer traffic*, and some additional traffic originating from residential zones inside the map, referred to as *inner traffic*. The probability of selecting a residential

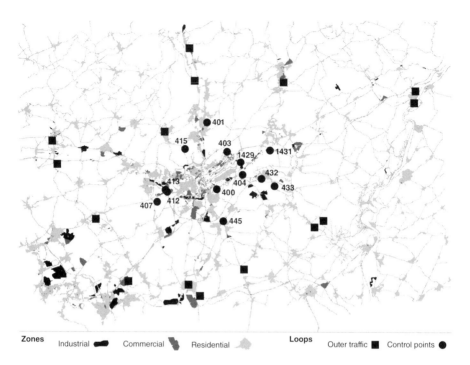

Zones   Industrial ▬   Commercial ◥   Residential ◿   **Loops**   Outer traffic ■   Control points ●

Figure 9.2. Simulation area with geographical zones and control loops.

zone is positively correlated with its surface. The inner traffic is defined as a fraction of the outer traffic using a parameter named *inner traffic ratio*.

The destination model (i.e., the probability of selecting one geographic zone as destination) is more complex and relies on the notions of *zone types*, *zone surface*, and *attractivity areas*.

The selection probability of a zone is a function of its surface and of its type (commercial, industrial, or residential). Each zone type is assigned an overall global probability of being selected as a destination type, noted P_T where $T \in \{R, C, I\}$ is the zone type (i.e., residential, commercial, or industrial). However, zones of the same type may exist in different locations, and some of them might be more attractive than others (e.g., a commercial zone in the city center may be more attractive than another commercial zone of equal surface outside the city). This effect is modeled by attractivity areas. Each attractivity area is defined for a specific zone type with geographic coordinates, a radius, and a probability. Coordinates and radius are set based on problem instance knowledge, but the probability is a tunable parameter. Each zone of the map either belongs to one attractivity area or to the *default area*, which represents the absence of any attractivity area. The probability $P(z)$ of a zone z to be selected can be formalized as

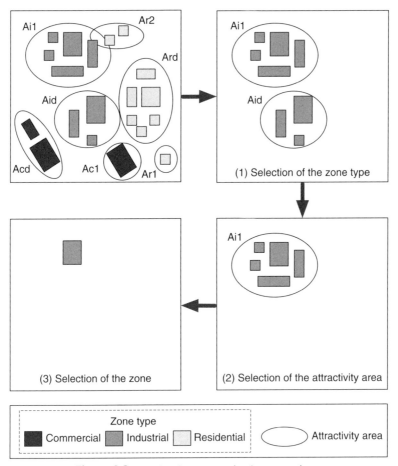

Figure 9.3. Destination zone selection procedure.

$$P(z) = P_T \times P(za) \times \frac{S(z)}{S(za)}, \tag{9.1}$$

where P_T is the probability of the zone type, $P(za)$ and, $S(za)$ are, respectively, the probability and surface of the attractivity area za to which the zone z was assigned, and $S(z)$ is the surface of zone z.

The example provided in Fig. 9.3 (top-left corner) presents the three *default* attractivity areas, Acd for commercial, Ard for residential, and Aid for industrial. Additionally, the illustrated map contains four attractivity areas, two residential (Ar1 and Ar2), one commercial (Ac1) and one industrial (Ai1), each of them having a probability.

The selection of a destination is done using a three-step probabilistic model. In the first step the zone type is chosen according to the zone type probability P_T. In the second step, one attractivity area or the *default* attractivity area of the same type is selected based on its probability, P_{T_i} or D_T. Finally, in the third and last step, one zone is chosen within the selected attractivity area with a probability $P(z)$ proportional to the zone surface.

Figure 9.3 illustrates the selection process of a destination zone in a simplified scenario. In step 1, the industrial zone type is chosen. Two attractivity areas of the industrial type remain, Ai1 and the default one Aid. Ai1 is then selected in step 2. Finally, in step 3 one of the five zones in Ai1 is selected as a destination.

After defining the origin and destination of each trip with the traffic demand model, the traffic assignment model generates the route between them. In VehILux a Dijkstra algorithm based on the shortest paths in time is used (based on the OSM input data).

Finally, the quality of the generated traffic is evaluated using the counting loops located inside the simulation area, which are used as control points (represented as numbered black circles in Fig. 9.2). The traffic generated by VehILux is then compared to the real traffic volume counts in these locations.

9.1.2   Optimization Problem Definition

In order to produce mobility patterns for a given environment, VehILux requires input data and parameters to be set. The map and counting information provide most of the needed information. Indeed, each zone given by the map is located and has a surface and a type. The various zone types are also given to the system as static information. Attractivity areas require more empirical knowledge on the considered area, so their position and radius is also given as static information.

All the other information in the system can be considered as tunable input parameters. The following parameters (Table 9.1) are thus considered as decision variables from an optimization problem point of view:

TABLE 9.1. Domain of the Variables
to Optimize

P_T	[1, 100]
D_T	[1, 100]
P_{T_i}	[1, 100]
InnerTrafficRatio	[1, 100]
ShiftingRatio	[1, 100]

P_T is the zone type attractivity assigned for each zone type T ranging from 1 to 100. Their sum equals to 100.

D_T is the default attractivity area probability for each zone type T. It ranges from 1 to 100.

P_{T_i} defines the attractivity of a conventional area of type T with index i. For each zone type a default attractivity area and one or more specific attractivity area(s) are set. It takes values between 1 and 100. The sum of default and conventional attractivity area probabilities for each zone type is 100.

InnerTrafficRatio is the inner traffic ratio that represents the amount of traffic originating from residential zones inside the simulation area as a percentage of the outer traffic (i.e., traffic generated from counting loops located at the border of the map). It ranges from 1 to 100.

ShiftingRatio is the shifting ratio that defines the percentage of vehicles that trip starts at hour h but ends at hour $h + 1$. Indeed, the model does not define a precise departure time for each vehicle trip but departures within 1-h time slots. The inner traffic ratio then permits one to simulate that some trips pass through the control point in the next hour.

The number of decision variables, and more precisely the number of attractivity area probabilities varies depending on the simulation area. For the considered Luxembourg scenario, one residential, one industrial, and three commercial attractivity areas are considered. The total number of decision variables is thus 13.

The quality of the generated flow is then evaluated by comparing the generated traffic counts with real traffic volume counts at the control points. Thirteen out of the 28 real-life traffic count locations positioned closer to the center of the region are reserved to validate the flow generated by the model.

The evaluation or fitness function F is the following:

$$F = \sum_{c=1}^{C} \sum_{t=1}^{T} |r_c(t) - c_c(t)|, \tag{9.2}$$

where $r_c(t)$ is the real traffic volume count at control point c in time slot t, $c_c(t)$ is the number of vehicles at control point c derived from the generated traffic flows in time slot t, C is the number of control points, and T is the number of time slots. The smaller this sum of absolute differences between the real traffic volume counts and the estimated ones is, the better the model estimated the real flow.

Traffic flows are generated independently for each 1-h time slot t and control point c [i.e., $c_c(t)$] as real traffic count data are typically collected on a per hour basis. As already mentioned, there is no precise departure time related to each origin–destination pair, except the 60-min slots (e.g., vehicle i departs from point a to point b between 9 and 10 a.m.). By default vehicles are supposed to arrive at their destinations in the same time slot. The shifting ratio SR, originally proposed in [6], removes this limitation by defining the ratio of vehicles whose trips are scheduled to start in time slot t, but will pass through the control point in the slot $t + 1$. The estimated number of vehicles that pass through control point c within time slot t [$c(t)$] is thus calculated as follows:

$$c_c(t) = p_c(t) \times (1 - \text{SR}) + p_c(t - 1) \times \text{SR}, \qquad (9.3)$$

where $p_c(t)$ is the number of all vehicles generated in time slot t that pass through control point c, $p_c(t - 1)$ is the number of vehicles generated in time slot $t - 1$ that pass through control point c in time slot t, and SR is the shifting ratio.

The objective is thus to use a single-objective optimization metaheuristic in order to fine-tune these 13 probabilities and obtain vehicular mobility traces that produce traffic counts as close as possible to the real ones. A formal definition of the problem follows:

$$s : \text{instance of the Graphstream simulation}$$
$$P_R = p_r \in \mathbb{R} \quad | \quad p_r \in P_T$$
$$P_C = p_c \in \mathbb{R} \quad | \quad p_c \in P_T$$
$$P_I = p_i \in \mathbb{R} \quad | \quad p_i \in P_T$$
$$D_R = d_r \in \mathbb{R} \quad | \quad d_r \in D_T$$
$$D_C = d_c \in \mathbb{R} \quad | \quad d_c \in D_T$$
$$D_I = d_i \in \mathbb{R} \quad | \quad d_i \in D_T$$
$$P_{R_1} = p_{r_1} \in \mathbb{R} \quad | \quad p_{r_1} \in P_{T_i}$$
$$P_{C_1} = p_{c_1} \in \mathbb{R} \quad | \quad p_{c_1} \in P_{T_i}$$
$$P_{C_2} = p_{c_2} \in \mathbb{R} \quad | \quad p_{c_2} \in P_{T_i}$$
$$P_{C_3} = p_{c_3} \in \mathbb{R} \quad | \quad p_{c_3} \in P_{T_i}$$
$$P_{I_1} = p_{i_1} \in \mathbb{R} \quad | \quad p_{i_1} \in P_{T_i}$$
$$\text{IR} = \text{ir} \in \mathbb{R} \quad | \quad \text{ir} \in \text{InnerTrafficRatio}$$
$$\text{SR} = \text{sr} \in \mathbb{R} \quad | \quad \text{sr} \in \text{ShiftingRatio}$$

with

$$PR + PC + PI = 100.0$$
$$DR + PR_1 = 100.0$$
$$DC + PC_1 + PC_2 + PC_3 = 100.0$$
$$DC + PC_1 = 100.0$$

$$\min F(PR, PC, PI, DR, DC, DI, PR_1, PC_1, PC_2, PC_3, PI_1, SR, IR) \qquad (9.4)$$

9.2 EXPERIMENTS

This section presents the experimental results obtained. Section 9.2.1 presents the configuration of the single-objective algorithms used, and their performance is analyzed in Section 9.2.2.

9.2.1 Algorithms Configuration

Similar to Chapter 8, this study deals with single-objective optimization. We have thus used the same four single-objective metaheuristics, that is, genGA, ssGA, cGA, and CCGA, to look for the best set of parameters for the VehILux mobility model defined in Section 9.1.2. The configuration of the algorithms is the one suggested by their authors, and it can be found in Chapter 5, except for the coevolutionary algorithm that considers 4 subpopulations of 25 individuals each. The termination condition is set to 8000 evaluations because of the computationally demanding fitness calculation. Solutions are encoded as real vectors of size 13. A normalization is used to ensure that the sum of all zone type probabilities PT is 100 and that the sum of attractivity area(s) and default attractivity area is also 100 for each type T.

In order to evaluate the VehILux mobility model parameters, experiments have been based on a detailed map of Luxembourg from OpenStreetMap [1], from which the corresponding road network graph and zones are extracted. It includes the roads length and speed limits and the information about the type, number, position, and surface of the zones. The surface of the considered area is 1700 km^2 (47×36 km). Traffic volume counts from 28 locations were obtained from [2]. As previously mentioned, 15 counting loop locations were selected as entering points and 13 as control points (see Fig. 9.2). For each control point, values corresponding to each hour were taken.

Two different instances have been tackled, the 11 h that was used in [6] to optimize the original VehILux model, ranging from 12 a.m. to 11 a.m., and a new smaller instance of only 3 h (from 6 a.m. to 9 a.m.). During this period (i.e., morning hours), most of the travel involves commuting, therefore, the entering points are selected from the locations positioned at the edges of the map.

9.2.2 Comparison of the Performance of the Algorithms

The performance of the algorithms is compared in Table 9.2. showing best and average fitness with standard deviation for all algorithms on both problem instances. Additionally, values shaded in dark gray represent the best obtained results, while the second best ones have a light gray background.

In the 3-h instance, the CCGA outperforms all other algorithms in both best solution found and average solution found. The second best solution is obtained by the ssGA while the cGA is second in terms of average solution.

In the 11-h instance, the best solution is still found by the CCGA, followed by the cGA. But the CCGA average solution quality is in second place, behind the genGA.

Statistical confidence in these results is here assessed using boxplots as shown in Fig. 9.4. In such boxplots, the bottom and top of the boxes represent

TABLE 9.2. Comparison of Algorithms on the 3- and 11-h Instances

Algorithm	3 h		11 h	
	Best fitness	Avg. fitness	Best fitness	Avg. fitness
genGA	4869	$4954.63_{\pm 43.62}$	14330	$14427.67_{\pm 55.08}$
ssGA	4858	$4991.27_{\pm 113.45}$	14341	$14502.17_{\pm 94.36}$
cGA	4865	$4950.80_{\pm 53.35}$	14326	$14441.50_{\pm 76.91}$
CCGA	4848	$4933.07_{\pm 86.74}$	14250	$14431.83_{\pm 106.04}$

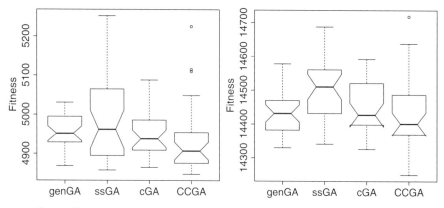

Figure 9.4. Fitness boxplot for the 3-h instance (*left*) and 11-h instance (*right*).

the lower and upper quartiles of the data distribution, respectively, while the line in-between represents the median. The whiskers are the lowest datum still within 1.5 IQR (interquartile range) of the lower quartile, and the highest datum still within 1.5 IQR of the upper quartile. The circles are data not included between the whiskers, that is, outliers. Finally, the notches in the boxes display the variability of the median between samples. If the notches of two boxes do not overlap, then it means that there is a statistically significant difference in the data with 95% confidence. In our case, it clearly appears that for both problem instances there is no statistical difference between the best algorithms since their notches overlap.

Figures 9.5 and 9.6 present the convergence of the four algorithms on the 3 and 11 h respectively. Such plots represent the best solution at every iteration of the algorithm averaged over the 30 independent runs.

In the 3-h instance, the ssGA presents the best initial convergence speed. However, it gets trapped in some local optima faster than the three other algo-

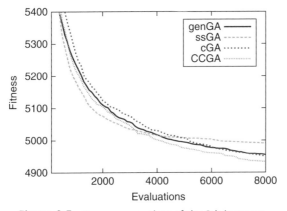

Figure 9.5. Convergence plots of the 3-h instance.

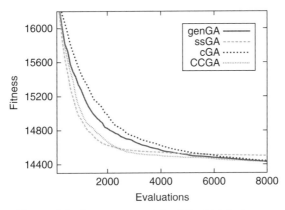

Figure 9.6. Convergence plots of the 11-h instance.

rithm as its convergence plot crosses the other three algorithm plots around 3000 function evaluations. The CCGA initially converges a bit slower but keeps converging for longer than the other algorithms and manages to reach the best average.

The ssGA behaves the same in the 11-h instance, with the best convergence speed but a fast flattening curve that exhibits some premature convergence. The CCGA is again very close and becomes best from 2200 evaluations. However, the genGA reaches the best average with a slower but more constant convergence, closely followed by the cGA. These have thus ensured a better solution diversity preservation. If using a higher number of evaluations was possible, based on this steeper convergence, we could expect a more significant average advantage for the genGA and cGA.

9.3 ANALYSIS OF RESULTS

After all experiments were performed, we obtain a set of 120 best solutions per problem instance (4 algorithms and 30 independent runs). In order to extract some additional knowledge on the solutions found, we first analyze the decision variables in these two best solution sets in Section 9.3.1. Then in Section 9.3.2 we study the best objective value found by the CCGA in both instances at the level of traffic control loops.

9.3.1 Analysis of the Decision Variables

In order to visually represent the variations in the 13 decision variables values found in the 120 best solutions, we provide boxplots in Figures 9.7 and 9.8 for the 3-h and 11-h instances, respectively.

In the 3-h boxplot, the first noticeable information that can be extracted is the relatively small range between the lower and upper quartiles of the data distribution for most of the variables. This shows that promising solutions are located in this limited region of the decision space. The smallest range is obtained with the inner traffic ratio (IR), with a range between 61.97 and 69.99. Only the industrial and residential attractivity areas probabilities feature a large range and thus variation in their values.

In terms of zone type probability, the industrial type (P_i) clearly dominates with a median at 64.77, compared to 31.65 for the residential (P_r) and 34.10 for the commercial (P_c). For the four commercial attractivity areas probability, both default and P_{c1} have a very low median attractivity, compensated with high probabilities for P_{c2} and P_{c3}. The industrial area has the highest attractivity of all, with a median probability of 87.16. Finally, residential probabilities are the most balanced.

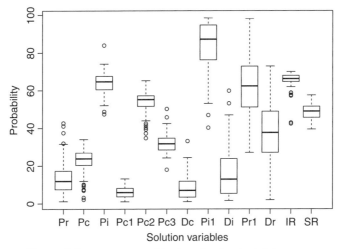

Figure 9.7. Decision variables boxplot for the 3-h instance.

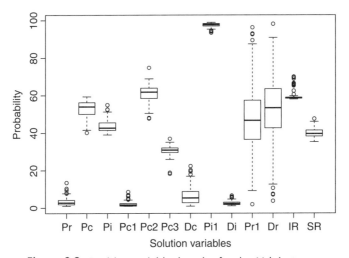

Figure 9.8. Decision variables boxplot for the 11-h instance.

When analyzing the 11-h instance boxplot, it appears that all the variable medians are very similar and their range of values is smaller than for the 3-h case, except for the residential attractivity probabilities. This also attests that the same promising decision space locations have been identified by all algorithms. The main difference with the 3-h instance is the commercial zone type probability increase, respectively, the industrial zone type probability decrease. This can be explained by the fact that in the 11-h instance, after 9 a.m. commercial areas will start attracting a lot of traffic. The same

TABLE 9.3. Decision Variable Values
of Best Solutions 3- and 11-h Instances
Found by the CCGA

Decision variable	Best 3 h	Best 11 h
P_R	1.1554	1.0000
P_C	28.1651	58.5880
P_I	70.6796	40.4120
D_R	36.0150	59.4788
D_C	6.2990	1.7655
D_I	2.5669	2.4094
P_{R_1}	63.9855	40.5213
P_{C_1}	6.2777	1.0704
P_{C_2}	53.6799	64.9543
P_{C_3}	33.7434	32.2099
P_{I_1}	97.4331	97.5906
IR	64.4731	58.4855
SR	51.5402	40.8842

difference is also observable between the global best solution in the 3-h and 11-h instances found by the CCGA, whose values are given in Table 9.3.

9.3.2 Analysis of the Objective Values

In this section we are interested in analyzing the objective values of the best solutions obtained during the optimization process. As previously mentioned, the fitness value F of a solution is equal to the sum of the total error in each of the 13 control loops. We thus propose to analyze the quality of the generated traffic in specific control loops.

Figure 9.9 graphically compares the real traffic counts with the VehILux counts from the overall best solution (i.e., CCGA) for the two scenarios. Four control loops out of the 13 are presented: 445, 403, 401, and 1431, which can be localized on the Luxembourg map in Figure 9.2.

It first appears that the generated flow generally follows the tendency of the real data. This is especially observable for the VehILux model on 11 h where the same peek hours are generated between 6 a.m. and 10 a.m. A few control loops, like 403, have less accurate values. One explanation can be the usage of the Dijkstra algorithm to compute shortest path in time for each trip, that is, from origin to destination. This might concentrate the vehicles flow on some paths to the expense of others where control loops might be located.

The selected four traffic counting loops are representative when comparing the accuracy of the 3-h traffic counts to the 11-h. Indeed, depending on the

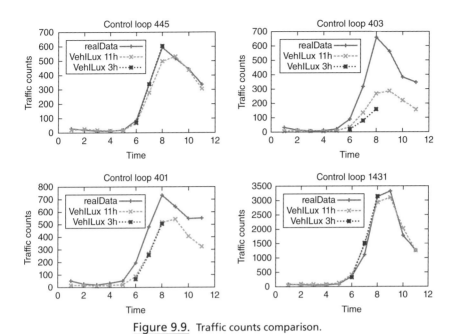

Figure 9.9. Traffic counts comparison.

TABLE 9.4. Traffic Counts per Control Loop for 3-h Instance and Similar 3-h Slot from 11-h Instance

Control Loop Number	3-h	11-h extract	Difference
1431	445	603	158
1429	248	1081	833
445	25	174	149
433	400	283	−117
415	111	103	−8
404	591	590	−1
432	268	304	36
407	434	370	−64
401	579	535	−44
400	135	191	56
403	809	628	−181
420	335	366	31
412	468	363	−105
Total	4848	5591	743

considered loop, the accuracy is similar, worse, or better. More details are provided in Table 9.4 where the error per loop for the 3-h instance and the same 3-h slot extracted from the 11-h instance are given. In addition, the last column provides the difference between these two, which is positive if the 3-h instance is better and negative if worse. Out of 13 control loops, 2 have almost similar accuracy, 5 are worse, and 6 are better. The highest improvement, 833, is obtained on loop 1429, which features a high traffic count with 1729 vehicles in 3 h.

This can be a consequence of the fitness function definition, which considers the sum of the absolute error per loop. The algorithm thus focuses on loops that can can be improved the most, that is, loops with high traffic, which might imply worsening other loops with lower traffic and thus lower improvement possibility. This can also be vizualized in Fig. 9.9 where the traffic generated in loop 1431 with very high traffic is improved and loop 403 with lower traffic is degraded. Normalizing the error per control loop could be investigated as a way to prevent this effect. Finally, the total error difference is 743 in favor of the 3-h instance. This means that considering shorter time frames indeed leads to better results, in our case to an improvement of 13%.

9.4 CONCLUSION

In this last experimental chapter, we have proposed an application of single-objective evolutionary algorithms to improve the accuracy of the VehILux vehicular mobility model. More precisely, VehILux parameters (i.e., probabilities) have been optimized in order to generate traffic flows that minimize the difference with real traffic counting data.

The CCGA found the best solution for the two problem instances considered, but, in general, no statistically significant difference could be found between the four EAs applied. Evidence of the good convergence speed of the CCGA was also provided.

An analysis of the decision variables range in the best solutions found has shown that very similar regions of the decision space have been identified by all four algorithms. Finally, the analysis of the overall best found solution by the CCGA in both problem instances has demonstrated that considering a smaller simulation time frame permits one to improve the mobility model accuracy.

REFERENCES

1. Openstreetmap. Available at `http://www.openstreetmap.org/`. Accessed July 2013.
2. Traffic volume counts in Luxembourg, Luxembourg ministry of transportation. Available at `http://www.pch.public.lu/trafic/comptage/`. Accessed July 2013.

3. F. Bai, N. Sadagopan, and A. Helmy. IMPORTANT: A framework to systematically analyze the impact of mobility on performance of routing protocols for adhoc networks. In *Proceedings of the 22nd Annual Joint Conference of the IEEE Computer and Communications Societies (INFOCOM)*, Vol. 2, pp. 825–835, 2003.

4. Y. Pigné, G. Danoy, and P. Bouvry. Sensivity analysis for a realistic vehicular mobility model. In *Proceedings of the First ACM International Symposium on Design and Analysis of Intelligent Vehicular Networks and Applications*, pp. 31–38. ACM, New York, 2011.

5. Y. Pigné, G. Danoy, and P. Bouvry. A vehicular mobility model based on real traffic counting data. In T. Strang, A. Festag, A. Vinel, R. Mehmood, C. Rico Garcia, and M. Röckl, Eds., *Proceedings of the 3rd International Conference on Communication Technologies for Vehicles*, Vol. 6596, pp. 131–142, Springer, Berlin and Heidelberg, 2011.

6. M. Seredynski, G. Danoy, M. Tabatabaei, P. Bouvry, and Y. Pigné. Generation of realistic mobility for vanets using genetic algorithms. In *Proceedings of the IEEE Congress on Evolutionary Computation (CEC)*, pp. 1–8. IEEE, New York, 2012.

7. S. Uppoor and M. Fiore. Large-scale urban vehicular mobility for networking research. In *Proceedings of the 3rd Vehicular Networking Conference (VNC), 2011 IEEE*, pp. 62–69, 2011.

10

SUMMARY AND DISCUSSION

This book gives an overview of most existing works dealing with optimization issues in mobile networks. Researchers in the field of ad hoc networks that are not familiarized with approximate optimization techniques, such as evolutionary algorithms, but that require the use of such tools in their everyday work will find it very useful. Four concrete examples, ranging from broadcasting algorithm to mobility model optimization, are given in order to show the interested researcher how to identify and define an optimization problem in the frame of ad hoc networks, as well as some hints on the way to address it.

We pay special attention to evolutionary algorithms (EAs), which is a broad family of well-known population-based optimization algorithms. In EAs, the population of solutions evolves thanks to the use of genetic operators, which combine the information of different solutions to generate new ones, and the survival of the fittest solutions.

The book is composed of two different parts. The first one is dedicated to introduce the reader in the field, as well as to provide a thorough review of the

Evolutionary Algorithms for Mobile Ad Hoc Networks, First Edition. Bernabé Dorronsoro, Patricia Ruiz, Grégoire Danoy, Yoann Pigné, and Pascal Bouvry.
© 2014 John Wiley & Sons, Inc. Published 2014 by John Wiley & Sons, Inc.

current state of the art. It starts with an overview of ad hoc networks, providing descriptions of the three main kinds of networks composing them, namely, mobile ad hoc networks, vehicular ad hoc networks, and sensor networks. The main existing technologies used in such networks are presented and discussed.

After presenting mobile networks, an introduction to evolutionary algorithms is provided in Chapter 2, for those that are not familiarized with these techniques. All the main components typically present in EAs are described, as well as four different kinds of EAs that differ on how the population of solutions is organized and managed. As we see throughout the book, it supposes a major influence of the performance of the algorithms, and they can be applied to any kind of EA. multi-objective optimization is also introduced in the chapter because many existing problems related to mobile networks are, indeed, multi-objective in nature.

Chapter 3 provides an extensive review on the application of EAs and other metaheuristics for a number of problems that have been identified in mobile ad hoc networks. First, a taxonomy of such techniques is given, depending on three main issues: (a) whether they are executed beforehand or during the network runtime, (b) the level of knowledge they require from the network, and (c) whether they are centralized or not. Then, we identify the main optimization problems that have been defined in the context of mobile networks in the literature, explaining the main existing metaheuristics that have been applied to solve them (paying special attention to EAs).

The last chapter of this first part is devoted to a presentation of the existing network and mobility simulators, as well as a description of the main existing models for emulating signal propagation and mobility patterns. This chapter is intended to help the reader in the choice of the most appropriate simulator(s) for his/her specific case.

The second part of the book focuses on the optimization of some relevant problems in the field of mobile ad hoc networks. It starts by presenting the proposed optimization framework in Chapter 5. It is a useful tool for researchers and engineers that deal with mobile networks. It is composed by a number of modules that can be easily plugged in or unplugged, and it can be used either for optimizing problems for mobile networks or for designing and validating new protocols and algorithms.

Chapter 6 studies the optimization of the parameters of a broadcasting protocol, according to the coverage achieved, the network use, and the time of the broadcasting process. Therefore, it has been solved with multi-objective optimization algorithms. A discussion considers the most appropriate way to build a representative set of the best nondominated solutions, which is an important process for the decision maker to have the most complete information on the problem. The obtained results, as well as the contribution of the different algorithms on the final set of solutions, are carefully analyzed.

An energy-efficient communication protocol is optimized in Chapter 7. As we saw throughout the book, mobile networks are typically composed by battery-powered devices, making the proposed problem highly relevant in this field. The problem is, again, multi-objective, and four different objectives were identified. However, one of the objectives, the time, was considered as a constraint in the optimization process, considering valid any solution that takes 2 s or less. Removing this objective makes easier both the optimization process and the interpretation of the results. A number of solutions were selected from the final set of nondominated configurations of the protocol, and they were carefully evaluated, compared, and analyzed on a wide set of networks.

Enhancing the network connectivity in the frame of VANETs is the target of Chapter . The goal is to create an underlying topology using the infrastructure composed by the road-side units to optimize the network connectivity (i.e., to minimize the distance between any two nodes, and maximizing the connectivity between devices). Additionally, the number of vehicles that communicate through the infrastructure should be minimized too in order to prevent the network congestion. Two different single-objective optimization problems are defined to solve a number of static network snapshots. The obtained results were used to assess the quality of a number of centralized and decentralized heuristics that we designed to solve the problem online. A realistic scenario was used for the experiments, which accurately reproduces the observed traffic in the city of Luxembourg.

In contrast of the previous chapters, focused on the optimization of communication protocols or the network topology, Chapter 9 presents an original approach that targets the optimization of a mobility model to make it as realistic as possible. It takes as an input data the information given by traffic counters located in Luxembourg. Some of these counters are chosen as traffic injection points, which are used by the mobility model to generate the mobility traces, using some geographical information to decide on the destination. The configuration of the mobility model is optimized to fit the observed data in the rest of the counters. The optimization problem is defined as a single-objective one, and the fitness function will be given by minimizing the difference between the real observed traffic and the generated one at every counter.

10.1   A NEW METHODOLOGY FOR OPTIMIZATION IN MOBILE AD HOC NETWORKS

After giving a general overview of the main works in the literature dealing with optimization issues in mobile networks, a new framework is proposed to help researchers in the field to tackle their problems and to guide them to successfully solve them. The framework, proposed in Chapter 5, has a simple architecture, composed of a number of modules that can be plugged in or unplugged according to need. These modules are used to specify the optimization algorithm(s) to use, the simulators, as well as their configurations, among others.

The framework is not intended for optimization purposes only. It can be used for designing and evaluating novel communication protocols or mobility patterns, which can be afterward optimized by plugging in the optimization module. We focus here on the use of metaheuristics, in particular, evolutionary algorithms, as optimization tools. This book shows how to apply them to tackle different problems in the field. The cases of optimal broadcasting, energy saving, network topology, and mobility traces generation were studied in a didactic way, so nonfamiliarized researchers can learn the techniques to apply them in their work.

Applying heavy optimization techniques as evolutionary algorithms for solving problems in mobile networks might seem counterintuitive because of the decentralized nature of these networks, as well as their limited resources. However, they can be really useful in this field. As we will see next, they are typically used in online or offline modes in the literature.

In the online cases, the optimization technique must be completely decentralized and can only make use of local knowledge of the network. Additionally, they cannot be computationally expensive because they will be executed in the network nodes. Ant colony optimization is typically used in such cases, generally to optimize the routing process and some of its variants (namely, multicast and multipath routing) [11, 16]. However, other metaheuristics, as GAs, were used online with local knowledge to solve problems related to node deployment [9, 18] and encouraging node cooperation [3].

The application of metaheuristics in offline mode makes sense, for instance, in the last step of the engineering process of protocols and algorithms that rely on a set of parameters to be tuned. They can be used in communication and topology control protocols, among others. They can also be used for the optimization of some of the components used in simulations to make them more realistic, as the mobility models, the signal propagation, and so forth. Notice that this optimization process generally requires the use of simulations to evaluate candidate solutions for guiding the search. These simulations are typically stochastic processes that require a number of repetitions in the evaluation process in order to look for meaningful results. Such experiments are run once to optimize the final solution, before it is implemented. Therefore, it is generally worth to carry out the computationally expensive experiments in order to find a nearly optimal result. In this book, some examples of the application of different EAs are given for the offline optimization of communication protocols (Chapters 6 and 7) and for making mobility models more realistic, as we do in Chapter 9 or [15]. Other examples can be found in the literature to optimize routing protocols [7, 17], to avoid selfishness [14], topology control, clustering [8], or security [13], among others.

Offline optimization techniques are also used in the literature for reverse engineering. In this case, the optimization algorithms are applied to solve the problem under some unrealistic assumptions, as the use of global knowledge, the lack of mobility, and the like. The designer then analyzes the obtained results, what will allow him/her to get new knowledge about the problem. Then this new acquired knowledge will be used in the design of the solution to the actual problem. The topology connectivity improvement shown in Chapter 8 is an example of this technique. Other examples can be found in the literature, where GAs are used for optimizing the topology connectivity, either by adjusting the transmission power for the nodes forming sensor networks [10] or by setting bypass links connecting distant devices in MANETs [1, 2] and VANETs [6, 12].

The proposed optimization framework can be used either for online and offline optimization modes. In this book, the offline mode is explored. We solve four different problems with EAs that evolve panmictic, cellular, and cooperative coevolutionary populations, in order to compare the performance of the different kinds of EAs. Online optimization algorithms can also be used in this framework, by implementing them in the optimization problem module. In the next two sections, we summarize our main findings on the performance of the different algorithms on the studied problems.

10.2 PERFORMANCE OF THE THREE ALGORITHMIC PROPOSALS

We briefly summarize in this section the behavior of the different algorithms on the four studied problems.

10.2.1 Broadcasting Protocol

The problem addressed in Chapter is to fine-tune the parameters of a broadcasting algorithm for an optimal performance. Three different objectives, in conflict with each other, were defined to measure the quality of solutions: the number of devices receiving the broadcasted message, the network use, and the time required by the process. Five parameters of the protocol are identified and optimized. This number is too low for the cooperative coevolutionary algorithm, which requires a number of variables in the different islands to apply the recombination operator. Therefore, we opted for discretizing the variables of the protocol for this algorithm.

Regarding the results, the cellular algorithm (i.e., CellDE) clearly outperformed the other ones. The panmictic algorithm (NSGA-II) outperforms the cooperative coevolutionary one (CCNSGA-II) in terms of accuracy, but the latter is statistically better according to the diversity of solutions found. The mentioned differences stand for the three network densities studied.

10.2.2   Energy-Efficient Communications

The obtained results for the energy-saving broadcasting protocol studied in Chapter 7 differ from those previously presented. In this case, NSGA-II generally outperforms CellDE in terms of accuracy of solutions, with the exception of the densest network, for which no significant differences were found between the two algorithms. Regarding the diversity of solutions in the Pareto front found, CellDE outperforms NSGA-II for all network densities.

Regarding CCNSGA-II, it is always significantly worse than the two compared algorithms in terms of accuracy, according to the metrics used. However, the algorithm contributes with a high number of solutions to the final Pareto front built from the solutions obtained in all experiments by the three algorithms. And this number grows with the network density: It provides 43, 67, and 76% of the solutions for the sparse, medium, and dense networks, respectively. Additionally, it provides high diversified Pareto fronts, as it outperforms NSGA-II for the three densities, and it is only worse than CellDE for the sparsest density. Therefore, we can say that the CCNSGA-II shows better exploration capabilities with respect to the other two algorithms.

10.2.3   Network Connectivity

Four single-objective genetic algorithms were used to solve the problem of improving the network connectivity introduced in Chapter : two of them with panmictic populations, a cellular one, and a cooperative coevolutionary GA. Two different fitness functions were used for the problem optimization, and similar conclusions were obtained for both of them. In general, the panmictic GAs outperform the others for the smallest (and less difficult) problem instances, but they perform poorly for the biggest ones, compared to the cGA and the CCGA. The reason is that using panmictic populations provide the algorithms with high convergence speed. This results in a premature loss of diversity in the population that in the most difficult problems favors the algorithms getting stuck in local optima. On the contrary, the GAs with structured population keep more diversity for longer, therefore, increasing the exploration capabilities of the algorithm. At this point, we would like to mention that, even when population diversity is preserved for a long time by the CCGA, the convergence speed it performs is as fast as for the panmictic algorithms.

Comparing the panmictic population GAs, genGA was outperforming ssGA in all cases when statistical differences were found, with the only exception of the largest problem using function F_2.

10.2.4   Vehicular Mobility

The last problem we tackle in the book is the optimization of the mobility model for VANETs in the scenario of Luxembourg. In this case, the objective is to minimize the difference between the real observed traffic and the simulated traffic in a number of predefined locations. Therefore, it is a single-objective optimization problem that has been solved with the same four GAs used for the network connectivity optimization problem.

The best algorithms were the CCGA and genGA for this problem. However, we did not find statistical confidence in most cases on the comparison of the algorithms. The only conclusion we could extract from these tests is that ssGA performs the worst for the large instance. Regarding the convergence speed, ssGA is the fastest algorithm, followed by CCGA, genGA, and cGA, in that order. An indication of the quick diversity loss in the population of ssGA is that it is the first one getting stuck in local optima. The cGA is the slowest compared algorithm, but it is able to find highly competitive results in all cases.

10.3   GLOBAL DISCUSSION ON THE PERFORMANCE OF THE ALGORITHMS

The choice of an accurate optimization algorithm for a given problem is not an easy task. There is a plethora of different kinds of metaheuristics in the literature, and it is very difficult to predict their behavior on a concrete problem. Additionally, there is not "a globally best" algorithm for all possible problems, as the *no free lunch theorem* [20] states. Therefore, it is an advisable practice to look for optimization algorithms that are shown to perform well for other problems with similar features to the addressed one. In this section, we try to give the reader some hints to choose an appropriate optimization algorithm, by discussing the performance of the different algorithms studied here for all problems.

TABLE 10.1. Ranking of Performance of Algorithms Used in This Book

	Single Objective			Multi-objective	
	Algorithm	Rank		Algorithm	Rank
1	cGA	3.21	1	CellDE	2.72
2	genGA	2.93	2	NSGA-II	1.89
3	ssGA	2.00	3	CCNSGA-II	1.39
4	CCGA	1.86			

Table 10.1 presents a ranking of the overall performance of the algorithms in the experiments made in the book. It was computed by applying the Friedman test to the presented average results of the algorithms in all problems (the higher the rank value the better the algorithm). In the case of the multi-objective algorithms, we are considering the results obtained for the three performance metrics studied to build the ranking. The test found statistical differences among the algorithms with 95% confidence. As we can see, the algorithms using the cellular populations are the ones performing the best for the studied problems. They are followed by the panmictic algorithms, and the cooperative coevolutionary one, in that order. This observation holds both for the single- and multi-objective problems.

We would like to emphasize at this point that, even when the cooperative coevolutionary algorithmic model was last in the presented rank, it performed well for the most complex problem instances, particularly in the case of the two single-objective problems (addressed in Chapters 8 and 9). In the next two sections, we will present some additional discussion on the performance of the algorithms for the single- and multi-objective problems, respectively.

10.3.1 Single-Objective Case

We first comment on the convergence speed of the algorithms for the single-objective problems. The algorithms implementing panmictic populations generally converge fast to an optimum. However, they might not be the best option to deal with multimodal problems, which are composed of a large number of local and global optimal solutions. The reason is that these algorithms are quickly loosing the population diversity, making it difficult to generate new solutions in other areas of the search space. Therefore, there is a need to look for an appropriate trade-off between the exploration and the exploitation performed by the algorithm in the search space [19].

Algorithms with structured populations generally provide better exploration capabilities than the equivalent panmictic ones. Consequently, they explore larger areas of the search space, exploiting the most promising ones. This way, the chances to find the optimal solution and/or avoiding getting stuck in local optimal ones are increased. However, they perform a slower convergence, therefore, requiring a higher effort to find the optimal solution with respect to panmictic algorithms (when they find it).

We observed that the studied cooperative coevolutionary algorithms converge as fast as the panmictic ones, but they still can effectively explore the search space. Indeed, these algorithms are among the most accurate ones for the biggest instances of most of the studied problems. However, their limitation mainly comes with the number of decision variables to optimize. This algorithmic model requires the decomposition of the problem into several smaller subproblems. When the problem is not easily decomposable, it is common practice to just split the chromosome into several smaller ones, which will be independently optimized in the islands. Therefore, the number of decision variables to optimize in every island must be high enough to allow the application of the evolutionary operators.

10.3.2 Multi-Objective Case

In the multi-objective case, it is difficult to extract conclusions about the performance of CCNSGA-II compared with the other algorithms. The reason is that the problems had to be discretized to be solved by CCNSGA-II due to the small number of decision variables of the original problem (only five variables). However, in previous works [4, 5], CCNSGA-II was shown to perform slightly worse than NSGA-II for a number of benchmark problems, but with the important advantage of being a parallel algorithm. Parallelizing multi-objective algorithms is not an easy task because normally information of the global population must be used to ensure a diverse set of solutions in the Pareto front approximation. The speedup of the algorithm was shown to be superlinear versus NSGA-II.

The particular case of the problems addressed in this book (in Chapters 6 and 7) confirm our previously published results: CCNSGA-II performs worse than NSGA-II in terms of accuracy of results, but it is better according to the diversity of solutions in the Pareto front, meaning that it is performing a better exploration of the search space. We checked the number of solutions that every algorithm contributes to the final Pareto fronts analyzed in the chapters, built from all solutions obtained by all the algorithms. In the case of DFCN optimization, CellDE is the algorithm providing more solutions, composing 47, 70, and 66% of the Pareto front (for the three densities, from the sparsest to the densest one), followed by NSGA-II, with 42, 30, and 34%, respectively, and CCNSGA-II, with 11, 0, and 0%. However, CCNSGA-II is the algorithm providing more solutions to the final Pareto front in the case of the AEDB optimization problem (except for the sparsest network): 43, 67, and 76% versus 50, 33, and 23% by NSGA-II and 5, 0, and 0% in the case of CellDE.

10.4 CONCLUSION

This last chapter provides an overall conclusion for this book. A brief summary of the contents of the book is first presented. Then, we discuss the novel methodology proposed to tackle optimization problems with metaheuristics in the frame of ad hoc networks. Finally, the performance of the three algorithmic classes studied (namely, panmictic, cellular, and cooperative coevolutionary) is discussed for the four problems addressed in the book, and their overall behavior on all the studied problems is also analyzed. Some hints are given in order to help the reader on the choice of the algorithm to use when solving similar problems.

REFERENCES

1. G. Danoy, E. Alba, and P. Bouvry. Optimal interconnection of ad hoc injection networks. *Journal of Interconnection Networks*, 9(3):277–297, 2008.
2. G. Danoy, B. Dorronsoro, and P. Bouvry. Overcoming partitioning in large ad hoc networks using genetic algorithms. In G. Raidl, F. Rothlauf, G. Squillero, R. Drechsler, T. Stuetzle, M. Birattari, C. B. Congdon, M. Middendorf, C. Blum, C. Cotta, P. Bosman, J. Grahl, J. Knowles, D. Corne, H.-G. Beyer, K. Stanley, J. F. Miller, J. van Hemert, T. Lenaerts, M. Ebner, J. Bacardit, M. O'Neill, M. Di Penta, B. Doerr, T. Jansen, R. Poli, and E. Alba *Proceedings of the 11th Annual Conference on Genetic and Evolutionary Computation (GECCO)*, pp. 1347–1354. ACM, New York, 2009.
3. Z. Dongmei, Z. Qu, Y. Yang, and X. Feng. A service negotiation mechanism in mobile ad hoc network. In *Proceedings of the 7th International Conference on Wireless Communications, Networking and Mobile Computing (WiCOM)*, pp. 1–4. IEEE, 2011.
4. B. Dorronsoro, G. Danoy, P. Bouvry, and A. J. Nebro. Multi-objective cooperative coevolutionary evolutionary algorithms for continuous and combinatorial optimization. In P. Bouvry, H. González-velez, and J. Kolodziej, Eds., *Intelligent Decision Systems in Large-Scale Distributed Environments*, Vol. 362 of *Studies in Computational Intelligence*, pp. 49–74. Springer, Berlin and Heidelberg, 2011.

5. B. Dorronsoro, G. Danoy, A. J. Nebro, and P. Bouvry. Achieving super-linear performance in parallel multi-objective evolutionary algorithms by means of cooperative coevolution. *Computers & Operations Research*, 40(6):1552–1563, 2013.

6. B. Dorronsoro, P. Ruiz, G. Danoy, P. Bouvry, and L. Tardón. Towards connectivity improvement in VANETs using bypass links. In *Proceedings of the IEEE Congress on Evolutionary Computation (CEC)*, pp. 2201–2208. IEEE, 2009.

7. J. García-Nieto, J. Toutouh, and E. Alba. Automatic tuning of communication protocols for vehicular ad hoc networks using metaheuristics. *Engineering Applications of Artificial Intelligence*, 23(5):795–805, 2010.

8. E. A. Khalil and B. A. Attea. Energy-aware evolutionary routing protocol for dynamic clustering of wireless sensor networks. *Swarm and Evolutionary Computation*, 1(4):195–203, 2011.

9. J. Kusyk, C. S. Sahin, M. U. Uyar, E. Urrea, and S. Gundry. Self-organization of nodes in mobile ad hoc networks using evolutionary games and genetic algorithms. *Journal of Advanced Research*, 2:253–264, 2011.

10. P. Ranganathan, A. Ranganathan, K. Berman, and A. Minai. Discovering adaptive heuristics for ad-hoc sensor networks by mining evolved optimal configurations. In *Proceedings of the IEEE Congress on Evolutionary Computation (CEC)*, pp. 3064–3070. IEEE, 2006.

11. M. Saleem, G. A. Di Caro, and M. Farooq. Swarm intelligence based routing protocol for wireless sensor networks: Survey and future directions. *Information Sciences*, 181(20):4597–4624, 2011.

12. J. Schleich, G. Danoy, B. Dorronsoro, and P. Bouvry. An overlay approach for optimising small-world properties in VANETs. In *Applications of Evolutionary Computation*, Vol. 7835 of *Lecture Notes in Computer Science*, pp. 32–41. Springer, Heidelberg, 2013.

13. S. Sen and J. A. Clark. Evolutionary computation techniques for intrusion detection in mobile ad hoc networks. *Computer Networks*, 55(15):3441–3457, 2011.

14. M. Seredynski, P. Bouvry, and M. A. Klopotek. Evolution of strategy driven behavior in ad hoc networks using a genetic algorithm. In *Proceedings of the IEEE International Parallel and Distributed Processing Symposium (IPDPS)*, pp. 1–8. IEEE, 2007.

15. M. Seredynski, G. Danoy, M. Tabatabaei, P. Bouvry, and Y. Pigné. Generation of realistic mobility for VANETs using genetic algorithms. In *Proceedings of the IEEE Congress on Evolutionary Computation (CEC)*, pp. 1–8. IEEE, 2012.

16. H. Shokrani and S. Jabbehdari. A survey of ant-based routing algorithms for mobile ad-hoc networks. In *Proceedings of the International Conference on Signal Processing Systems*, pp. 323–329. IEEE Computer Society, Los Alamitos, 2009.

17. J. Toutouh, J. García-Nieto, and E. Alba. Intelligent OLSR routing protocol optimization for VANETs. *IEEE Transactions on Vehicular Technology*, 61(4):1884–1894, 2012.

18. E. Urrea, C. S. Şahin, I. Hökelek, M. I. Uyar, M. Conner, G. Bertoli, and C. Pizzo. Bio-inspired topology control for knowledge sharing mobile agents. *Ad Hoc Networks*, 7(4):677–689, 2009.

19. M. Črepinšek, S.-H. Liu, and M. Mernik. Exploration and exploitation in evolutionary algorithms: A survey. *ACM Computing Surveys*, 45(3): 35:1–35:33, 2013.

20. D. H. Wolpert and W. G. Macready. No free lunch theorems for optimization. *IEEE Transactions on Evolutionary Computation*, 1(1):67–82, 1997.

INDEX

Evolutionary Algorithms for Mobile Ad Hoc Networks, First Edition. Bernabé Dorronsoro,
Patricia Ruiz, Grégoire Danoy, Yoann Pigné, and Pascal Bouvry.
© 2014 John Wiley & Sons, Inc. Published 2014 by John Wiley & Sons, Inc.